Chinese Junks on the Pacific

New Perspectives on Maritime History and Nautical Archaeology

UNIVERSITY PRESS OF FLORIDA

Florida A&M University, Tallahassee
Florida Atlantic University, Boca Raton
Florida Gulf Coast University, Ft. Myers
Florida International University, Miami
Florida State University, Tallahassee
New College of Florida, Sarasota
University of Central Florida, Orlando
University of Florida, Gainesville
University of North Florida, Jacksonville
University of South Florida, Tampa
University of West Florida, Pensacola

Hans K. Van Tilburg

Foreword by James C. Bradford and Gene Allen Smith, Series Editors

University Press of Florida
Gainesville · Tallahassee · Tampa · Boca Raton
Pensacola · Orlando · Miami · Jacksonville · Ft. Myers · Sarasota

Chinese Junks on the Pacific

Views from a Different Deck

First cloth printing, 2007
First paperback printing, 2013

Library of Congress Cataloging-in-Publication Data
Van Tilburg, Hans.
Chinese junks on the Pacific : views from a different deck /
Hans K. Van Tilburg ; foreword by James C. Bradford and
Gene A. Smith.
p. cm.—(New perspectives on maritime history and nautical
archaeology)
Includes bibliographical references and index.
ISBN 978-0-8130-3053-1 (cloth: alk. paper)
ISBN 978-0-8130-4921-2 (pbk.)
1. Junks. 2. Seafaring life—China. 3. Seafaring life—Pacific
Area. 4. Sailors—China—Travel. 5. China—Naval history.
I. Title.
VM101.V35 2007
910.9164—dc22   2007001299

The University Press of Florida is the scholarly publishing
agency for the State University System of Florida, comprising
Florida A&M University, Florida Atlantic University, Florida
Gulf Coast University, Florida International University, Florida
State University, New College of Florida, University of Central
Florida, University of Florida, University of North Florida, Uni-
versity of South Florida, and University of West Florida.

University Press of Florida
15 Northwest 15th Street
Gainesville, FL 32611-2079
http://www.upf.com

This book is dedicated to my father, Richard Van Tilburg,
who introduced me to the sea when I was eight years old
on board the sloop *Brunhilde.*

Contents

Illustrations

Tables

Foreword

Water is unquestionably the most important natural feature on earth. By volume, the world's oceans compose 99 percent of the planet's living space; in fact, the surface of the Pacific Ocean alone is larger than the combined surface area of all land bodies. So vital to life is water that NASA looks for signs of water as carefully as it does for air when testing whether moons or planets can sustain life. The story of human development is inextricably linked to the oceans, seas, lakes, and rivers that dominate the earth's surface. The University Press of Florida's series New Perspectives on Maritime History and Nautical Archaeology is devoted to exploring the significance of the earth's water while providing lively and important books that cover the spectrum of maritime history and nautical archaeology broadly defined. The series includes works that focus on the role of canals, rivers, lakes, and oceans in history; on the economic, military, and political use of those waters; and upon the people, communities, and industries that support maritime endeavors. Limited by neither geography nor time, volumes in the series contribute to the overall understanding of maritime history and can be read with profit by both general readers and specialists.

To date, there have been few studies of East Asian watercraft, certainly far fewer than of European, Mediterranean, or North American. All but one of the studies focus on river and coastal craft and virtually ignore the oceangoing junks of China. The single study of oceangoing junks focuses on the technical design and construction of the vessels themselves and ignores artistic and cultural details, their sailing qualities, and the extended voyages they undertook. Nor have there been many studies of the impact of vessels from one culture on foreigners, especially when those craft are viewed outside their native land. Thus this study of Chinese junks and the reception they received upon their arrival in Canada and the United States during the first half of the twentieth century adds significantly to understanding both the junks themselves and the impact of things foreign on the American imagination.

Using terminology exact enough for specialists, yet clear to a general reader, Hans Van Tilburg presents the first analysis in a Western language of the construction characteristics and operation of seagoing sailing junks. His account of the voyages of the junks from Asia to California also details conditions on these transpacific voyages at the end of the sailing era. Drawing on the fields of history, naval/maritime architecture, anthropology, and popular culture, Van Tilburg deftly places the junks in a cultural context by analyzing the reaction to those vessels by early twentieth-century Americans as reflected in newspaper articles and brochures published to promote visits to the vessels on both the Pacific and Atlantic coasts of the United States. The ways in which owners sought to "market" the ten sailing junks as tourist attractions also provide insights into early twentieth-century advertising and the promotion of leisure activities.

Van Tilburg eschews the labels *traditional* and *modern* when analyzing the ten vessels. Most were built for oceanic commerce, not as yachts or to serve as floating residences. Few were hybrid designs incorporating rudders or diesel engines. All appear to have been built by Chinese shipwrights using familiar patterns and methods of construction. Van Tilburg acknowledges that ten vessels form too small a sample to allow conclusive statements about oceangoing sailing junks as a class of ships or to develop categories of such vessels as others have done for riverine and coastal junks.

Equally important is the way in which Van Tilburg places the ten junks squarely in historical and cultural context. After analyzing the design and construction of the junks and describing their transpacific voyages, he tells an interesting story of popular American culture, how promoters financed their enterprises and tried to attract crowds, how newspapers reported such activities, and how popular reaction reflected the American view of the "mysterious" East. Most Americans viewed the vessels as curiosities worthy of only cursory examination, and none of the ships became the object of scholarly attention.

Thus, Hans Van Tilburg brings to the junks a long overdue examination, and in doing so he has produced a work of value to individuals in a variety of academic disciplines.

James C. Bradford
Gene A. Smith
Series editors

Preface and Acknowledgments

This eclectic work has grown slowly and in pieces over a number of years, first as a master's thesis at East Carolina University, and then as a Ph.D. dissertation at the University of Hawai'i. As such, many thoughtful scholars and colleagues have contributed much along the way. I would like to acknowledge the great assistance of Dr. Jerry Bentley and Dr. David Chappell, and the whole advisory committee at the university's history department. The subject of coastal studies in China is quite broad, and obviously the present work just scratches the surface. But professors in the UH history department unfailing welcomed the new perspective on nautical technology. Also, I would like to thank Dr. William Still Jr. and the maritime history and nautical archaeology faculty at East Carolina University for encouraging and supporting an interest in East Asia that stretched far beyond the realm of more usual thesis topics.

This study of ten voyages crosses bridges between several related disciplines, such as history, cultural anthropology, ethnographic studies, and maritime archaeology. These voyages can be seen from multiple perspectives. But the variety of analyses all come back to a single central object, a single event—the junks themselves carrying their crews across the ocean. For firsthand accounts I am indebted to the crew members of the *Free China*, who are soon to be featured in other documentaries as well. I wish them the best of luck in all their endeavors.

Images of historic junks are rare, and the curators and photo archivists of various institutions are too many to mention. A number of images come from published works, in some cases works that are out of print and by publishers which are out of business. Every effort has been made to locate the appropriate sources and individuals. If any images have been printed in error, please contact the publishers or the author.

Finally, to my wife, Maria, and daughter, Sabina, you have given me support for years beyond anything I could have expected or even deserve. I am sorry to say I am working on another book.

Slowly.

chapter 1

Junks, Not Just Floating Wood

Beginning in 1905, a handful of traditional Chinese sailing vessels, known as junks, sailed from China to North America across the Pacific. As a whole, these were not part of the modern export market of Chinese-built vessels seen commonly in today's marinas, craft specifically made in Hong Kong and Taiwan for West Coast yachtsmen and others; nor were most of these sailing vessels representative of modern hybrid wooden boat construction in China, incorporating European rudders and diesel engines and other features. The junks that sailed eastward across the Pacific were versions of true historical working vessels from the China coast. The arrival of these vessels allowed observers to catch a fleeting glimpse and gain some feeling for the nautical technology and seafaring culture of the Chinese people. Or they should have, if viewers back then had realized what had sailed into their view. For a host of reasons, though, many people almost totally misunderstood what they were seeing, misplacing the historical significance of the special features of these Asian vessels. This was true one hundred years ago, and in some surprising ways is still true today.

Historically, European travelers to East Asia had long observed that China possessed more ships than any other country in the world. China is now noted by many scholars as having had a significant maritime influence over the regions of East and Southeast Asia, and confirmed contacts as far west as Africa and the Red Sea. The Chinese economic giant dominated regional maritime trade for hundreds of years, and this included much trade under sail. Yet, if a survey of maritime history texts is any indication, solid details of Chinese maritime history and particularly the special advances in

Chinese nautical technology seem almost nonexistent. This seems a strange contradiction. What do we really know of Chinese sailing vessels?

What we do know has usually been limited to the work of a very small group of nautical specialists, old China hands who translated a small part of the existing technical data. Recently, though, Chinese ships have come into public view again. There is a resurgence in interest regarding the story of Admiral Zheng He and the Chinese armadas of the early fifteenth century, one usually focusing on the reportedly fantastic dimensions of the largest of the vessels involved, the "treasure galleons," or *baochuan*. This resurgence of interest in the epic Ming dynasty voyages has served to focus some attention on Chinese nautical technology. Notably though, that interest is limited to a specific, isolated period some six hundred years ago. There has not been much awareness of the much longer history of Chinese seafaring. There is more to the story.

Broadening our understanding of the evolution of nautical technology in China, seeing events like the Ming voyages in context, and recognizing that Chinese sailing traditions and constructions extended well into the nineteenth and twentieth centuries would help expand our view of East Asian seafaring. After all, large junks on long ocean passages were not inexplicable and rare phenomena of legendary times, but working vessels built in response to our common environment, the sea. Broadening the study of Chinese junks allows us to better understand comparisons between vessel designs across regions and through time. What are the differences between fifteenth- and nineteenth-century Chinese sailing craft? Between Chinese and western ships? European and American nautical experts found Chinese ship design to be highly advanced. Oddly, though, their technical treatises had little effect on public opinion. Why are we only now learning about Chinese ships built six hundred years ago? The Chinese have been very involved in seafaring for a very long time, but we foreigners have been slow to see the outlines of maritime history and nautical technology in China. Why did we ever turn away?

There are a number of reasons why Chinese junks have remained in the dark to us. Early twentieth-century observers in America typically regarded Chinese sailing junks as quaint and unwieldy creations constructed in the fashion of sea monsters, general appraisals including a mixture of surprise and contempt. Their views were recorded in articles and brochures published during the arrivals of the junks described here, an interesting genre of tourist literature. Sailing junks were generally assigned by the public to the vague time frame of "ancient," no matter when they were built. There existed a feeling that such sailing ships had changed little over the centuries,

even the millennia. It also seemed that, while these craft may have once succeeded in distant voyages, those that built them had little knowledge of the
art of ship construction, hence the stagnation of the design of these "ancient"
junks. The English term *junk* itself is obviously not likely to win praise in the
West. But what did these junks represent? What can we now say of some of
the last remaining Chinese working sailing vessels? Were they really representative of centuries of unchanging design? Or did the human tendency to
contrast "our" progress against "their" apparent backwardness obscure the
more dynamic nature of their evolution?

In order to answer these and other related questions, this book focuses
on a selection of ten Chinese junks that crossed the Pacific Ocean and were
displayed and documented, to greater or lesser degrees, in North America.
This is a focused study of a small sample of Chinese junks from the perspective of a foreign maritime scholar. As it turns out, the vessels featured here
represent some of the last commercial sailing junks of China, and certain
elements of their construction portray technological patterns developed
over centuries. There are presently few shipwrights who still possess the
knowledge of how to construct a sailing junk with the Chinese-style rudder
and masts stepped in Chinese fashion. While wooden boat construction still
continues, most if not all are fitted with diesel engines and numerous other
modern modifications. Evolution in design and use is natural, but these recent features radically change the overall construction of the original sailing
vessel. The transpacific junks presented here incorporate certain features no
longer seen anywhere else.

These junks that found their way to scattered ports in North America
were complex craft. Most represented successful regional designs of boats
tried and proven on long sailing voyages. Most seemed to have very little
trouble crossing the thousands of miles of ocean on their way to American
ports, where sometimes shocked spectators stood in astonishment at their
arrival. Observers' reactions provide an important source of information on
these junks, and also on the reasons why we know so little about them. Some
of these Chinese ships achieved a certain amount of local fame. Crowds
welcomed them in ports like Victoria, San Francisco, Los Angeles, Portland,
and San Diego, though often more as bizarre objects of fancy than as vessels
of any overt historical, technical, or anthropological interest. Some of them
served as public floating museums, displaying a variety of gruesome weaponry and other artifacts.

The majority of these ten junks eventually rotted, sank, or were scrapped.
Only two remain relatively intact. There has been no prior systematic study
of these ships, nor of their transpacific journeys. Few organized efforts were

made to preserve these vessels. This work attempts to reverse this oversight by examining these junks and voyages with two basic tasks in mind: first, to ascertain the historical significance of the vessels themselves by placing them within the known typology of Chinese ship construction for seagoing junks, in other words to explore the physical analysis of their construction; and second, to interpret the historical contexts of their overseas journeys. Where did they come from and what happened to them after they arrived? The answer to these questions involves an interdisciplinary approach, borrowing tools from the related disciplines of history, cultural anthropology, ethnographic studies, and maritime archaeology.

The physical analysis of these junks involves the technical description of Chinese ship construction. Changes in junk construction over time can be better understood once the basic elements of junk construction are defined. These basic elements are described in a combination of documentary and archaeological evidence. There is more to the analysis of ships, though, than simply the inventory of ship parts, or the repetition of length, beam, and draft measurements. Considering the complex nature of ship construction, the vessel *as a cultural artifact* can be read as a kind of text containing historical information. Yes, there is valuable technical information, but there is social and economic and even political information as well. The physical artifact of the sailing ship represents an expression of seafaring culture, for its construction encompasses numerous modifications and concessions to social and economic and political realities, in addition to the physical environment. This is a major hypothesis that serves as a foundation for this study: Chinese junks, and wooden sailing vessels in general, are more than merely machines for transportation; they are complex technological and cultural (and even political and economic) artifacts. As such, their form can be read as a kind of document of the past. Interpretation of the physical features of a ship allows a glimpse into a maritime lifestyle, a realm with no easy counterpart on land. This particular approach is borrowed from the field of material culture studies. Interpreting objects as documents provides one way of revealing meaning in material culture that might otherwise be lost in the trivialization of display.[1] Thus the physical analysis of these selected ships may be significant in two ways: first, as specific technical examples of historical ship types, transportation in the context of nautical evolution, and second, as cultural artifacts in and of themselves, symbols of meaning for a seafaring society.

A selection of ten junks does not provide a large enough sample for the development of a distinct typology of Chinese seagoing vessels. The technical analysis, therefore, must rely on available information and attempt to merge the small sample with the existing classifications. This involves a great deal of piecing together of scattered references and heavy reliance on a few certain documents, for unfortunately the most detailed sources available feature river junks and not coastal and ocean types. One exception to this rule is G.R.G. Worcester's *A Classification of the Principal Chinese Sea-Going Junks (South of the Yangtze)*. It is the only known detailed attempt to categorize historic ocean-sailing junks, albeit only for a specific period and given location. Worcester's *Classification* provides a helpful technical framework for understanding these ten vessels.

The second broad task of this investigation involves understanding the particular historical circumstances of the transpacific voyages. These selected vessels may not have been the first craft to have made the voyage from East Asia across the Pacific, nor were they the only Chinese-built vessels on the West Coast. There is after all a nineteenth-century history of Chinese maritime activity in the Americas, as well as of Japanese junks landing on American shores. Where do the recorded transpacific voyages fall within this context? And what influences color the historical interpretation of these exotic arrivals? Much of the primary information recorded about these distant arrivals naturally reflects the specific social and political context of the times. Western attitudes toward their Asian neighbors were strained by a number of cultural and economic forces. The newspaper and journal articles that commented on the successful crossings contain a great deal of cultural baggage concerning how certain observers on the American coast viewed the maritime history and technological achievements of the Chinese, or of any nonwestern culture. As this second line of investigation involves different perceptions of differing cultures, the methodology employed here involves more ethnohistorical interpretation. Do descriptions of these vessels tell us more about Chinese maritime history, or more about American perceptions of a distant Asian Other? Understanding the historical setting for these voyages makes it easier to see why American public perceptions of Chinese ships differ so widely from those of maritime historians and nautical specialists.

The format for this study progresses through differing themes involving these junks. Following this introductory chapter, chapter 2 provides the overviews of the historical stories, as much description of the individual voyages as is possible from the existing sources. Chapter 3 establishes the basic construction data used to analyze these specific vessels, and then examines each in as much depth as possible, ending with some broader historical interpretations of the physical forms. Chapter 4 moves from the realm of nautical technology into the related fields of cultural history, seafaring folklore, and maritime popular religion, focusing on the "nonfunctional" features of the junks. Chapter 5 examines the historical settings of these junks in China, the Pacific, and the American West Coast, seeking in the historical context the roots of our misunderstandings of these vessels. Chapter 6 looks at these perceptions directly, through the analysis of public documents such as published articles and newspaper stories, and the complications of perception and display. Finally, chapter 7 offers a few general conclusions. A partial Chinese-English glossary, admittedly incomplete, offers some assistance for parts of the junk discussion, and hints at the possibilities for further comparative analysis of historical nautical terms.

Obviously, the ability to remain intellectually flexible when working between the related but separate academic disciplines of history, anthropology, and archaeology is crucial to this work. This is a broad-reaching study, attempting far more than is justified with such a small sample and such limited documentation. Primary and secondary written materials, oral traditions, paintings, and photographs are juxtaposed with construction details and archaeological site investigations. Flexibility is most necessary simply because there are very few thorough treatments of the subject, and a variety of sources must be considered. Hopefully this book may shed some light on the general question of how history and anthropology might be combined in the investigation of the human past. Ten Chinese junks offer a sample candidate for this hybrid approach.

It is tempting to label these transpacific junks as examples of *traditional* Chinese ship construction, and indeed that term is used within the study, but this must be accompanied with caution in a work that overtly examines the concept of traditional Chinese ship design itself. The term *traditional* can be problematic, particularly when mistaken for a fixed and unchanging measure of a foreign culture, a definition forever frozen as an artificial snapshot. Wooden sailing vessels, composed of many different individual features, fall into a broad continuum between extremes of very established "old" and very introductory "new" features. Innovations in ship design emerge locally, or are adopted from foreign sources, or spring from a combination of these two or other influences. Instead of simply claiming that some junks are traditional while others are not, junk construction and design evolution might be better understood broken down into component features. Some features reflect common Chinese usage over a long period of time, while others are comparatively new. For instance, hull shape and the use of internal partitions known as bulkheads extend far into the Chinese past, but features such as standing rigging or upright capstans, both of which find use on junks in the nineteenth century, do not. The nature of specific construction features, and the combination of these features themselves, changes over time. The comparison is not one of a traditional junk versus a nontraditional junk, but varying combinations of older and newer features on junks, which as a group change over time.

The main hypothesis here is that these junks are representative of historic and significant Chinese sailing designs, and that by examining these vessels and these voyages in a careful manner, it is possible to contribute to our knowledge of East Asian maritime history in the Pacific, to gain an insight into the much larger picture of Chinese nautical technology and its evolution, and to begin to understand how it is that we know so little about Chinese ships. The ten junks that sailed into our western awareness serve as the primary documents. The task ahead is to explore how such documents can be read, and, following that, to reveal what they have to say.

A Note on Sources

There are simply very few places to go for a truly accurate and contextualized view of Chinese *oceangoing* junks. This includes Chinese and western sources, thus the importance of working with more contemporary examples and looking backward into the past, assessing their significance. Invariably the rare article or treatise on Chinese junks falls under the oriental heading or "Far East." The question is asked "Far from what?" The answer is "Far from everything familiar to us." Thousands of years of maritime activity in Arabia and South Asia are often condensed into a one-page treatment of the ubiquitous dhow, itself a type of misnomer. And the millennia of maritime history in East and Southeast Asia, likewise, appear often as a single treatment of the generic junk, another misnomer. There is no single junk, as there is no single China during the long dynastic period. Symptomatic to this perhaps, neither *dhow* nor *junk* are terms truly native to their appropriate regions. *Dhow* is a Swahili term for local vessels, from the mixture of Bantu and Arabic; *junk* comes from Southeast Asia via Portugal, a term for local Southeast Asian vessels.

Chinese shipwrights were the first to develop the median rudder, the balanced rudder, and transverse interior bulkheads. Chinese mariners may have been the first to use the compass for navigation. Chinese vessels featured some very advanced hydrodynamic designs and efficient airfoil sails. What excludes them from more extensive coverage in the general maritime texts?

What has and has not been written about any given topic, such as Chinese maritime history, is a telling statement in its own right. Researchers such as

Leonard Blussé, Jennifer Cushman, Gang Deng, Robert Antony, Sarasin Viraphol, and others have all contributed greatly to our general understanding of the Chinese maritime realm, but frankly a detailed treatment based on Chinese maritime technology, on the kind of technological evolution so well represented for the West in the studied progression from ancient Mediterranean vessels to Viking longships to oceanic galleons, does not exist for the East Asian world. Only a rare few sources, including those based on archaeological studies of Song–Ming period shipwrecks, attempt to make a detailed study of Chinese ship construction available to anyone, let alone westerners. The pickings are, indeed, scarce. But where does one begin to investigate the evolution of Chinese junks?

In general, documentary sources on Chinese junks can be divided into several basic categories: first, rare individual articles in western nautical journals, chiefly from the 1920s and 1930s, focusing on ship construction; second, a few chapters included in larger works by modern historians of maritime China, featuring information on the economic role in overseas trade, or recent technical summaries of archaeological findings, such as Sean McGrail's comprehensive *Boats of the World*; third, brief firsthand descriptions by westerners who encountered or traveled on Chinese junks in the nineteenth and early twentieth centuries; fourth, the very rare monographs produced by scholars specializing in East Asia and nautical technology, such as G. R. G. Worcester and Joseph Needham; fifth, Chinese language secondary sources, and sixth, miscellaneous works. Interestingly, in all of these categories, photographs of vessels and shipyards in China are very rare. Newspaper articles are not included in categories here, being more a matter for the historical ethnographers than for the historians of maritime technology.

What seems to be missing are primary documents recorded by the generations of maritime Chinese themselves regarding traditional coastal commercial sailing junks. The reason Chinese records on private commercial vessels are so scarce is a matter of some speculation. Merchants, fishermen, and sailors who went overseas and had contact with foreign cultures did not form the most respectable class of Chinese elite. Private shipping was often not a high priority to the official chroniclers of the Confucian Chinese Empire. And sailors in not only the Chinese culture but in many cultures the world over are not usually noted as being among the first ranks of the literate. In the words of Paul Chow, navigator of the junk *Free China*, "We were the first generation of fishermen to read and write."[2]

Individual articles from western journals capture a small portion of detailed junk data. These articles range from the mid-nineteenth century to the late twentieth century. Most of them, though, originate from the 1920s and 1930s. In the nineteenth century, not only the treaty ports opened to foreign trade on the coast, but some interior areas of China as well, were carved into spheres of foreign influence. Major imperial offices, such as the Chinese Maritime Customs Service, were placed under foreign control, though these did make a clear effort to serve the imperial structure. The Service was acquainted with some of the junks, but could not hope to fully comprehend or control domestic shipping. Sir Robert Hart, in 1873, stated, "Of native trade in the interior, and the movement of native produce and foreign goods along the coast in Chinese junks, we know nothing."[3] The rare firsthand articles on Chinese junks, then, date to this period and the decades that followed. Illustrations in these articles range from none to fair, though not many ventured measured plans. There are few photographs from these early years.

Nautical chapters in larger works, sometimes included as a side note in broader histories of maritime China, feature information on ship construction from several modern scholars. Until recently the intention of these works was not to inspect individual examples of junks, nor to lay bare the technological evolution that created the complex artifact of the vessel, but to shed light on the maritime relationships and realities of the social and economic and political past in Asia. That is no small task, and such efforts open a large and fertile subject area for research. Discussion of the types of ships involved, while not extensive, is therefore well fixed in historical context. Familiarity with nautical technology might require this somewhat specific historical background. Jennifer Wayne Cushman, in her *Fields from the Sea: Chinese Junk Trade with Siam during the Late Eighteenth and Early Nineteenth Centuries,* deals directly with the long-distance coastal merchant vessels involved in the junk trade to Southeast Asia. Cushman devotes a chapter entitled "Chinese Maritime Sailing Vessels" to the broad discussion of junk classification.

Only a few years ago comparative summaries of the recent archaeological studies of Chinese shipwrecks were nonexistent. With the recent publication of Sean McGrail's *Boats of the World* and specific works by other authors this is now changing. The number of underwater sites and information on hull structure and artifact remains now contribute directly to our understanding of maritime China. McGrail devotes almost fifty pages of his substantial work to Chinese junks, covering a wide range of years and perspectives, and summarizing the most fruitful of the studies. The majority of wreck sites are from a China hundreds of years in the past. Can these inform the examination of nineteenth- and twentieth-century junks?

Primary impressions by nineteenth-century travelers, western observers in China who witnessed, recorded, and sometimes sailed on Chinese ships, make up another type of source. Western missionaries, diplomats, and merchant adventurers found themselves very early on in close contact with coastal populations. Their journals and reports reveal much that has not yet come to light in any other form. Their observations provide important clues to what life was like within the junk trade, and their descriptions of the vessels add to the body of data. This remains true no matter that some of their observations were more influenced by cultural bias than others. It is often the case that initial impressions of the totally unfamiliar tell us as much about the observer (if not more) than of the observed.

There are a number of specialized monographs that focus specifically on the nautical technology of Chinese vessels, though not many deal systematically with the topic. The majority are sketchbooks, notes on vessels casually observed and equally casually commented upon, meant for quick and easy consumption in the West. Only a few works truly delve into the subject with a passion. One of the best known monumental works on the subject of ancient Chinese vessels is Joseph Needham's *Nautics* volume in his immense *Science and Civilization in China.* This is one of only two works to include any photographs of historic Chinese junks in serious analysis. Needham's scope begins with the very origins of seafaring in Asia and stretches all the way to the twentieth century. Within this broad spectrum, sailing junks within the past several hundred years occupy only a minor segment at the end. The theoretical treatment of elements of nautical technology, however, is solidly laid forth, and his contributions have yet to be paralleled. His work was completed before many of the more recent archaeological studies made their debut.

George Raleigh Gray Worcester, a sailor by profession (midshipman in the Royal Navy), served for thirty years as the river inspector at Shanghai for the Chinese Maritime Customs Service. The inspector general at the time, Sir Frederick Maze, released him to survey Chinese maritime technology inland up the Yangzi River. Eight years of fieldwork culminated in three years of detention in a Japanese interment camp for both the river inspector and his wife. He later published five definitive works on Chinese junks of the Yangzi Basin, supervised the construction of the Maze collection of junk models, and served for seven years as the editor for *The Mariner's Mirror.*[4] He is generally recognized as the single authority on traditional Chinese sailing vessels of the early twentieth century, with one important restriction. His work attempts to be comprehensive for a single large region only, focusing, as it states, on the junks and sampans of the Yangzi River, not seagoing coastal junks (though fortunately he includes the Fuzhou pole junk in this category as a vessel frequenting the lower reaches of the waterway).

Oddly enough, there are only a few scarce Chinese nautical sources that describe in detail the types of traditional sailing junks in China in the nineteenth century. It becomes quickly obvious, though, when searching for specific material on the nineteenth-century junks, that ship construction in China during this period meant, for most concerned, the construction of a modern steam navy, under the direction of Li Hongzhang and other modernizers responding to the foreign threat. Such emphasis addressed the most critical issue of the period, strengthening the country in the face of western pressure. The design of wooden sailing vessels at this time, long taken for granted, was understandably completely overshadowed. In the words of Joseph Needham, "systematic nautical treatises did not arise in Chinese culture, or at least did not get into print."[5] However, there is much more in China to be learned. This work only begins to consider the Chinese language sources relevant to the nineteenth- and twentieth-century study of junks. Chinese researchers, much more familiar with the subject, will no doubt find much that is either lacking or incorrect within these pages—and hopefully correct these oversights in future publications.

For historical significance and information on activities and settings for these Chinese vessels, the above sources are absolute necessities. Most contribute little, though, by way of real information on the actual construction process of the junk itself. The basic reasons for this are common to cultures far beyond China's borders. Traditional vessels of seafaring people were typically never built by plans or documents, but by "eye," the knowledge being passed from person to person within a closed guild or community of shipwrights. This was as much art form as industrial enterprise. China is certainly not alone in this respect. For western vessels, this situation only began to change in the eighteenth century, when a conscious effort was made to inject scientific construction techniques into the previously closed and closely guarded art of the shipwrights. This situation changed later for China, an empire that had not seen the need for such an effort until the attempt was made to establish a modern steamship yard at Fuzhou in the mid-nineteenth century. As with other seafaring cultures, no one is absolutely certain how historic junks in China were really built, for few people recorded details before there seemed to be a reason to intentionally and carefully record such things.

Junk construction is at heart a statement of maritime culture, the vessel itself the best real document of the past practices of the Chinese seafaring population. Junks are technological artifacts, cultural wonders, and much more. What can be said of the state of scholarship on Chinese junks? This study is not just an introductory technical analysis of nineteenth-century vessels, but a work that recognizes that what we know about these junks is inextricably linked to our social environment, both past and present. Our understanding seems to mirror the state of scholarship on other vernacular vessels—incomplete at best, but hopefully showing signs of improving in the eleventh hour. As Worcester pointed out, such glimpses of a historic seafaring world are becoming exceedingly rare. "Although I have sometimes written in the present tense, it must be understood that everything in these pages concerns the Old China, the China that has gone for ever. . . ."[6]

chapter 2

The Journeys Across the Pacific

The Pacific Ocean encompasses over 69 million square miles. It is the largest, deepest ocean in the world, fringed by at least eleven separate seas, stretching some 9,300 nautical miles from Panama to Mindanao. The populations in this study, East Asia and America, are only two of many cultures brought into contact by the sea highways within this wide region. And it is the ship, the tool of contact on, in, and across the Pacific, which is of particular interest here. The technology of the sailing junks served as the bridge between the distant shores. The ocean at once unites cultures in a maritime encounter and serves as a kind of barrier or filter, removing the vessels that failed to complete the crossing.[1]

For any mariner attempting to sail eastward across the ocean, the route will include weeks of variable weather and long stretches of isolation. Of course, some paths are better than others. The route eastward across the North Pacific pioneered by Spanish mariners in 1564 proved useful for hundreds of years. This involved running north past Japan and turning east near latitude 40 degrees north, taking advantage of the prevailing westerlies and currents in the North Pacific. This is still the most dependable and fastest crossing available.[2] When viewed properly with a globe, the great circle course from southern China to the western coast of North America appears much more of a straight and direct route than the inherently distorted spherical projections on flat surfaces, such as with the common Mercator representations. The great circle route swings northward in close contact with the eastern coast of Japan.

For Europeans, successful Pacific crossings began in 1521, when Magellan's small Spanish fleet staggered northwestward from the Strait of Magellan and, via Guam, into Portuguese territory in the East Indies. Magellan's circumnavigation did not represent a reliable and easily achieved passage, though, but a story of luck and survival. Storms, disease, and starvation would continue to make such long westward-bound voyages a hazard for many a sailor. The ships might be able to withstand the journey, but often their human passengers could not.

Then the Spanish navigator Andrés de Urdaneta discovered his way back to New Spain by sailing eastward across the Pacific in 1564. This made the complete circumnavigation of the globe unnecessary, and avoided transgressing into what was, by Papal decree, Portuguese territory in Southeast Asia. Urdaneta sailed with the clockwise rotation of the prevailing North Pacific high–pressure system, running up the western Pacific past Japan, crossing at about 40 degrees north latitude, and then due south along the American coastline. He discovered the North Pacific "express route," highlighted by winds and currents favorable to the Pacific region round trip. In short order the Manila galleon route was established as a fairly regular Pacific trade route for more than two hundred years. The Chinese may have already been aware of this current, now called the Kuroshio, as early as the fourth century B.C., during the Warring States period.[3]

Historians in the Pacific are of course well aware that indigenous voyagers had already blazed long maritime highways between remote landfalls. Pacific Islander migration, as outlined in current Lapita pottery theory, occurred much earlier and over a much longer expanse of time than the Manila galleon trade.[4] It is postulated that much of the journey followed a route eastward along the equatorial latitudes, or in other words *into* the prevailing winds. Explorers may have taken advantage of seasonal weather variations to progress eastward, and then could always rely on normal weather patterns to return home. Wayfinding targeted groups of islands, whole archipelagos, rather than individual islands or points in the ocean, and included an intimate knowledge of sea states, reefs, weather, stars, and birdlife. These migrations from Southeast Asia eastward utilizing Pacific voyaging canoes are among the boldest examples of seafaring in human history. The oral and archaeological traces of indigenous Pacific voyaging paint a picture that matches, if not exceeds, the scale of western voyages of Pacific exploration, such as those conducted by Bougainville, Kruzenstern, Vancouver, and Cook.

Compared to these events and explorations, very little is said concerning incidental Chinese junk voyages into or across the Pacific. Regional histories place China's maritime sphere of influence in East and Southeast Asia, and from there westward across the Indian Ocean. The Pacific seemed to be the edge of the world, from which Chinese voyagers could not return. But some Chinese Pacific voyages did take place.

Circumstantial evidence suggests the possibility of Chinese maritime activity in the Pacific as early as the Shang dynasty in 1200 B.C. There are other intriguing clues, but such material is rare and controversial at best. When it comes to asking what is really known about Chinese Pacific crossings, historic examples of ten Chinese junks beginning in 1905 provide a much more solid foundation for research than distant legend. So why have these more recent passages not been investigated? They were not "firsts," they did not open a new passage, but crossed in the wake of others. They were sailing in a time when steamships were the preferred mode of transportation. The realities of anti-Chinese fervor in America, chaotic social conditions in China, and the underlying fact that the Chinese imperial government did not aggressively seek overseas maritime colonies combined to muddy the waters. This last attitude was in distinct contrast to the way that some European nations, particularly England, evolved to dominate maritime trade. In China most of the overseas contacts had been matters for private merchants, not concerns for state-supported missions. Most of the Pacific crossings were conducted in vessels built by families or small groups of private merchants investing in their own livelihoods. The kind of coastal trade they were engaged in, dominated by seafaring Chinese far from the imperial capital, had little of official nature about it. Scholars of Chinese maritime history point out that few details are known about any aspect of overseas private trade, this being "largely a result of a long denial by the elite class in China of private overseas trade activities."[5]

If records on overseas voyages originating from China seem scarce, the subset of Pacific junk crossings is smaller still. Existing documentation comes mainly in the form of popular media notices upon their arrivals on the West Coast. There is little that is reliable or scientific about it. Records regarding the voyages of these transpacific vessels are unevenly distributed. They mainly consist of widely scattered newspaper articles and brief notice in secondary sources. Only ten junks of the list in table 1, marked by asterisks, provide enough, or indeed any, information for inclusion in this study. And not all ten of the selected vessels succeeded in making it to the far shore.

Crossing the Pacific was no small task, and a successful crossing must have been cause for celebration. Typhoons, or tropical storms at or near hurricane strength, threaten the North Pacific from June to November, most

Table 1. Historic Junks Voyaging in the Pacific

Name	Destination	Year	Disposition
unknown	San Francisco	1849	unknown
unknown (5)[1]	Baja, Mexico	1850	wrecked
unknown (8)	Mendocino	1852	unknown
unknown (2)	Monterey	1854	unknown
Whang Ho *	San Francisco	1905	unknown
Ning Po *	San Diego	1912	abandoned in Catalina
Amoy *	Victoria	1922	sunk in Pamlico Sound
Fou Po II *	Moloka'i	1935	wrecked in Moloka'i
Hummel Hummel *	San Pedro	1938	beached in Papua
Sea Dragon *	San Francisco	1939	lost at sea
Tai Ping	Vancouver	1939	unknown
Cheng Ho *	Tahiti	1939	beached in Papeete
Mon Lei *	San Francisco	1947	unknown in Manhattan
Free China *	San Francisco	1955	San Francisco yard
High Tea	San Francisco	1959	unknown
Golden Lotus	Auckland	1961	unknown
One Step	Sydney	1964	wrecked
Beihai junk *	Portland	1989	Portland park

Note: [1]Numbers in parentheses indicate number of junks reported in that year.

during August and September. Conditions on board wooden sailing vessels can be appalling, especially if those vessels are said to be among the oldest wooden ships left afloat in the world. Sometimes the sources capture these realities, but in general we need to peer between the lines and imagine life on board these groaning wooden ships and beneath creaking, snapping sails. This is the human side to the story of these crossings.

Perspectives on Ship Histories

Sometimes maritime narratives rely too frequently on individual ship descriptions alone, the dates for building, launching, statistics and plans, horsepower of the marine plant, when in service, when laid up—facts repeated in a variety of different formats. Notice the way we write about the *Titanic* or *Bismarck*. Such portrayal essentially amounts to an individual life history of what is, after all, an inanimate object. This is not an attempt to avoid social comment, but an honest byproduct of our romantic attachment to seafaring topics. It is a mark of the importance of *The Ship* to seafaring cultures—but there is little in the way of larger historical treatment. As one historian has put it, such works risk being categorized as "popular history, in which complex processes are ignored in favor of antiquarianism—

amassing facts without significant interpretation—or reduced to single dramatic moments."[6] Shipwrecks are always popular. Of course, nautical converts, of whom I am admittedly one, relish the anthropomorphic approach to the histories of individual floating objects. Nonetheless, I have to agree with the impression that ship histories often lack significant theoretical treatment or historical context.

Why restrict ourselves to a single ship, or focus only on those most famous and/or tragic of stories? Archaeologists have, for a long time, realized the importance of the commonplace and more mundane objects, the typical working craft, usually taken for granted. These reflect the experiences of the majority, not just the first-class, upper-deck elite. Carefully measured drawings of barges and colliers and lumber schooners in archaeological reports have an important place in the study of the past. But as often as not, they are sketches of only the artifacts, devoid of all occupants. In short, there is nobody on board, the human element is missing. Yet it is exactly that human element that infuses ships with history, with meaning. A dinghy is a dinghy. But Captain William Bligh's open boat voyage of some thirty-six hundred miles to salvation in the Dutch East Indies is a story. Rusting metal is not very interesting to most, until the name *Titanic* is emblazoned on the stern. The *Mayflower*, the *Golden Hind*, the U.S.S. *Arizona*, these are ships that stand as cultural symbols, interpreted within the nation-building context. We package our history in them.

This, then, is where we begin this study, with the packages of the junk stories, the less-than-glamorous vessels and the sailors who brought them across the largest ocean in the world. Unlike the above-named ships, these packages are not automatically a part of American or European history. They were Chinese artifacts, though the majority of the crews that transported these junks were usually American. It is no coincidence that the junks best represented in western records were manned by westerners. Even when crews were mixed, Americans were usually in charge. Their stories, then, are not purely Chinese, but are relegated to the Pacific Basin, to a dynamic multicultural region joined by the water highway. These junks function as transnational and transcultural tools, freely purchased, traded, or stolen by seafaring peoples between China and America. This is part of the nature of the maritime world. For these artifacts, borders have little meaning. The junks have significance for both Chinese and American people.

Overall, it is how these junks were used that imparts the most obvious meanings for the public that received them. Their Pacific voyage stands out as the predominant feature for their western audiences, previous incarnations being of less interest to observers at the time. A machine for sustenance will be appraised with respect, often being granted anthropological or technological importance; a carnival ride will be an object of no serious consequence. What happened to the vessels' significance in the journey across the Pacific? What then to make of these Chinese junks from across the seas?

Stories of the Voyages

THE *WHANG HO*

The story of the *Whang Ho,* though light on details about the ship itself, gives us a strange and amusing tale about the way Chinese junks were used by western businessmen. Reports vary as to the exact origins of the *Whang Ho.* Some say that the junk was built new in Shanghai by order of an American citizen, W. M. Milne, an entrepreneur from Southern California who knew a good entertainment scheme when he saw one. With his ties to the movie industry, Milne was familiar with promoting opportunities as tourist attractions.[7] He brought the junk over to America for exhibition purposes, wanting an exact replica of an authentic Chinese war junk. Other reports state that Milne purchased the quite used one-hundred-plus-year-old *Whang Ho* directly from the viceroy of Nanjing himself, and then ran into trouble when the Chinese government refused to allow the *Whang Ho* to depart native waters.[8] The price for war junks of this period, including their complete outfit of cannon and rifles, was estimated at 8,000 Mexican dollars.[9]

Questions in the United States revolved around whether the war junk was truly an official vessel of the Chinese imperial government and would be vouched for by the same. Should the *Whang Ho* receive honors the same way any vessel representing a sovereign nation should? Or was the junk, officially registered by no one, a foreign maverick subject to detention, confiscation, and destruction? After all, American authorities were on the lookout for Chinese vessels coming into American waters illegally, and all needed to be clearly identified. The history of anti-Chinese agitation on the West Coast during the decades near the turn of the century is well known. Chinese immigration, for a host of reasons, was not welcomed by Americans.

However the dilemma was settled, the vessel set out in 1906 under the command of Captain Mark Allen Graham, formerly an officer of the steamship *Roanoke.* Not much is known about the crossing itself, except that it was said to be as thrilling as some of the voyages of the adventurous Sir Francis Drake, and that Milne, who was on board, was able to bring it to a successful conclusion only after suffering imminent disaster at every moment. The *Whang Ho* arrived at San Pedro in October. She made the port of San Francisco under sail on December 8, 1906, and was taken under tow by the steam schooner *Aurelia* at least as far north as Portland, Oregon, for an extended stay of approximately one year.[10]

Milne planned to exploit the exotic nature of such a vessel to its fullest, but apparently the public was not as cooperative about the venture, and the vessel did not meet the earning expectations of her managers. Plans were then laid for the *Whang Ho* to continue on to Coney Island, New York, by way of the Strait of Magellan, in search of more profitable pastures. The *Whang Ho* Company, founded in San Francisco, obtained sufficient financial backing, and Captain Graham was given charge of the trip into the Atlantic. The junk set out from Portland on January 4, 1908, arriving to provision for the long voyage in San Francisco later that same month. Here begin the details of the strange demise of the rare Chinese war junk.

Allegedly Captain Graham, after having passed the entrance to the harbor, slipped over the side and made his escape by small boat. A warrant was later issued for his arrest, brought by one of the stockholders of the *Whang Ho* Company. He was eventually placed on trial for felony embezzlement. Exactly why he abandoned the junk may never be known. There was some comment at the time, though, that old vessels like the *Whang Ho*, especially when tremendously over-insured, had a nasty habit of disappearing without a trace. Indeed, that would be one method of making the ship pay, a method familiar to shipowners past and present. The *Whang Ho*, continuing onward, encountered heavy seas near Cape Horn. With its huge rudder damaged, it turned back for repairs at Papeete, Tahiti.[11] The crew immediately deserted, apparently displeased with the junk and her voyage, and returned to America on the steamer *Mariposa*. A new crew assembled for the *Whang Ho*, and a Captain Helms signed on for $2,000 to complete the journey, and once again the junk set out for New York in May of 1908.[12]

For several months there were no reports of any sightings of the *Whang Ho*, and the junk was placed on the overdue list in a number of locations. It was not until November, when the British steamer *Moana* arrived in Victoria, that news surfaced. *Whang Ho* had been picked up by a cutter and towed to Thursday Island, the junk itself in a dismantled condition. One source reports that from there the *Whang Ho* made passage to Sydney, Australia, arriving at the end of 1908 and again causing a stir amid shipping circles.[13] The final disposition for this wayward ship, the proper ending to the story, remains unknown.

THE *NING PO*

Though not many are aware of the significance of some rotting timbers on Catalina Island, the remains of one of the most historic transpacific Chinese vessels rest buried in the mud some few miles off the Los Angeles coastline. The *Ning Po* was a 138-foot, 500-ton, Fuzhou-style coastal Chinese cargo vessel. When the *Ning Po* arrived on the West Coast in 1913, she became the most exotic vessel from the East, serving as a floating museum for a while. What sold the most tickets were stories of bizarre tortures, blood flowing in the scuppers, rebel heads bouncing across the decks, etc. A local pirate celebrity, the *Ning Po* is still the subject of museum displays and short articles. The story of this junk has been told continuously for almost one hundred years. Yet, as is all too common, it has become difficult to separate fact from fiction. The exact balance between the two remains unknown. Some journalists stated, "Garbled and ludicrous stories . . . have so taxed the credibility of readers that her true history has been as much obscured as are her splintery remains."[14]

There is little enough certainty about the origins of this particular vessel. G.R.G. Worcester, customs inspector for the maritime service in Shanghai, recorded several large Fujian craft, similar pole junks, in the early decades of the twentieth century as having been more than 150 years old, a testimony to their extremely heavy, overbuilt construction. It is not too incredible, therefore, to suggest that the junk was indeed built in the eighteenth century. If western secondary sources quoting oral testimony at the time can be believed, the *Ning Po* was built either in 1753 or 1806, under the name *Kin Tai Fong*.[15] Most sources report the 1753 date, stating that the junk was built in Fuzhou, China.[16] The junk was described as being the fastest, best-equipped Chinese vessel on the coast. Apparently, soon after being launched, the *Kin Tai Fong* turned smuggler and slaver, allegedly taking part in a rebellion against the government in 1796, a time when pirates were particularly active in southern China. Next, she was seized for smuggling silk and opium and slave girls, and again for piracy in 1806, and again in 1814 and in 1823. It is said that 960 slave girls could be fitted below decks for the trip to Canton, a measure of volume generally unfamiliar to maritime historians.[17] In 1834, the *Kin Tai Fong* was reportedly confiscated by Lord Napier for smuggling and slaving activity. In 1841, she began her seven-year stint of serving the imperial government as a prison ship. Reportedly, 158 rebels, whom the government found too expensive to feed, were summarily executed during this time, hence the grisly tales of blood running in the scuppers and heads bouncing across the decks. In 1861 she was seized by *Taiping* rebels, heavenly warriors fighting against the imperial army and confounding western missionaries with their homegrown brand of Christianity, and converted into a fast transport. Retaken by English forces, her name was changed (reportedly) by General Charles George "Chinese" Gordon, one of several western figures involved in aiding the imperial government against the massive social uprising in southern China. She became the *Ning Po,* named after a major coastal city. In 1864 she fought in the battle of Nanjing.[18]

The story weaves back to outright piracy, holding that for some years after 1884 the *Ning Po* made a pretty good living preying on wealthy European tourists in and around Hong Kong. Lured by fine cuisine and the prospect of an enchanting moonlight tour of the local islands, unsuspecting passengers soon found themselves robbed of all personal belongings, including clothing, and quickly set ashore on some out-of-the-way spot. British authorities soon sent the Royal Navy after the literal tourist trap. A sister ship, the *Kwang Su,* was sunk by the H.M.S. *Challenger,* and this apparently was enough to convince the *Ning Po*'s crew that further resistance was futile when they were overhauled by the H.M.S. *Westgate.*[19] The crew was imprisoned, and the vessel was sold in Hong Kong. Exactly how many owners the *Ning Po* had is hard to say; certainly she outlived some of them. The amount of truth in the story, well-worn and generally unreferenced, is also difficult to ascertain.

In 1911 she was captured by Chinese revolutionaries in Hankow, and the following year sold to a group of American tourists for $50,000. The express purpose was to sail her to America and place her on exhibit at various ports.[20] Two attempts were made to cross the Pacific. After having been damaged in a couple of typhoons, abandoned by a mutinous crew, and towed back to port after yet another storm, the *Ning Po* finally succeeded in crossing the Pacific under the able command of German captain Jes Toft and a fourteen-man crew of Scandinavian and Chinese sailors. The captain received his orders from none other than William M. Milne of Pasadena, who had found himself another junk after the demise of the *Whang Ho.* The intention was to bring the vessel over in good time for the 1915 Panama-Pacific Exposition in San Francisco.

The junk made the run from Yokohama, Japan, to San Pedro, California, along the North Pacific express route, 40 degrees north, in a relatively fast fifty-eight days, December 12, 1912, to February 19, 1913. The passage was not easy. Storms split the main boom, cracked water casks, and opened seams in the aging hull. When she was spotted off the coast by the steamer *Honolulu,* crowds in Southern California prepared themselves for her arrival. In response to a hail from the steamer offering to transfer food, Captain Toft reportedly answered "send us a keg of beer!"[21] Hundreds of curious onlookers met the Chinese ship, yet the junk did not stay long. The *Ning Po* left the Port of San Pedro on February 22 for a more picturesque and publicly accessible setting moored off Venice, California, where it was open to the public for 25 cents per person. She was towed to San Diego briefly, to test the tourist waters there. Later she returned to San Pedro, after supposedly putting out under tow from the steamer *Shoshone* bound for San Francisco, a voyage she never completed.[22]

Thus she began her career as a floating attraction and museum of bizarre torture implements in Los Angeles, Long Beach, and San Diego. The junk arrived well stocked on the West Coast for such a role, boasting beheading swords, starvation cages, rusting ancient cannon, pikes, spears, a beheading block, and even a makeshift "dungeon" in the stern. It seems that the show, though, was not as successful as the backers had wished. Faced initially with a tonnage tax on the order of $600–$800, and then with a civil court claim for back wages of $450 due the crew, the slowing trickle of two-bit customers proved inadequate. Milne expressed his intentions of voyaging through the Panama Canal and on to better venues on the eastern seaboard, much like he had planned for the *Whang Ho* years earlier. From there it would be onward to all the principal ports of Europe. These plans were laid before November 18, though, when the junk *Ning Po* parted her anchor chain and went onto the rocks in a storm off Dead Man's Island.

Following the grounding, Milne quickly arrived from Pasadena. Together with First Officer Albert Wiborg, who narrowly escaped the shipwreck, they managed to haul ashore as many curios and relics as possible.[23] The junk sank in shallow water, the upper decks still exposed. Hardhat divers and the salvage tug *Crescent* managed, after four days of work, to refloat the vessel, and she was taken to the Fulton and Woodley Shipbuilding Yard at Mormon Island, and then hauled out at Craig Shipbuilding Company in Long Beach for completion of the extensive repairs to her wooden form.

By this point Milne had had enough of the *Ning Po* and its related expenses, and in 1914 he sold her to the Meteor Boat Company of Los Angeles. The Meteor Company was run by Walter Hubbard, a Los Angeles auto dealer, and Charles Lochard, later manager of the Los Angeles Angels baseball team.[24] She re-entered her career in the entertainment business when the Meteor Company opened her for visitors at the municipal dock in Long Beach. "Outside of its very great age and interesting points of construction, the ship's contents, though gruesome, would have a great educational value to the ordinary person."[25] An even larger collection of destructive implements, many of dubious antiquity and authenticity, came on board from various and sundry collections.

The *Ning Po* briefly appeared moored at Catalina Island, twenty-six miles off the Los Angeles coastline. Her first port of call on Catalina was Avalon Harbor itself, where a Mr. Knowles put on "special dinners and novelty entertainment."[26] These included an appetizing multicultural combination of chop suey, noodles, and Knowles's own special tamales. It is not clear exactly what constituted the entertainment on board, but complaints about the noise soon forced the junk to be moved to nearby Lover's Cove. Pre-Prohibition days in Catalina saw a struggle between the "wets" and the "drys." And the old junk *Ning Po* was not dry. In 1915 the *Ning Po* was towed south again to San Diego, where numerous visitors once more dropped two bits and paid their respects.

Following World War I, the junk again made the trip to Catalina Island. This time tourists had to make the trek from Avalon to the harbor at the Isthmus, where the *Ning Po* was slowly settling in the mud. Going back into the floating bar and restaurant business was not an option, however. The passage of the Prohibition amendment in 1919 doomed that trade for the *Ning Po.* Instead she became a backdrop for Hollywood movies.[27] Her superstructure was rebuilt a number of times, offering a changing set for many a swashbuckling epic.

As of 1919, the island of Catalina itself had become the property of William Wrigley Jr., of Wrigley chewing gum fame. This privatization doomed the Meteor Company and sealed the fate of the *Ning Po.* William Wrigley later did look into the cost of saving the old junk, but the $9,000 price tag was considered too high.

The old junk, at this point, began to literally sink into oblivion. Sheltered at Cat Harbor on the far side of the island, a bay with other relics from the age of sail deteriorating alongside, the *Ning Po* had come to rest at last. Abandoned, deck and hull timbers were scavenged by curiosity seekers and yachtsmen looking for a quick supply of tropical woods. For years the *Ning Po* furnished the Boy Scouts of America with camphor wood for all kinds of carving projects, such as bowls, boxes, and napkin rings. Some of these carvings were later exhibited at the Chicago World's Fair in 1934. During one last Hollywood production in 1935, fire ships drifting in the not-so-predictable breezes moved out of control and ran into the slumbering hulk of the *Ning Po,* burning the topsides to the waterline. Not a group to give up lightly, the Boy Scouts continued hauling chunks of wood off the wreck well into the 1950s. Pieces of the mainmast were distributed to every scout at the

Figure 1. Captain Waard, with his wife, son, and three crew members of the junk *Amoy.* (From Borden, *Sea Quest*)

1953 Jamboree in Newport Beach.[28] What is left of the ship is a wreck covered with mud off Ballast Point at Cat Harbor, along with an assortment of artifacts on display at the maritime museum in Avalon, Catalina Island. The *Ning Po* was probably, at one time, the oldest vessel in the world. The remains of the lower hull are covered by two feet of mud, the site being exposed at low tide, awaiting the maritime archaeologists.

THE *AMOY*

The *Amoy* provides us with another junk brought to the West Coast by enterprising Americans and Chinese. This time the coast received an authentic Amoy fishing vessel. The sea captain George Waard, who reportedly had come to have a great respect for the construction and seaworthiness of Chinese junks, had the twenty-three-ton, three-masted, sixty-five-foot vessel built at Amoy, China, in 1921.[29] Waard, a Canadian naturalized citizen of Dutch origin, had served on a variety of vessels, both steam and sail. He had, as well, spent years in show business, beginning about 1913 in China.[30] It took three months to build the junk by hand, no power tools being used in the construction. After the junk was completed in Amoy, she was sailed to Shanghai. A course was mapped out northward to Hakodate, Japan, and then across the Pacific at about the 42nd or 43rd parallel. Captain Waard set out from Shanghai at 5:00 p.m. on June 21, 1921, with his Chinese wife, son

Robert (Bobbie), and a four-person crew. *Amoy*'s crew consisted of George Kavalchuck (a former Shanghai River policeman), Chan Tai, Loo Fook, and Wong Fook.[31]

Contrary weather forced the vessel into port several times on the passage to Japan, and repairs were made at Hakodate, including the purchasing of two new anchors. Leaving Japan on July 18, the junk was forced to the southeast to dodge another typhoon.[32] On July 30 the freighter *Ben Avos* was sighted and positions compared. Then a series of gales forced the junk up to 54 degrees north, finally fetching up at Attu Island in the Aleutian chain. The large passenger steamer *Empress of Canada* was sighted, and Captain Waard attempted to contact her via semaphore, but the small wooden craft had no luck trying to gain the larger vessel's attention. On August 6 a gale carried away the rudder, and the crew jury-rigged a temporary replacement. On August 9 the *Amoy* reached English Bay on Atka Island, where the crew members were soon advised by an East Indian–registered schooner to find another harbor.[33] The *Amoy* was then advised by a U.S. revenue cutter to make for Dutch Harbor, where the captain managed to obtain bolts for further repair of the rudder. These bolts soon snapped in a gale the junk encountered near Unimak Pass, and yet another makeshift repair job managed to carry the vessel all the way to her final destination.

The *Amoy* could make between six and seven knots (seven and eight miles) per hour with a good breeze. Her peak run was recorded at 180 miles in a single day, but usually the averages were well below that figure. Often the junk would proceed twenty-five miles to the east, only to drift back fifty miles to the west during the night's calms. On August 29 she put in to Unalaska for repairs to the rudder, and here George Kavalchuck left the vessel for reasons not well explained.[34] From there the *Amoy* had a relatively uneventful passage to her destination, except for a near collision with the Japanese steamer *Taketoyo Maru* in the fog while only hours outside the safety of the harbor.

Captain Waard and his crew arrived in Victoria Harbor from Shanghai on September 20, 1922, after a passage of three months, "as dry as on the day of her launching, with not a drop of water in her."[35] In a sense it was a return to Captain Waard's home, as he had been brought to British Columbia by his Dutch parents when only a child, first going to sea at the age of twelve on board a sealing ship out of Victoria.

The tale of the passage is recounted in rather bold terms by the papers of the times. The fantastic journey was said to match the greatest thrills imaginable, but with misfortune sailing close in the wake of the sturdy craft. The rudder, after all, broke three times while typhoons pushed the vessel far to the north, where the *Amoy* alternately labored heavily or was becalmed in the Bering Sea. High latitudes and contrary weather in the North Pacific challenged the *Amoy,* stretching the passage out by as much as an additional month.

The *Amoy* received a huge reception as hundreds lined the causeway at her arrival and then visited the junk. Seven hundred in the first day alone queued up to see the ship, and thousands more in the coming weeks. The overseas Chinese in British Columbia came in great numbers as well, all being allowed access. Hollywood stars Douglas Fairbanks and Mary Pickford, honeymooning at the time in Victoria, went on board as well.[36] Visitors were entertained with stories of the passage, and shown the huge snakeskin left over from a struggle with an unwanted stowaway. Captain Waard remained at his post and gladly recounted the tales for the nominal fee of 25 cents, collected by his wife. "Through the livelong day naught came from his lips but a continual stream of tales of the transpacific trip, praise of his sturdy craft, anecdotes of his long sea experiences and interesting sketches of life in the Far East."[37] These were the captain's tales of the roughest trip Waard had ever made. "There was nothing but a succession of calms and typhoons. The calms were the most annoying, tearing, smashing everything to pieces, making absolutely no headway. Then another storm would come along. We had a gale every Sunday."[38] Much of the amazement expressed by the media of the day revolved around comparisons of the junk's voyage with the accomplishments of the Vikings and/or Christopher Columbus, whichever suited best.

The *Amoy* proceeded south, eventually making San Francisco Bay. It is likely that the junk called at additional ports, such as Nanaimo and Bellingham and Eureka, along the way, though that is not recorded. It is recorded that the *Amoy* called at Vancouver, Seattle, and Portland on her way to California. Much of what seemed to drive the itinerary was the perceived profitability of the various stops. Papers had previously noted that "should cruising of this nature prove profitable it is probable that it will be prolonged indefinitely, to extend to Portland, San Francisco, the Panama Canal and up the Atlantic Coast."[39] And this is exactly what the *Amoy* seemed to be doing. Following a long stay at San Francisco Bay near Vallejo, the junk continued to Los Angeles, and then through the Panama Canal to the West Indies, spending months among the islands and South American ports.[40] Finally Captain Waard took the *Amoy* up the East Coast to Bridgeport, Connecticut, where he sold her to Alfred Nilson, who had signed on board in San Francisco as part of the crew. Alfred Nilson and his wife raised a family of three boys on board the *Amoy,* sailing her for twenty more years on the

East Coast. The junk was a familiar sight at New Rochelle, New York. Some sources report that Waard sold her to Leroy Lewis, head of the H. J. Lewis Oyster Company.[41] Perhaps Leroy Lewis was the actual owner, and Alfred Nilson the captain. One way or another, though, George Waard had ended his time with the *Amoy.* Had her profitability run out? Had he finally grown tired of talking? Or had he grown weary of life at sea itself? Captain Waard is reported as having traveled back to Vancouver Island, where he spent the rest of his days on a ranch.

In 1926 the *Amoy* was still in show business, so to speak. Leroy Lewis, along with Captain Nilson and his wife, and Benjamin Whiting, a native of Panama, set out on a three-year round-the-world cruise from Stratford, Connecticut, in May.[42] Several months later, on August 10, the *Amoy* was detained by the U.S. Coast Guard in New York. Captain Nilson had flown the Chinese flag to dress the boat up, though the U.S. flag remained aloft as well, a breach of protocol. The Chinese students on board were held under suspicion until they were able to produce passports.[43] One source places the *Amoy* on display at New York harbor in 1938, immediately before the New York World's Fair. Apparently the junk was again sold and finally sank in North Carolina's Pamlico Sound in the 1960s, as reported by David Nilson, grandson of Alfred Nilson.[44]

THE *FOU PO II*

The French enterprise of sailing on board Chinese junks (*Fou Po I* and *Fou Po II*) involves deliberate anthropological investigations into migration routes in the Pacific, rather than American storytelling for two bits a pop. The central figure in this enterprise was the maritime ethnographer and former French navy officer Captain Eric De Bisschop, whose experience included several experimental voyages throughout the Pacific.[45] Following his travels on the *Fou Po II,* De Bisschop built a double-hulled voyaging canoe in Hawai'i, the *Kaimiloa,* and sailed to France. He is sometimes regarded as the father of the modern sailing catamarans. In 1956, with the intention of challenging Thor Heyerdahl's controversial theories of westward Pacific migration, De Bisschop attempted an eastward and upwind passage from Tahiti to South America on a voyaging raft, the *Tahiti Nui.* But before all these adventures, he sailed on board Chinese-built junks.

In 1935 De Bisschop, following the loss of the junk *Fou Po I* on a reef off Taiwan in a typhoon, had a second junk built in Amoy. The *Fou Po II* was a forty-foot, three-masted Amoy fishing vessel design, in appearance not unlike the *Amoy.* De Bisschop had sailed for several years out of Ningbo and Amoy in the early 1930s. As an accomplished mariner, he felt that the junk design was extremely seaworthy, an "embodiment of the knowledge of the ages."[46] With the backing of the Societe Francaise de Geographie, De Bisschop and his crewmate, Joseph Tatiboet, set out to sail along the migration route, as it was understood then, of the ancient Polynesians, tracing their route from the Philippines to the Dutch East Indies, the north and northwest coasts of Australia, the shores of Papua, and the Solomon, Santa Cruz, Gilbert, and Marshall archipelagos.

The junk and her crew cruised along the projected routes for months. The *Fou Po II*, intending to put in to Jaluit in the Marshall Islands for careening and repairs to the rudder, was then detained by Japanese officials on suspicion of espionage. Pre-war tension surrounding Japanese military installations in the Pacific was high. Convincing the local governor of the innocent nature of their investigations (De Bisschop conducted hydrographic observations and multiple navigational fixes in order to study the equatorial countercurrents) took some doing, but the *Fou Po II* was finally released to go on her way. After twenty-five days of cruising about in the western Pacific, the two men then decided to make their way to Hawai'i. On this leg of the voyage, the *Fou Po II* averaged a respectable 110 miles per day. Heading north, though, added hundreds of miles to their passage. De Bisschop relied on extra provisions. Unfortunately, Japanese officials on Jaluit had broken open the sealed emergency rations carried deep in the bilges of the junk. The rotten food was discovered at sea, with two thousand miles left to go for Hawai'i, and all of it had to be jettisoned. De Bisschop and Tatiboet were soon reduced to the very meager rations of curry powder and tallow. Some of their last energy reserves were used up hauling the large rudder on board and making repairs at sea. The discovery of half a cracker made for a happy event, a noted celebration of De Bisschop's birthday during the passage.

Eventually, the junk made it into the steamer lanes some one hundred miles northeast of the Hawaiian island of Moloka'i. The two had barely enough strength to wave and shout weakly for help, but these gestures were interpreted by those on board a passing steamer as friendly greetings, and were reported as such upon the steamer's arrival at Honolulu. The following day the two voyagers finally sighted Moloka'i Island. Veering trade winds and currents kept the weakened men in position off Kalaupapa, rather than forwarding the junk on with all speed to Honolulu. With no charts or knowledge of the reefs offshore, De Bisschop took a bearing on what he believed to be a ship riding at anchor and attempted to make his entrance to the safety of the harbor. Rather than a ship, though, the vessel sighted was the nineteenth-century wreck of the supply schooner, which had serviced the leper settlement at Kalaupapa, only to have run upon the reef.[47] By luck, the *Fou Po II* made it past the reef and dropped anchor, and a canoe of four Hawaiians later arrived and brought the nearly unconscious men ashore.

The *Fou Po II*, at anchor and unmanned, later blew onto the nearby reef and broke apart. All the papers, records, and photographs of three years' work were completely lost. The wreck site of the Amoy-style sailing junk in Hawai'i has never been located. De Bisschop, though, would continue his interest in Chinese vessels (see *Cheng Ho* below).

THE *HUMMEL HUMMEL*

The voyage of the *Hummel Hummel* differs as well from the several earlier examples of floating museums and tourist attractions. The small junk carried out its Pacific voyaging as a pleasure cruiser under private ownership. Dr. E. Allen Petersen, an osteopath from Los Angeles, and his Japanese American wife, Tani, discovered the well-used vessel on the Whangpoo River, tied up to the French Bund, and purchased her for $250. Dr. Petersen had previously served as a physician during the bombing of Shanghai in the summer of 1937, and had made two voyages from San Francisco to Australia and Manila on the bark *Moshulu* in 1919. The *Hummel Hummel* was a small, thirty-six-foot, two-masted, Ningbo-style fishing junk.[48] Responding to his boyhood dream, the Petersens cleaned and provisioned the vessel for the first leg of the voyage to Japan, and took on board as crew two Russian sailors, twenty-five-year-old Nick Perminoff and twenty-one-year-old Victor Ermoloff, who had escaped the revolution in their home country. On April 28, 1938, the junk, blending in easily with the many local craft, slipped past American and Japanese warships and made its way down the Yangzi River toward the sea.

The small vessel took over a month to make the trip to Japan, experiencing rain, fog, storms, headwinds, and calms continuously. "Every Sunday we had stormy weather, ending in a calm and thick fog."[49] On their passage the crew witnessed an apparently abandoned dismasted Japanese fishing junk drift by. Following landfall at the island of Oshima, the Chinese junk hugged the coast on its way toward Yokohama. Dr. Petersen had received warnings from Japanese fishermen about inadvertently being carried out to sea by the strong Japanese current.[50]

The junk went into dry dock for thorough repairs in Japan. The old *Hummel Hummel* was recaulked, repainted, ballasted with three tons of iron and sand, and outfitted with additional water tanks for the long Pacific passage. On July 12, vessel and crew set out for San Pedro, California. For the remainder of that month the junk averaged fifty-eight miles per day, reaching within three hundred miles of the Aleutian Islands. On the fifty-fourth day from Japan, the junk caught sight of the Swedish tanker *Sveaborg*, and Dr.

Figure 2. Dr. E. Allen Petersen and Tani Petersen, owners of the junk *Hummel Hummel,* ready for more distant passages. (From Petersen, *Hummel Hummel*)

Petersen was able to check his position. Newspapers and sacks containing fresh fruit, vegetables, and two legs of pork were passed down to the small wooden craft bobbing next to the tanker. Twenty days later one of the Russian crewmen suddenly reported hearing a cow, and soon Fort Bragg on the Northern Californian coast emerged from the fog. By-passing the Golden Gate, the *Hummel Hummel* made it into San Pedro on October 3 after sailing eighty-five days from Shanghai.

The layover in Southern California was only temporary, though, and after more ballast and provisions were put on board, the junk set out once again, this time for Callao, Peru. The Russian passengers, without passports or visas, were detained in California by immigration officials, while claiming that Dr. Petersen reneged on his promise of wages earned. The Petersens, alone on board, encountered ninety days of squalls and headwinds before crossing the equator, during which the copper bottom paint wore off and teredo worms began to decimate the wooden keel and hull.[51] Repairs at Pimentel, Peru, included replacing most of the keel, the whole rudder, and a number of bottom hull planks.

At this point the Petersens cancelled their plans for continuing to beat into the Humboldt Current, and changed course for the South Pacific islands. Soon the junk made Fatu Hiva in the Marquesas, followed by a twenty-one-day passage to Pago Pago. The Petersens continued to voyage among the islands until word of the attack on Pearl Harbor reached them. At Samarai Island, the entry point for southeastern Papua, they left the junk under a canopy of palm fronds.[52] Dr. Petersen enlisted with Australia's New Guinea Volunteers for the duration of World War II. The final disposition of the Ningbo-type junk *Hummel Hummel* is unknown.

THE *SEA DRAGON*

Richard Halliburton, the well-known adventurer, author, and lecturer, became famous for his daring travels and self-promoting style. He had swum the Hellespont, been imprisoned on Devil's Island, trekked through Egypt and Siberia, and accomplished any number of exciting and daring deeds. Perhaps more importantly, Halliburton never seemed to grow weary of telling people all about them. His final exploit involved attempting to cross the Pacific on a Chinese junk, one he had custom built for the project in late 1938. He would not escape this last adventure.

This particular voyage originated with the planning for the 1939 World's Fair in San Francisco, when fair promoters convinced Halliburton to hire a junk and bring it across for exhibition, Chinese crew and all.[53] To Halliburton's mind, such a stunt would emulate the alleged tale of the outraged

Figure 3. Richard Halliburton, explorer and director of the *Sea Dragon* project, and the oversized dragon on the stern quarter of his junk. (From Root, *Halliburton*)

Chinese warlord, who in 1875 sent a small fleet of war junks to avenge the wrongs done to Chinese laborers overseas. The seven war junks reportedly made landfall at Monterey, instead of San Francisco, and the town proved so hospitable to the sailors that the vessels were sunk or broken up, the misguided migrants joining with Monterey's early Chinese community.[54] Is this story a fanciful myth? Researchers in California have cited the legend as basically unsubstantiated. Only the *Monterey Gazette* of February 19, 1864, makes passing mention of a similar "rumored approach of a hostile fleet from China." Nonetheless, the Halliburton Trans-Pacific Chinese Junk Expedition Incorporated of San Francisco sold shares, principally to four wealthy New England families, and the junk was launched from Hong Kong's Wharf No. 2 in January 1939. The four families also supplied an inexperienced crew.[55]

The corporation had searched for a used junk to purchase, inspecting the aging fleets in Ningbo, Shanghai, Wenzhou, Fuzhou, and Amoy, but many of those places were dead harbors, all junks having fled the very immediate threat of the Japanese invading forces. Junks were already being sunk by the thousands in the Asian Pacific war. Having a new vessel built was the last and more expensive option for the Halliburton project.

The tall, seventy-five-foot, Wenchow-style, three-masted junk named *Sea Dragon,* built speedily at Fat Kau's shipyard in Kowloon, featured experimental western alterations, such as shrouds to support the masts, a modern steel rudder, and an inboard diesel engine. Her design was criticized by Asians and Europeans alike. Chinese mariners warned against the breaching of the familiar watertight bulkheads, a change necessary to accommodate the engine and propeller shaft. Western nautical experts found the tall, top-heavy craft too unstable. Halliburton, though, eternally pressed for money, had a strict schedule to meet in order not to lose his berth at the upcoming World's Fair. Having insured the vessel with Lloyd's of London, and somehow obtained a letter from the Japanese navy that would *in theory* allow the junk safe passage beyond blockading ships offshore, the junk and Halliburton's crew set out across the Pacific on February 4, 1939. The crew armed itself as best they could against the pirates who operated off the Chinese coast in the complete absence of any coast guard. Shotguns were easily accessible, and American flags decorated both sides of the hull. The crew consisted of Halliburton, Captain John Welch, Engineer Henry von Fehren, an assortment of six Americans (either hitchhikers in East Asia or seamen set ashore), a cook, two kittens, two puppies, and a Portuguese cabin boy. The departure was accompanied by fireworks, gongs, and cheers from both the wharf and the American liner *President Coolidge.*

Three days later, despite the sendoff, the *Sea Dragon* was back at Hong Kong. One crew member was put ashore and hospitalized, another suffered appendicitis, and a third had a broken ankle. The cabin boy resigned. Even the kittens got put off the boat.[56] A professional mate was hired, likewise an assistant engineer and a Chinese crew, and on March 3 the junk set out once again. To make up for lost time, a course was laid in for a brief call at Midway Island, a remote atoll at the time being developed into an American naval air facility, skipping any lengthy stopover among the main islands of Hawai'i.

What happened to the *Sea Dragon* has been a mystery for sixty years. The brief and grim final radio message was received on March 24, 1939, hinting at the poor conditions in the North Pacific. "Southerly Gales, rain squalls, lee rail underwater . . . wet bunks, hard tack, bully beef. Having wonderful time, wish you were here instead of me."[57]

Many doubted at first that this disappearance was anything more than another publicity stunt, and thought that Halliburton would arrive sailing triumphantly into San Francisco Bay with yet more harrowing tales to tell. The U.S. Coast Guard refused to conduct a search over what was, possibly, just simple radio failure. Eleven days later, on April 4, Halliburton's parents petitioned the secretary of the Navy to begin search operations. After a month, the U.S.S. *Astoria,* on its way back from Yokohama, combed 108,000 square miles without finding a trace of the *Sea Dragon.*[58] Captain Charles Jokstad of the liner *President Pierce,* an old friend of Halliburton, was the first to file a sighting of probable wreckage. He reported the remains of the rudder two thousand miles out at sea, a *year* after the loss.[59] Five years later a wooden keel and attached frames drifted ashore at Pacific Beach, California. No one knew if it came from the *Sea Dragon.* Some speculated that Halliburton was cast onto a coral beach with Amelia Earhart, who had vanished in 1938.

THE *MON LEI*

There is very little available information on the junk *Mon Lei.* As an indication of the confusion over the age of junks (or over details of American history), one source suggests incorrectly that this vessel was one of the oldest ever to visit the port of New York. The fifty-foot, Swatow-type junk was believed to have been built in 1850 in central China. In 1938 the *Mon Lei* completed the passage from Hong Kong to San Francisco in eighty-three days with a crew of eight.[60] According to another secondary source, the *Mon Lei,* sponsored by Robert Ripley of *Ripley's Believe It or Not!* fame, made the voyage in 1942.[61] Newspaper accounts state that Ripley purchased the junk, which had been built for a Chinese warlord, in Florida. This was following the junk's own escape from China to America shortly after Pearl Harbor.[62] Maritime enthusiasts remember the ornate interior decorated with dragon carvings, ornate teak sculptures, and oriental rugs.[63] Fittings for a Chinese warlord?

The *Mon Lei* was given to Mystic Seaport Museum in Connecticut in the mid-1950s, but was never officially owned by that institution.[64] The junk was said to have been taken out of their collection when all non–New England vessels were purged. Following this, the vessel appeared on tour advertising *Mon Lei* Beer in the 1960s. The vessel was last heard of based at a marina in Manhattan in the 1970s.[65]

THE *CHENG HO*

The *Cheng Ho* exemplifies a scientific function not unlike the *Fou Po II.* Here we have an example of a large junk being built for scientific use in the Pacific and around the world, something more rightly called an updated, modern version of a junk yacht. It is difficult to say now how much of the *Cheng Ho*'s construction reflected long-standing Chinese designs, taking into consideration the numerous modifications. The completed *Cheng Ho* would feature refrigeration, air conditioning, luxury accommodations, a botanist's laboratory, twin diesel engines, electricity, and modern plumbing.[66]

The first attempt to build what was called at the time the Queen of Junks was a collaborative affair. A number of international sportsmen, including Count Ilya Tolstoy, grandson of the Russian novelist, supported a project under the title "Ning Po Junk Expedition."[67] The project goal was to undertake a voyage from Hong Kong to the Paris Fair of 1937 by way of the Suez, and a large Chinese junk was needed. Thomas Kilkenny traveled to Hong Kong to oversee the construction of the project's vessel in the 1930s. Exactly why this project failed is unclear, but financial backing did not materialize. Kilkenny eventually went into teak ship construction in China, building pleasure yachts for American buyers.

By 1939 Kilkenny did find a solid backer for the Chinese junk project, when Mrs. Ann Archbold of New York, daughter of the late John D. Archbold and aunt to Richard Archbold, who had explored New Guinea by plane, commissioned Kilkenny to build a deluxe junk for scientific expeditions, such as botanical surveys by the Fairchild Tropical Garden Association, seeking new plant species. Kilkenny's vessel was built to Lloyd's specifications at the well-known shipyard of Ah King in Hong Kong. The overall shape or lines were taken from a one hundred-year-old salt junk. It was thought the design of the junk *Cheng Ho* reflected the mighty treasure ships or *baochuan* of the early Ming dynasty.[68] No plans or examples of these vessels have ever been discovered, and the *baochuan* had no known overt connection to salt barges, so it is hard to take this claim very seriously. Nevertheless, shrouds were added to the masts, a modern western rudder took the place of the Chinese design, and twin 110-horsepower diesel engines dominated the holds. The 106-foot, 154-ton Ningbo-style junk was, therefore, a hybrid design. The modern junk had an eight-knot cruising speed and a range of five thousand nautical miles.[69] Named after the famous fifteenth-century Ming dynasty admiral Cheng Ho (Zheng He), the Fairchild Tropical Garden Expedition's junk got under way late in 1939. With rumors of a Pacific war buzzing in the air, the expedition was seen as the last chance to gather flora and fauna among the islands in Southeast Asia. It was surely one of the last great colonial scientific expeditions to a pre-war Pacific, featuring as well a flare for the historic and exotic. On board were Captain Kilkenny, aristocrat Mrs. Archbold and her personal nurse, Marian, botanist David Fairchild and assistants, photographers, and a Chinese crew, known only as engineer Mo So, boatswain Ah Gunn, Ah Fook, Fo Tai, Kai, Han, Sin, Sing, and cabin boys Jack and Sam.[70]

The vessel first rendezvoused in Manila Harbor to meet the arriving scientists, following the junk's ceremonial launching on October 15. From there leisurely months were spent cruising among Southeast Asia and the little-visited ports scattered among the many islands. The *Cheng Ho* headed south by way of Zamboanga to the eastern Celebes. On February 25 an engine fire broke out, and the junk was briefly disabled. Temporarily repaired, from there she cruised to Soembawa, Lombok, Bali, and west to Soerabaya in Java, where a month of refit completed work on the vessel. Turning east to Makassar, the route then led across the Banda Sea to Ceranam and Amboina.

The scientific venture officially ended when the junk was forcibly detained in Amboina, when it was learned that Germany had invaded Holland. All entry permits to Indonesian ports were summarily cancelled, and cablegrams arrived from the Philippines ordering the *Cheng Ho* to return to the Philippines. The scientist crew, of course, continued their collecting work as they headed north via Ternate and Zamboanga, where the expedition sadly disbanded on June 16, 1940, five months after departing from there. "We bade the loyal Chinese crew farewell, and as their kindly faces smiled down on us for the last time we wondered what would become of them when they got back to Hong Kong."[71] The junk continued on to Cebu, where, after an overhaul, Mrs. Archbold arranged for a new captain and crew. Captain Ellis Skofield then turned eastward to Fiji, arriving later that year.[72]

Another biological sampling expedition, this time to the islands of the central Pacific, was sponsored by Mrs. Archbold and Harvard University. Otto Degener, having enjoyed semi-retirement on a coral beach on O'ahu, traveled to meet the vessel in Suva. The botanist and his Hawaiian-born Filipino assistant, Emilio Ordonez, boarded in November 1940.[73] The crew consisted of "two white boys, a Samoan chief who had performed the intricate sword dance in a well known motion picture, and a fine group of better-class Filipinos."[74] All was not harmony, though, on board the Chinese-built vessel. Stories of tension and mutiny on the passage from Cebu to Suva were rife. Captain Skofield, formerly a master of missionary vessels in the Philippines, apparently had no great love for non-Caucasian crews. "Labor trouble" jeopardized the cruise, and by Christmas 1940 the voyage was over. Otto Degener stayed on in Vanua Levu, while Mrs. Archbold made for Hawai'i, suffering further from various thefts, mutinies, and desertions. She made the decision, in the months before the Japanese attack on O'ahu in December 1941, to sell the *Cheng Ho* to the U.S. Navy for one dollar. The stately *Cheng Ho* then became inshore patrol vessel 1X-52 for the duration of the conflict.[75] Such quickly requisitioned irregular craft in the Hawaiian Islands (consisting chiefly of Japanese-built fishing sampans) were operated by the U.S. Coast Guard as yard vessels and antisubmarine warfare boats. There are no reports of these units ever engaging the enemy, but the servicemen did manage to make an extra buck or two from the excellent fishing in island waters during the war years.[76]

The Chinese junk was taken into the American military service on July 23, 1941, under its original name and outfitted with one 3-inch, 23 caliber gun on deck.[77] The *Cheng Ho* became a station ship of the fourteenth naval district at Pearl Harbor. She was taken out of service on January 18, 1946, and stricken from the navy register on February 25 of that same year. The navy's intentions at the time they originally purchased the junk from Mrs. Ann Archbold were to turn her over to the naval academy at Annapolis: "in compliance with the wishes of the President [Franklin Delano Roosevelt] the *Cheng Ho* will be restored to her original condition as opportunity permits, and the vessel sent to the Naval Academy . . . when conditions warrant."[78] This never happened due to lack of immediate need and lack of available tugs, among other reasons. The proposed transfer to Annapolis was indefinitely deferred in June 1945. Similarly, a plan to load the junk on a landing ship for transport in December fell through. The junk was transferred instead to the War Shipping Administration for disposal. There is no obvious explanation as to why the Naval Academy or FDR was involved with the history of the *Cheng Ho.*

Following the war, the junk was brought back to commercial use as part of the Cheng Ho Trading and Exploring Company, operated by none other than Eric De Bisschop, the French scientist who had arrived emaciated at Moloka'i on board the junk *Fou Po II*, and Otto Degener. She sailed between Tahiti and Hawai'i carrying passengers and cargo. Eventually the *Cheng Ho*, with new engines and renamed the *Hiro*, settled permanently into the inter-island trade in French Polynesia. The *Hiro* had become a copra trader. As of 1955 she was still sailing between the Leeward Islands, Tahiti, and the Tuamotus.[79] She may have ended her days on a beach near Papeete.

THE *FREE CHINA*

Here is the best recorded example of a commercial Chinese sailing vessel crossing the Pacific to the West Coast, and a rare story of adventure overseas. The *Free China*, a Fujian cargo vessel, was entered in a European yacht race, and crossed the Pacific from Taiwan to San Francisco in 1955. Although the story was an international feature, and numerous newspaper and maga-

Figure 4. The transpacific crew of the *Free China*, only hours away from stepping ashore at San Francisco. (Courtesy of the San Francisco Maritime National Historic Park, B7.17)

zine articles and spots on television programs covered the arrival for a brief time, it is a story that has not been well disseminated, and never published in extensive detail. The event quickly receded into obscurity. There was no *place* in the American landscape for the *Free China*.

Fortunately, the original crew of Taiwanese fishermen who brought the old junk across the Pacific are still available for interviews, and their photo albums and even 16mm film footage are intact.[80] In fact, even though the craft has been somewhat altered since arriving on the West Coast, the junk *Free China* herself is still in existence. She is likely the oldest Chinese-built sailing junk still in seaworthy condition.

The story really begins with Paul Chow's decision to join in a transatlantic yacht race and leave behind the island of Taiwan. Chow, originally from a high-ranking mandarin family in northern China, had been forced to leave the mainland following the Communist victory over Republican forces. The United Nations Rehabilitation and Relief Administration (UNRRA) trained him in modern fisheries work, and he was hired by the Fisheries Rehabilitation Administration.[81] Many of his friends in the Fisheries Administration in Taiwan were in similar circumstances, newly trained exiles from the Chinese mainland.

The attitude of the United Nations, though ultimately one of philanthropy and goodwill, was somewhat narrow. In assessing a country that had been possibly responsible for more technological invention than any other in the field of fishing, having been fishing for literally thousands of years, the UNRRA found that "The Chinese paid little or no attention to the importance of fishing [meaning undoubtedly *modern* fishing], which was carried out by the inhabitants of the various islands and provinces along the coast in small wooden craft . . . there were no big capital combines to handle the trade."[82] The United Nations proposed the construction of a fleet of two hundred modern diesel-driven fishing trawlers, complete with radar. In 1946 six of these fishing vessels crossed the Pacific under their own power and arrived in Shanghai. The Taiwanese fishermen who took up the UN call would, incidentally, send one of their own vessels back the other way, the *Free China.*

The long-range effect of this postwar assistance had both positive and negative outcomes. New technologies and methods were imported to China and the catch increased, but ultimately the disappearance of old traditions and wooden sailing junks was hastened. It is fortunate that the new recruits in this cultural exchange happened to be dedicated to saving a bit of the old patterns in the form of a sailing junk. It was this group of Taiwanese seamen as Paul Chow describes them, "the first generation of Chinese fishermen who could read and write," who would procure and outfit the junk *Free China* and bring her to the United States during the years immediately following the Communist establishment of the People's Republic of China.[83]

In September of 1954, between long fishing trips out to the Philippine Islands or far into the South China Sea, Paul Chow sent a letter to the New York Yacht Club race committee, suggesting that they accept a Chinese junk into the transatlantic race from New York to Sweden scheduled for June 1955. Surprisingly enough, they accepted, and Taiwanese Fisheries officials and local politicians were supportive enough to offer 45,000 yuen toward the project.[84] Yet everything hinged on actually finding a sailing junk.

Tension at this time between Taiwan and the mainland was extreme, and there were few places they could actually look for a possible junk candidate. One trip in January 1955 was attempted on board a navy landing craft to the small island of Tachen, immediately off the coast of the Chinese mainland. Seeking a junk was a worthy pursuit, but one worth risking life and limb in

dangerous territory? The effort failed due to continued fierce fighting between Taiwanese and Communist forces. Upon their eventual return to the
dock at Keelung, however, they observed the raked masts of a transient sailing junk nearby.

The owner of the junk, a salt fish trader from Fujian Province by the name
of Lian Yi-Kwai, was eventually located. The junk had arrived from Matsu Island; the load of salted ribbon fish in the holds was collateral for the owner's
gambling habits while in Taiwan. The eighty-foot, two-masted *Sheng Xiao
Li* (the junk's registered name *Victory, Piety, Profit*) was locally known as a
Fuzhou flat head junk, also called a pole junk by some.[85] She was of inde-
terminate age, having been apprehended numerous times for smuggling on
the Chinese coast, each time being outfitted with a new set of registration
papers, a new name, and auctioned off to a new owner.[86] Her current documents reported her being built in 1948, though by all other accounts (and by
the appearance of the junk herself) she was at least half a century old, if not
older. Lian Yi-Kwai, having become aware of the news coverage of the group
of Chinese adventurers fervently seeking a junk for an upcoming overseas
race, was in an excellent bargaining position. He never flinched from his
price of 46,000 yuen, about $1,150 U.S. at the time.[87] Paul Chow and his im-
mediate partner, Loo-Chi Hu, purchased the junk on February 17, 1955, and
work began to refit the vessel for the Pacific journey.

The story of the race and the project of launching a sailing junk on a
worldwide tour became a well-known cause for an island nation in the
throes of an all-out struggle against the Communist mainland. Donations
from the army, navy, governor, Rotary Club, Fisheries Administration, etc.,
brought needed supplies to the effort. Rotten planking was replaced, decks
recaulked, sails refashioned, all ropes and lines refurbished, and provisions
and spare equipment gathered. The traditional "Eight Fairies Crossing the
Sea" and the Phoenix and Sea Serpent designs were repainted on the hull.
Chiang Kai-Shek's son, Chiang Ching-Kuo, arranged a photo session with
the crew. The Ministry of Communication even appointed a committee to
do a feasibility study on sailing a Chinese junk across the Pacific. In Paul
Chow's words, "They devoted half of their time in arguing how [we] should
cook. Then for the rest of the evening, they took turns reminiscing old sea
stories one after the other."[88] The committee eventually split on the opinion
of whether or not the junk would make it across the Pacific. Bets were taken,
and no final decision reached.

Meanwhile, Paul Chow and his friends in the Fisheries Rehabilitation
Administration (FRA) fishing fleet continued their work. The most difficult
barrier to overcome proved to be obtaining exit passes from Taiwan and

visas for America. At this point the American vice-consul in Taiwan, Calvin Mehlert, became connected to the project. He would eventually replace one of the members and travel across the Pacific with the *Free China*, acting as the American liaison and also capturing the voyage on 16mm film. Reno Chia-Lin Chen, originally from Nanjing, sailed as purser; Benny Chia-Cheng Hsu of Swamei served as coxswain; Marco Yu-Lin Chung from Beijing was elected skipper; "Huloo" Loo-Chi Hu from Yangzhou was the rigging master and doctor; and Paul Chuan-Chun Chow was navigator/radio operator and owner. All had joined the FRA as deckhands and had quickly become captains. The fact that none of them had any real experience on sailing vessels of any type did not seem to strike them as worthy of particular concern.[89]

On March 8, 1955, the junk was launched under her new name, *Free China*. The mayor's wife, unused to western launching ceremonies, pitched a bottle of French champagne at the junk as if it were a baseball. The bottle bounced off the hull and smashed on the ground. This was the first western launching anyone had ever seen, and so it was considered normal as far as ceremonies went. Following immediately was the Chinese tradition of firecrackers at auspicious events, and then the junk moved down the launching ways and into the water. After a short shakedown cruise in the harbor, in which the original captain, or *lao da* ("big one"), manned the helm exclusively, the crew felt ready. The *Free China* slipped her lines and departed Keelung, Taiwan, on April 4, 1955.

The consequences of lack of experience appeared when first hoisting the mainsail. The six-man crew, considerably reduced from the normal complement of fifteen, had difficulties handling the heavy batten lug mainsail, which swept out of control over the cabin, breaking lashings and bolts and knocking the ship's compass over the side. Communication broke down as to how to handle the rigging. "Actually the Big One had told us the name of each line. They were in Foochow dialect. None of us could comprehend what he was saying. Huloo insisted to stick to the names he had learned from the junk sailors from Ningpo, which was a different dialect; Hsu Chia-Cheng went by his Swatow names, which he could not even pronounce."[90] This highlights the specialized nature of sailing skills in any culture. Lack of proper spares, jammed halyards, a dead radio, and broken lines combined to force the junk back to Keelung after only a few days. It was a true shakedown cruise—things shook.

On April 16 the junk left the dock again, this time accompanied temporarily by the M/V *Yu Hsiang* and with a guest junk captain and official observers on board as far as nearby Wu Ren Dao (No Man's Island). Taiwanese officials were clearly worried over the safety of the fishermen, as well as the potential

of a public relations disaster. After minor repairs at the island, the observers were transferred back to the escort vessel, and the *Free China* set course
for Okinawa in the face of approaching Hurricane Annie. In deteriorating
weather the tiller and all spares soon snapped. The disabled junk radioed
for tow to Okinawa.[91] Officials from Taiwan ordered the junk abandoned
when the rescue vessel *Chungking Victory* arrived on scene, but the crew
refused. Upon reaching Naha, officials again ordered the junk confiscated
and the crew repatriated back to Taiwan. Yet, according to Calvin Mehlert,
a properly registered Chinese vessel that had never been abandoned, now in
refuge at an American military base, came under the exclusive jurisdiction
of the immediate captain. Mehlert, the American vice-consul, proved helpful in freeing the junk from the legal morass. Incidentally, Mehlert's friends
at Naha included Captain Kilkenny, formerly of the luxury junk yacht *Cheng
Ho*, who advised the *Free China*'s crew to make for Hong Kong and have the
interior of the vessel decorated with expensive oriental carvings. This was
not done. The crew again refused to obey instruction from Taiwan and stuck
with the junk.

After six days in Naha, the *Free China* set out for Japan. The Kuroshio
Current assisted this passage, adding some forty to fifty miles per day to
the log. On May 13 they arrived in Yokohama harbor. A parade of vessels,
quarantine, immigration, customs, newspapers, soon made their way to
the anchored junk. Ambassadors, Chinese organizations of Yokohama, and
cheering schoolchildren met the vessel at the dock. Further repairs were
made in Japan. A steel gallows frame was constructed for the heavy mainsail.
Shrouds were added to the rig design after much debate. One month later,
the crew and vessel were ready for the Pacific, and the vessel departed on
June 17. During this time any real expectations of making the July deadline
for the transatlantic race came and went. The race itself ceased being the
incentive for the journey.[92]

The passage from Yokohama to San Francisco lasted fifty-four days, and
was relatively uneventful. Two Pacific storms were encountered; Marco
Chung was briefly knocked overboard by the tiller; and one of the two chickens was sacrificed for Paul Chow's birthday.[93] Passing whales also caused
some anxiety to the small wooden craft, but the ship emerged unscathed
from the curious pods. The junk averaged a steady five to seven knots on
this last leg.[94] The whole voyage from Taiwan lasted 112 days. Reported by
American vessels outside San Francisco Bay, the *Free China* received a Coast
Guard cutter escort from the Farallon Islands and under the Golden Gate
Bridge. Hundreds of local San Franciscans and other spectators met the *Free
China*, and T. K. Chang, the Consul General to Nationalist China, brought

the crew a bouquet of yellow chrysanthemums as the junk docked at Pier 43 on August 8, 1955.

"The first Chinese junk to enter San Francisco Bay in a century—or, maybe ever—did so yesterday," read the local papers.[95] Customs agents, along with chamber of commerce, immigration, and quarantine officials, made their usual appearance. Celebrations in Taiwan mirrored those across the Pacific. Almost twelve thousand Chinese had joined a contest to guess the exact arrival time of the junk, and twenty-seven winners had to participate in a separate drawing for their prizes of pen and pencil sets.[96] Meanwhile, the *Free China*'s crew met with officials from the Six Companies of San Francisco's Chinatown, the "founding fathers" of the business community. And although Paul Chow and the others still expressed their desire to continue what was now seen as a round-the-world cruise, they had run out of funds. What exactly to do with the wooden junk, badly in need of serious overhaul, became the immediate question.

First they sailed the old vessel over to China Camp in Marin County, where a feisty, pistol-wielding, Chinese expletive–spewing local character known as Mrs. Quan, who lived at the historic site of the nineteenth-century California Chinese fishing village, promised to look after the craft.[97] Unable to find funds to complete the needed overhaul, Paul Chow had the ship's title transferred to the Chinese Consolidated Benevolent Association, the Six Companies, in November of 1955.[98] The *Free China*, meanwhile, ended up abandoned and on the rocks at China Camp. Inquiries were made into the possibility of the National Maritime Museum in San Francisco accepting responsibility for the ship. The Maritime Museum at first tentatively accepted the gift, agreeing to preserve the historic vessel.[99] But the museum, not wanting to burden itself with another expense, in the end declined full responsibility and transferred legal ownership to a small group of volunteers. This group, associated with the museum, undertook to care for the foreign junk out of sheer love of maritime tradition and vernacular vessels. In 1956 the junk was rescued from seventeen months of abandonment at China Camp and towed to the Alameda shipyard in the East Bay. There it was hauled out of the water. America's National Maritime Museum passed the torch, stating, "Although our group has kept the vessel out of the water and under partial surveillance, the junk has deteriorated and her condition is not good. Like you, we are interested in seeing the *Free China* eventually restored to good condition, even though we ourselves may not be in a position to do so."[100]

The ship spent the next four years at the Alameda shipyard. Following a period of being abandoned there for firewood, the vessel was put back into shape. After much work the junk was refloated and taken to the Oakland Dock and Warehouse Company, where she remained for three more years.[101] A number of local maritime notables, such as Harry Dring, the maritime museum supervisor, Max Lemke, a San Francisco insurance agent, and Henry Rusk, a naval architect, assisted Reno Chen and Paul Chow in making the junk seaworthy again, and then in keeping the aging wooden vessel afloat.[102] In this way the *Free China* was transferred from the crew to private ownership by Californians, and she remained in the Bay Area.

The *Free China* underwent considerable renovation over a period of many years in the San Francisco Bay. The keel was deepened, a modern steel rudder replaced the larger wooden Chinese version, and bulkheads were removed so that a Volvo diesel engine could be fitted into the hull. Moved down to Oyster Point marina in 1966, the old smuggling vessel finally found herself surrounded by modern harbor facilities and behind locked gates. When Harry Dring became too old to care for the junk, she was sold in 1989 to local Bay Area resident Govinda Dalton. Without financial support, nor any guidance on historic preservation, Dalton was free to alter the privately owned vessel in any way he saw fit. The foremast was removed and the high oval stern with its ornate designs was cut away with a chainsaw. (At least pilfering by the Boy Scouts of America was not involved.) The *Free China*, now renamed *Golden Dragon*, remains hauled out of the water and up on blocks at the Bethel Island Boatyard near Sacramento, California.

But what of the crew? Marco Chung, after returning to Taiwan, has retired from a career in business and now lives in Hacienda Heights, California. Paul Chow recently retired as professor emeritus of physics at California State University, Northridge, and is currently writing a book about the voyage, *The Junk Story.* Loo-Chi Hu ended up working for the UN Food and Agriculture Organization, becoming an advisor to New Zealand fisheries. He now teaches Tai Chi Chuan in Christchurch, New Zealand, and has constructed a detailed model of the *Free China.* Benny Hsu studied marine biology at the University of Washington. Unfortunately he was killed in an automobile accident in 1969. Reno Chen, after working in the electronics industry in the Bay Area, has retired and lives in Palo Alto, California. Calvin Mehlert continued his career in the Foreign Service, serving in Taiwan, Bangkok, London, Warsaw, Monrovia, Liberia, and Washington, D.C. He currently lives in Camp Connell, California, and is editing the 16mm footage from the Pacific crossing.[103] In 1995 they met in San Francisco for the fiftieth anniversary of their voyage. Their story will not be forgotten.

THE BEIHAI JUNK

This last example of a Chinese working junk did not cross the Pacific under her own power, though she sailed in China as well as the Pacific Northwest. The Beihai junk was shipped on board a modern container vessel across the ocean. Nonetheless, the construction features contribute to this study in important ways, and the events that followed her arrival mirror the pattern of neglect and disuse seen in other voyages. The Beihai junk was encountered by the author during a research trip to the West Coast in August 2000. Though it is representative of traditional fishing junks, it was never intended to fulfill its traditional role, being built purposefully for an American museum. Today it is slowly falling apart amid Oregon's blackberry bushes.

In 1989, Guy Lasalle Jr., an Oregon native who worked in southern China, was commissioned by the Portland Children's Museum to find a sailing junk for a planned exhibition called "Homes on the Move."[104] With his connections to a fishing village at Beihai, Guy Lasalle located some of the last remaining shipwrights who still remembered how to construct traditional junks, and in three months the hand-built sailing junk was launched. No plans were used in the construction, as the junk masters in response to questions merely sketched shapes temporarily in the sand.[105] The shipwrights themselves were Chinese mariners previously exiled from their homes in Vietnam during the border wars between the two countries, and resettled in a permanent UN-created refugee camp at Beihai. There the Chinese government had supplied the infrastructure for the community to continue fishing and building wooden vessels, mainly motorized trawlers. There was a certain measure of pride in being asked to construct an old-style fishing junk for an American museum, in saving a part of the local maritime heritage.

Guy Lasalle himself became interested in junks while a student at Lewis and Clark College. With his partner, Michelle Loh, Lasalle formed Dragon Junks Ltd., a company with the aim of importing junks to the west. The Beihai junk was the first vessel brought over.[106]

The junk from Beihai (no name was ever associated with it) is an eight-ton, two-masted sailing vessel about thirty-five feet long, built of local Chinese hardwoods. In style it is most closely associated with types like the Kotak chuan, a common type of fishing boat in the local district near Beihai, though it combines elements of other vessels in the region.[107] It is, according to Guy Lasalle, one of the very last sailing junks built in the area.

In Portland the rare vessel went on display at the Children's Museum, with a ladder installed for visitors to climb up onto the deck and a railing for safety's sake encircling the topsides. The exhibit lasted between March and

July 1991. After five months in the yard of the museum, on display beside a felt Mongolian yurt and a bright silver American Airstream trailer, the wooden boat was transported by the Museum to a storage yard belonging to Portland's Urban Forestry Division. There, at Delta Park East, the Beihai junk sat unattended and open to the weather for fifteen years, until being purchased back from the museum by Guy Lasalle Jr. in 2006. All of the junk's rigging and associated artifacts were held in storage at the museum.

THE SAMPLE OF TEN JUNKS

These vessels, a portion of the incidental junk traffic between the Asian and American coastlines, are united by a common thread. They are samples, to varying degrees, of the long traditions of junk construction in China. Some are fairly consistent representations of long-standing designs, and others are mixed bags of fanciful creations, combining elements from various regions in less than successful ways. All represent a kind of bridge between our western understanding of the Chinese past and the mostly unwritten history of the coastal Chinese shipwrights and sailors. Each junk is an opportunity for us to glimpse a part of that past.

Most of these vessels were brought across the Pacific under the auspices of American or European control. Even the *Free China* voyage, with Vice-Consul Calvin Mehlert on board, benefitted from westerners associated with the project from the early stages. This may also serve as partial explanation as to why these and not other voyages have been better documented and remembered. The nature of the event itself, the arrival on foreign shores of Chinese sailing vessels, lends a bias toward the sample. For about a century between the gold rush in California and the conclusion of World War II in the Pacific, Chinese immigration to America was discouraged, if not outright banned. Anti-Chinese sentiment ran high in the western states. Any Chinese migrants arriving on the coast in their own junks would have had little incentive to make official entry or otherwise bring notice to their journey. Concerning the selected vessels in this study, American involvement sets these junks apart from other purely Chinese voyages that may or may not have contacted the Americas in the past.

Given the general lack of distribution of knowledge on Chinese wooden ship construction, it can be difficult to accurately describe the junks themselves. The first step in the evaluation of these vessels is to examine the appropriate literature. How do we know what little we do know about Chinese junks, and how do we begin taking a serious look at these voyagers?

chapter 3

Reading the Junks Themselves

Besides simply labeling these vessels as junks, what really are they? What do they convey to us besides stories of adventures on the high seas? By combining the sample of Chinese junks that crossed the Pacific with what is currently known about Chinese junk construction, we can better evaluate these vessels from a technological standpoint. This involves delving into the existing historical and archaeological results and comparing this to the current sample's photographs and artifacts. If there is one rule of thumb when it comes to assessing Chinese junks, it is that they are quite unlike western vessels in many different ways. These differences center around critical components of ship construction: fastening systems, hull construction, sail rig, and rudder design. The unfamiliar nature of all of these components would have a profound effect on the western perceptions of these transpacific junks.

Language itself can be misleading. Although *junk* is used throughout this study for convenience, the term itself ultimately proves to be unsatisfactory. What can be said about a generic term applied to the multitude of Chinese vessel designs, many of which predate all the ships European seafarers later built? That we lack the language capable of discriminating among the varieties of junks has not helped matters. *Junk* is a word like piracy, which in the western languages finds frequent use yet somehow remains fairly undefined. No one is even sure of the origins of the term *junk*, though it is suspected that Portuguese voyagers, encountering Javanese mariners in Southeast Asia, were informed that local boats were called *djonq*, or in Portuguese *junco*, and, hence, adopted the word for any East Asian vessel, no matter the size or design.[1] It is a term, then, associated with the East India Trading

Companies as much as Chinese sailing vessels. It is nonspecific. What, for example, is the difference between a junk and a sampan?

The English word *junk* also referred in the historic sailing world to over-ripe pieces of salt beef, as well as the most obvious reference denoting useless scrap of any type. A term more apt to specifically denote nothing in particular is hard to imagine. As defined for the West, a junk is "a native sailing vessel common to Far Eastern seas, especially used by the Chinese and Javanese."[2] The dictionary's brief entry ends quickly, and moves on to the definition of "ship," meaning the western ship, stretching out to nine pages. Naturally, the Chinese have always been much more precise in their terminology, at the very least attaching a regional marker to *chuan*, or boat, denoting location, as in for instance *fuchuan*, or Fujian boat, and *guangchuan*, or Guangzhou boat.

Inadequate language marks the whole investigation of Chinese junks. This is, in fact, a more general phenomenon applicable to the wider maritime field. For English nautical words and expressions, many owe their origins to a multiplicity of Greek, Spanish, French, Dutch, Scandinavian, and East Indian words. This is a natural reflection of the fluid-like nature of the maritime experience. Maritime terminology sometimes seems a separate language unto itself, and is therefore the proper subject for specialized dictionaries.[3] This necessity has particularly baffled researchers in Chinese maritime history, for the abundance of terms used in the technical description of Chinese junks often existed only in spoken dialect, not written form. Shipwrights in China did not devote their time to scholarship, and the literary class did not engage in the building and handling of ships. "At best scholars could only make commentaries on technical terms which even their predecessors had perhaps only half understood. So although Chinese encyclopedias . . . generally contain sections devoted to shipping terms, it is noticeable that the majority of these concern types of boats and ships long obsolete."[4] Even Worcester's decades of extensive research met with such difficulties, since "even the finest shipwrights and sea-captains with whom he worked, could not write, nor could any members of their crews or families. It is clear, then, that there are certainly many spoken craft terms for which no written forms exist at all."[5] The Chinese nautical lexicons that are easily accessible, such as the *Yinghan hanghai cidian* (English-Chinese Maritime Dictionary), feature modern sea terminology and have little or nothing to do with the sailing of wooden junks.

There is no need here to attempt the immense task of an analysis of all Chinese ship construction, which might not even be possible. That junks are complex and have undergone change over time is the basic assumption, and one cannot pigeonhole junks into any simple one-word definition. For some types, a detailed analysis, though rare, is available, and there is no need to repeat that work here. What is needed, though, is to engage in enough analysis of Chinese junk features to be able to analyze these ten examples within this work. Junk construction and design must be understood enough to be able to place these examples within the larger Chinese maritime context. Are they what we say they are? Are they vessels that represent long established Chinese features? Are they "traditional"? Where do they fall in that continuum between static design and dynamic change? And having classified them, what does such knowledge mean for their historical significance?

Remembering Patterns in Junk Construction

In assessing the physical nature of these junks, certain specific elements of Chinese ship construction must first be examined. Do we know what constitutes long established Chinese construction features, and what are the more recently introduced changes? Here we must draw principally from the results of recent archaeological work, as well as information from scattered secondary sources, for a glimpse of what was only recorded by the builders in the form of the actual object.

For intelligent yet illiterate shipwrights who never had time to take the imperial examinations, the construction features themselves are the "documents" of the skills of coastal Chinese craftsmen. Learning to read these documents is a way of eliciting maritime history from the material culture. During the Song dynasty, Fujian Province was noted as unsurpassed in the construction of seagoing vessels, referring to a body of knowledge and level of activity encompassing many styles of regional ocean junks, not just an individual version.[6] Regional features common to many different designs find expression in junk hulls and fasteners, masts and sails, and rudder designs. Thus the basic features described here are at somewhat of a general level and sometimes do not address specific elements of individual craft in complete detail. Local stylistic variations have introduced certain changes to junk designs. By first discussing what we know of regional construction, and then looking at the examples of transpacific junks, we can attempt to understand the difference between regional and local features, and what makes a junk a junk.

In assessing junk construction, it is helpful to adopt a perspective from material culture studies that features patterns and languages, specific designs and their interpretation. In 1989 the Smithsonian Institution hosted a conference entitled "History from Things: The Use of Objects in Understanding the Past." This led to the collection *History from Things: Essays on Material Culture*, edited by Steven Lubar and W. David Kingery, addressing the many ways that objects are shaped and in turn reflect human beliefs, behavior, and history. Within this context, Lubar examined the industrial revolution, reading the changes in political culture through the shifting technological patterns of machine evolution. "In technological artifacts, style reflects the cultural values of the people who invent, shape, and use them. . . . The nature of patterns . . . provide[s] a grammar not of the finished products, but of the cognitive strategies, a series of mental templates to guide the work of design."[7] Lubar makes explicit use of language as metaphor for understanding technological patterns over time. The approach stems from Christopher Alexander's 1977 work *A Pattern Language*, developing insight into the human design process in urban planning. For Alexander the language of architectural patterns answers basic problems, such as where to locate doors, or which windows are compatible with what rooms. Pattern language provides designs that have been proven successful in the past and adopted. It is a way of revealing the evolution of human designs, initially applied to the field of architecture. Junks are not simply machines in the sense of Lubar's industrial revolution, they are the transport and storage and working/living platform for Chinese fishermen and merchants. They are not fixed homes, but dwellings on the move. They are human-designed artifacts that have evolved over time in response to multiple needs and influences, artifacts from a period before the distinct division between machine industry and artistic craftsmanship. Can the perspective of pattern and language assist in the understanding of Chinese junks?

Adhesion to established patterns in the construction of vessels made it possible for shipwrights to measure their product, to define and judge their creation, and most importantly to assure themselves that the boat would float. Alexander's *A Pattern Language* emphasizes that "In designing their environments, people always rely on certain languages which, like the languages we speak, allow them to articulate and communicate an infinite variety of designs within a formal system which gives them coherence."[8] In the pattern and language approach, patterns for junks were the successful combinations of hull shape, rudder design, fastening technology, and propulsion. These designs "spoke" to the Chinese shipwright: this transom with these sails makes a Fujian fishing vessel, that hull shape is a northern design, those rudders belong to southern coastal traders, etc.

Others have noted that ship designs and shipwrights themselves tend to remain very conservative for most of history. Was the shipwright's language a cautious one? The cost for failure, for experimentation with radical and possibly nonfunctioning designs at sea, was high indeed. Vessels vanished with their crews. Mediterranean galleys existed into the sixteenth century, and the basic design of the full-rigged western sailing ship remained essentially unchanged for hundreds of years. The introduction of steam power itself was a slow process unwelcome by many and marred by sometimes spectacular failures. Once shipwrights developed a language of successful designs, these had a tendency to remain fixed, perhaps changing only slowly if at all. Alexander states that "many of the patterns are archetypal, so deeply rooted in the nature of things that it seems likely that they will be a part of human nature, and human action, as much in five hundred years as they are today."[9]

More recently others have challenged this generality as it applies to the maritime world, this type of received theory. Vessel design obviously does change through time, and at certain periods may prove quite dynamic relative to other eras. A reliance on the language pattern approach would suggest the former rather than the latter, that vessel designs and components persist through time and change only slowly. Radical design changes are not a part of the existing pattern but a break in it, a change in the language. The two perspectives may not really be mutually exclusive at all. Ship construction might evolve slowly as patterns are tested and perpetuated, until conditions external to this natural development force a change. At the beginning of the Ming dynasty in the fourteenth century, the Maritime Ban prohibited the private construction of oceangoing vessels of a certain size. The first Ming emperor, following upon almost one hundred years of foreign (Mongol) rule of China during the Yuan dynasty, severely curtailed foreign contact overseas by making the private construction of large seagoing vessels with more than three masts an offense punishable by exile or death. This prohibition, only slowly relaxed over the years, had a devastating impact on merchants, seafarers, and shipwrights. Many took up permanent residence in overseas Chinese communities in Southeast Asia. In the early years of the Tokugawa Shogunate in Japan an imperial edict proscribed open ocean junk designs in lieu of coastal vessels with unwieldy rudders, an unfortunate choice for many Japanese seafarers who later found themselves adrift and castaway on the currents of the Pacific. Steam-powered warships forced a complete revision of maritime construction in East Asia. There are instances where design change can be external and dynamic. Given our strong connection to proven patterns, such design change might be actively resisted. Is this the case with the junks? First the question must be answered: what is the baseline language of the junk, the patterns of the construction features?

Recent archaeological work provides some of the most concrete data for a summary of junk construction characteristics, many of these sites being examples of Chinese ships from Song, Yuan, and Ming dynastic periods (Song, 960–1279 A.D.; Yuan, 1279–1368 A.D.; Ming, 1368–1644 A.D.), roughly equivalent in time to Europe's medieval age. Sean McGrail's *Boats of the World* currently provides an excellent overview of construction analysis based on site work, as does Geoff Wade's *The Pre-Modern East Asian Maritime Realm: An Overview of European-Language Studies* for the variety of sites being explored. Such work represents a reversal of previous trends, a new emphasis on understanding junk construction from firsthand evidence. Have Song to Ming period junk characteristics continued into the nineteenth and twentieth centuries? If so, this would seem to suggest truly well-established patterns within the language of the junk masters, their interpretation of successful patterns. The following table presents a brief listing of the major contemporary discoveries and projects. It is admittedly incomplete in that it only includes sites of probable oceangoing Chinese vessels where at least a trace of hull or wood structure has been reported, but it combines the basics from McGrail's *Boats of the World*; Jeremy Green's

Table 2. Chinese-Style Shipwreck Sites

Site name	Location	Date	Notes
Quanzhou vessel 1 (Houzhou harbor)	Fujian Province, China	1277 A.D.	Excavated 1974 and documented in detail by Song Shipwreck Committee and others, almost full length of hull above turn of the bilge and bulkheads intact. Now on display in Quanzhou Museum.
Quanzhou vessel 2 (Fashi)	Fujian Province, China	1100–1200 A.D.	Excavated 1982, estimated original length 23 meters. Now on display in Quanzhou Museum.
Shinan vessel	Southwestern coast of Korea	1323–1367 A.D.	Excavated 1976–1982 and documented in detail. Chinese-style vessel built in southern China, hull and bulkheads intact and lifted in sections.
Penglai vessel 1 (Dengzhou port)	Shandong Province, China	1376 A.D.	Discovered 1984, found during dredging operations. Remains consist of keel, stem, planking, framing, bulkheads, mast steps, rudder seating, anchors, rigging, etc.

continued

Table 2—*Continued*

Site name	Location	Date	Notes
Ningbo vessel	Zhejiang Province, China	900–1200 A.D.	Partially excavated 1988, discovered along ancient wharf. Half of hull intact, transom bow and stern missing.
Baijiao vessel	Fujian Province, China	900–1200 A.D.	Investigated in 1990–1992 by joint China-Australia program, one of three sites surveyed near Dinghai village.
Suizhong vessel	Bohai Bay, Liaoning Province	1100–1300 A.D.	Investigated between 1992 and 1994, only a trace of wooden structure left, but a full cargo of porcelain and iron products of the Yuan dynasty.
Penglai vessel 2	Shandong Province, China	1271–1368 A.D.	Discovered 2005, possibly the remains of a warship from the Yuan dynasty.
Lena Shoal vessel	Palawan Island, Philippines	Late 1400s A.D.	Discovered in 1997, investigated by joint Philippine National Museum and Franck Goddio team.
Turiang vessel	Singapore Strait, Malaysia	1305–1370 A.D.	Discovered in 1998, indication from wood type and fastening system that vessel is Chinese in origin. Multinational cargo.
Bakau vessel	Karimata Strait, Indonesia	1403–1440 A.D.	Investigated in 1999, no identifiable keel (may be flat-bottom), hull remaining with traces of bulkheads.
Santa Cruz vessel	Zambales, Philippines	1400s A.D.	Excavated in 2000, a trade junk of the Ming dynasty.
Takashima vessel	Takashima Island, Japan	1281 A.D.	Discovered in 2001, appears to be scattered remains of a thirteenth-century Mongol invasion ship, built in Fujian Province.
Tanjung vessel	Coast of Sabah, Borneo	1000s A.D.	Investigated in 2003. Ship's temperate climate pine and fir or cedar timbers indicate probable Chinese origin.
Penglai vessel 2	Shandong Province, China	1271–1368 A.D.	Discovered 2005, possibly the remains of a warship from the Yuan dynasty.

chapter entitled "Arabia to China: The Oriental Traditions" in *The Earliest Ships*; *Bulletin of the Australian Institute for Maritime Archaeology*; Wade's *The Pre-Modern East Asian Maritime Realm*; and Yu Weichao et al., *Sunken Treasures: Underwater Archaeology in China.*

Of these projects, three have produced substantial documentation, adding significantly to our current understanding of Chinese-built seagoing junks: the Quanzhou vessel discovered at Houzhou harbor, the Shinan vessel, and the fourteenth-century wreck at Penglai near Dengzhou port.[10] A number of other junks with Southeast Asian features (for example, dowels instead of iron nails) have been located in Malaysian waters and the Gulf of Thailand, providing important clues to the differences between Chinese and Southeast Asian vessels. Others in Southeast Asia exhibit features of a "South China Sea" tradition, a hybrid combination of Chinese and Southeast Asian details (not included in above list). As overseas Chinese communities in Southeast Asia were active in maritime trade, and Chinese trade goods and export ceramics are ubiquitous in the region, there is some difficulty in drawing a strict distinction between Chinese and Southeast Asian vessels. The comparative results of Song–Ming period Chinese junk archaeology are due to the work of the Quanzhou Museum of Overseas Communication History in Fujian Province, and researchers such as Li Guoqing, Jeremy Green, Lin Shimin, Zhang Wei, Donald Keith, Zae Guen Kim, Michael Flecker, and many others.

The following sections combine documentary and some ethnographic information with data from the archaeological projects listed above. This is a summary of some of the major features or patterns of junk construction. Further details about specific sites and features can be found through the references.

MAIN PATTERNS: HULL, BULKHEAD AND FRAMES, PLANKING,
AND KEEL

Overall, the Chinese junk hull is quite different from contemporary hull construction known in the West. Influential nautical scholars have postulated that the design of vessels, from the very beginning of shipbuilding in China, has been along totally different lines compared to western vessels. In approaching these early variations, nautical researchers have divided ship construction into several divergent directions. Four basic roots of shipbuilding are recognized by maritime ethnographers: rafts, skin boats, bark boats, and log boats. While western vessels are considered descendants of log boats, such as dug-out canoes, Chinese junks developed, in the existing assessment, from bamboo raft traditions.[11] Even details such as the internal bulkheads of Chinese junks are seen as possible representations of the internal dividing septum of bamboo, the material used for many oceangoing rafts in China up until recent years. Others still maintain the possibility of the junk design coming from the dug-out boat tradition.[12] Some even hold out the theory that junks and sampans are the offspring of an as-yet-undiscovered twin-hulled log catamaran.[13] In short, an accurate picture of the origins of junk design is less understood than the evolution of western boats, but the final form has been typically associated with the very building material for the ancient sailing rafts, "a natural model ubiquitous in East Asia, the longitudinally split bamboo."[14] This issue has particular significance not only regarding the shape of the vessel, but over the internal structure as well. The rounded form of the hull reflects the curved bamboo stem and the solid interior bulkheads the bamboo's dividing septa.

Hull Shape

Results from current archaeological work provide an overview of hull shape from a broad span of Chinese history. In general, junk hulls had a broad, rounded profile, flaring sides and transom or flat sterns perpendicular to the main axis of the ship. (See the glossary for some of these technical definitions.) The bow featured relatively sharp lines underwater, yet a smaller transom above the waterline.[15] Plan views of the hull shape reveal another difference between Chinese and European vessels. The classic form of the wooden European sailing ship, at least from the time of the sixteenth century onward, has been very bluff or rounded (as opposed to sharp or pointed) at the bow—in other words, the widest point of the hull was forward of the midsection of the vessel. In sixteenth-century documents this shape was sometimes compared to that of a fish swimming through the water, the fanciful hybrid of a thick-headed cod with a long mackerel tail. Chinese junks, by comparison, feature the widest point aft of the midsection of the hull. The form to be emulated, according to Joseph Needham's analysis, was not the fish, but the duck, which floats on the water and not in it.[16] Modern racing yachts are now built along the latter design, the Chinese hull shape in plan view (top down) with the widest beam aft of midships. The most advanced hull shapes today emulate long-established Chinese designs, not European models. Reconstructed lines from the Quanzhou shipwreck confirm Needham's and others' observations.[17]

Within these general parameters, the pattern of Chinese hull shape from the Song dynasty to the twentieth century seems to remain fairly constant, but there is a great deal of variety within the broad criteria for such generalities as "transom sterns" or "sharp waterline with transom bows." Local-

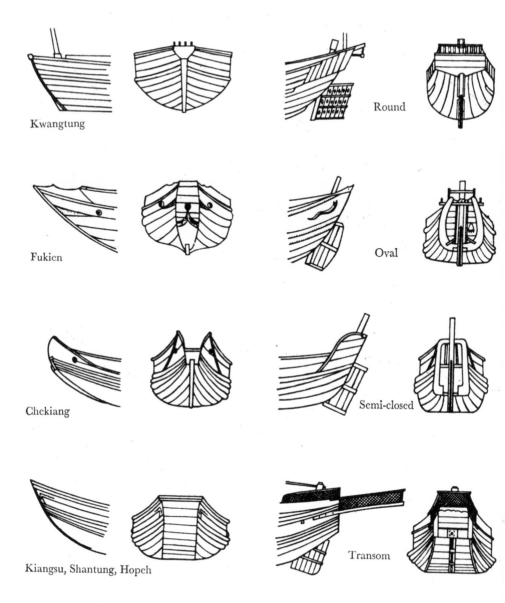

Kwangtung

Round

Fukien

Oval

Chekiang

Semi-closed

Kiangsu, Shantung, Hopeh

Transom

Figure 5. General regional distinctions in Chinese junk bow (*left*) and stern (*right*) construction. (From *Sail and Sweep in China,* by G.R.G. Worcester, London, 1966; courtesy of the Science Museum/Science & Society Picture Library)

ized patterns of square or oval transom sterns, bows with wings versus flush deck transom bows, etc., were recorded by a number of nineteenth- and twentieth-century observers. Many of these designs can be generalized into regional categories of either northern or southern influences.

Bulkheads and Frames

The use of watertight bulkheads, solid partitions perpendicular to the main axis, which in China extend as far back as the late Han dynasty (second century A.D.), is one of the most significant contributions to the field of nautical design.[18] Bulkheads, and the inherent increase in structural integrity and safety, were not adopted by the West until the creation of large, iron-hulled steamships such as the *Great Eastern* in the nineteenth century. The junk's hull gains its strength through the combination of multiple interior bulkheads and partial frames or wooden "ribs" adjacent to those bulkheads. Site work on several of the Song dynasty wrecks reveals small limber holes through the bulkheads, drainage holes located on centerline allowing bilge water to flow from each compartment. Cargo spaces are thus solid but not completely watertight.[19] Presumably flooding between compartments could be controlled, perhaps by plugging the limber hole.

Transverse bulkheads in the Quanzhou, Shinan, and Penglai vessels were numerous, up to thirteen within the hull and spaced on an average between five and six and one-half feet apart.[20] This may not be true for all junk styles, or all periods. Some twentieth-century Asian junks had nonuniform bulkhead spacing determined by the need to separate functional areas: living quarters, fish holds, cargo holds, etc.[21] L-shaped flat iron brackets, known as *gua ju* nails, were used to brace the bulkheads, connecting them directly to the primary hull planking. The brackets were recessed into the bulkheads (on the side opposite the partial frames), and the bracket feet were recessed into the outside of the planking.

Partial or half-frames were associated with each bulkhead, by all indications fitted into the hull after the planks were in place. In the Quanzhou 1 example, each frame set forward of midships was placed on the aft side of the bulkhead, and each aft of midships placed forward of the bulkhead.[22] Additional internal stringers, riders, clamps, or other longitudinal timbers do not appear in the Song to Ming ship examples (at least not in the lower hull), as these would interfere with the *gua ju* nail and bulkhead/half-frame construction.

In contrast to this tradition of internal bulkheads, general European construction built ships essentially as strong hollow shells, void of internal structure that would interfere with cargo space or the operation of naval ordnance on long, open gun decks. Hull planks were attached to a previously assembled skeleton of narrowly spaced frames or ribs, and seams along the planks were caulked. Longitudinal timbers ran the length of the western hull, particularly along the lower areas of the bilges and keel.

In the western vessel, strengthening longitudinals are widely distributed around the entire hull surface, but are concentrated at the keel, the deck line, and the bilges, the lower hull interior spaces where the ship's bottom meets the sides. The deck is devoid of longitudinals. The longitudinals and frames form a "cage" that determines and maintains the shape of the vessel. The cage is anchored to the keel and deck-edge strength members. In the junk, the arrangement is almost reversed. Most of the heavy fore-and-aft timbers are in the sides, often at the deck line, and in the deck and upper works themselves. The relatively thin bottom planking is analogous to the equally thin deck planking of the western craft. Unlike the western craft, which is built up from its keel, the junk is "hung" from its deck.[23]

There is a clear understanding of the stresses involved in building wooden sailing vessels of the western design, and these stresses ultimately limit the size of western vessels to a little over three hundred feet long, the size of the largest wooden sailing cargo schooners ever built in the late nineteenth and early twentieth centuries. The precise knowledge of the stresses involved in the designs of junks, so unlike western vessels, is not as clear. The structural components familiar in western vessels, such as keelsons, clamps, and shelves, were simply absent in the Chinese junk. Instead, on junks "the upper planks of the sides are enormously thickened. Generally described as wales, these thick upper planks may be single or multiple, full vessel-length or partial, and are commonly rounded wooden trunks squared off on the inside."[24] These partially finished planks or logs can be seen along the upper hulls of many different junks. In short, both western and Chinese vessels faced similar stresses at sea, but the Chinese came to very different design solutions than the West.

Such different engineering principles might place the Chinese hull design outside the familiar parameters of western wooden ship construction. Limitations to the hollow shell design of western ships might not apply to Chinese junks. The remains of a Chinese warship off Japan's Kyushu Island, lost during the attempted Mongol invasion in 1281 A.D., suggest an original overall length of 230 feet, twice the size of European vessels of the same period. The anchor stock alone was twenty-three feet long.[25] The subsurface investigations of vessel remnants at Takashima reveal diagonal or angled iron nailing patterns (square nails), a possible transom piece, and two partial interior bulkheads (one over eighteen feet in width) patterned with the characteristic V-shaped hull profile.[26] Findings so far suggest the hasty construction of a large war fleet, rather than the more carefully fitted features of normal junks.

Marco Polo's observations, contemporaneous with the Mongol invasion attempts, describe Chinese ships with four to six masts, crews of up to three hundred sailors, and sixty cabins on deck for traveling merchants.[27] Ibn Battuta, the Muslim traveler to China in the fourteenth century, reported Chinese ships manned by six hundred sailors and four hundred marines.[28] Admiral Zheng He's treasure ships of the early Ming dynasty, the backbone of China's armadas that in the early fifteenth century crossed the Indian Ocean to the Red Sea and beyond, were recorded in the Chinese historical record as being well over four hundred feet in length. That may well be an exaggeration or error, but those making the case for significantly shorter *baochuan* based on technical limitations of western wooden construction alone should take the differing construction methods into account.[29]

Planking

Hull planks were edge-joined to each other using rabbeted laps and angled iron nails, as well as attached directly to the transverse or perpendicular bulkheads. The main visual evidence of edge nailing in photographs of junks are rows of triangular notches, usually filled with Chinese caulking compound. The continuing use of this fastening method has been well documented in recent years. The alignment of hull planks, also called strakes, reflected both the smooth edge-joined surface (carvel—Penglai 1 wreck) and the individually overlapping strake style (clinker—Shinan wreck). For the Quanzhou 1 wreck, both clinker and carvel styles applied. Several strakes were carvel-built with rabbeted edges, and then the hull "section" was itself rabbeted and lapped over the adjoining section, to produce a combination clinker/carvel hull construction.[30] Scarfs, or the joints where the ends of hull strakes met, were located at bulkhead positions. Most of the archaeological samples featured a single layer of hull planking, but the Quanzhou 1 shipwreck had a second, thinner outer layer, aligned to maintain its carvel/clinker hull design.

Caulking technologies, methods of sealing the narrow gaps between hull planks as well as plugging nail holes, have long been an important feature for successful junk construction. Such things as sap and tar and hot pitch have been used by a variety of seafaring cultures. The Chinese caulking material has in the past been made up of a mixture of lime (from oyster shells), tree resin such as tung oil, and a fiber medium such as copra or cotton or pounded hemp. This mixture, known as *chunam*, has been recorded at least as early as the thirteenth century by observers such as Marco Polo, and it shows up in the archaeological context as well.[31] *Chunam* was used on the Bakau wreck (early 1400s), the Quanzhou 1 wreck (1277), and others. Missionaries in the mid-eighteenth century remarked on the material, noting it lacked the nauseous smell of tar, and also "there is no danger of fire, as there is in our vessels wherein so much pitch and tar are used. . . . Tho' the sea run very high, and the vessel was deeply laden, yet by the strength of its planks, and goodness of its caulking, it made very little water."[32]

This same type of caulking was used on the *Free China*, built sometime in the late nineteenth century. Scraps of fishing net had been used as the binder. *Chunam* was still in use in the 1980s, as evident in the Beihai junk built for the Portland Museum. It has often been described as cement-like, and its rigidity and inability to flex, according to some sources, leads to increased leakage.[33] It is essentially the same compound used by the brine-works engineers of Sichuan for piping and other containers.[34] In fact, *chunam* is still in use today, being applied to modern fishing trawlers. Currently it is generally composed of such elements as crushed shell, lime, linseed or tung oil, and a variety of thickening agents, such as crushed bamboo, sand, or asphalt.[35] Several tree species, such as *paulownia* and *firmiana*, have been described as wood oil, or *tung* trees.

Keel

Much past discussion surrounding Chinese hulls and seafaring abilities has centered on the absence or presence of the junk's keel. The keel, and also the deeper relatively V-shaped cross section of hull, are more suited for deep water or oceanic voyaging; while the more rounded and flat-bottomed "keelless" hull shape is more suited to coastal and river navigation. The first stabilizes vessels in the open sea, minimizing leeward drift, and the second allows operations over shallow shoals and tidal mudflats. The description in *Science and Civilization* features flat-bottomed vessels that coincide well with the raft root origin theory for all junks. Needham's attention to "the oldest and least modified types" deals only with raft-junk designs from specific early periods, subsets of junks lacking any structures similar to stern post, keel, and stem post. "In the most classical types there is no stem either, but a rectangular transom bow. The hull may be compared to the half of a hollow cylinder bent upwards towards each end, and there terminated by final partitions—like nothing so much as a piece of bamboo slit along its length."[36]

Needham's massive work *Science and Civilization in China* was completed before more recent archaeological discoveries, namely Song dynasty vessels and others excavated during the 1980s in joint cooperation between the Australian Institute for Maritime Archaeology and the Beijing National Museum. These projects discovered the remains of substantial seagoing vessels with V-shaped hulls (or "rounded bottom" in McGrail's terminology) and keels, and provided new data for a more complete understanding of regional variations. These junks were much better adapted to true ocean sailing, more suitable to the deeper bays and harbors of the southern Chinese coastline.[37]

Chinese keels on southern coast seagoing junks were often made up of three individual sections, a fore, middle, and aft keel piece.[38] The relationship between the lengths of these sections was a major factor in the overall shape of the hull. In fact, one method that Chinese scholars have used to define styles of junks is based on various ratios of keel section length to hull width, overall length, mast diameter, etc.[39] Distinct oceangoing keels and deeper V-shaped hull profiles of southern coastal junk designs appear in vessel remains at Quanzhou 1, Quanzhou 2, Shinan, and Ningbo. McGrail, in *Boats of the World,* finds that in general Song to Ming dynasty junks have aft keels inclined upward at about 10 degrees from the main keel, and fore keels inclined upward at about 20 degrees. Keel sections are joined by complex horizontal scarfs.[40] The hull transitions between the main and fore keel were generally angular, rather than smooth. This gave most of the vessels studied a fore-and-aft rocker, a main keel that was not flat. Unfortunately, information on the selected junks in this study does not always provide dimensions of any types of keels.

Whether Chinese junks had or did not have keels is really a question of junk capability at open ocean voyaging. Unfortunately, it is not always clear what the acceptable western definition of keel is when used in reference to Chinese junks. While relatively flat-bottomed junks do not feature the pronounced western design, the center plank is often up to 50 percent thicker than surrounding hull strakes, and is often labeled a keel, in Chinese the *longgu,* or Dragon Spine. This is the case with the Penglai 1 shipwreck discovered in 1984.[41] The dictionary definition of the keel is "the lowest and principal timber of a wooden ship . . . which extends the whole length of the vessel," but is not necessarily the timber "to which the stem, sternpost, and ribs or timbers of the vessel are attached."[42] Nonetheless, western specialists are most familiar with keels that feature a flat run from upright stem and stern posts. Chinese junks with axial rudders at transom sterns and transom bows have no stem or stern posts. Three-part keels are joined at specific angles. This seems to have caused some confusion. In short, whether the observer chose to label a particular junk as either having or not having a keel depended more on subjective perceptions of Chinese history rather than broader scientific data. It may be easier to categorize the junk form with the raft tradition if one focuses on post–Ming dynasty shallow water craft and downplays China's ocean voyaging past. Historically, the Chinese have built both V-shaped hulls with keels and flat-bottomed vessels with relatively minor or no keels, each for its own purpose and geographic suitability. During certain periods oceangoing designs were severely restricted, but recent archeological work has put to rest the idea that Chinese junks were never built for open ocean passages.

Gang Deng describes the V-shaped hull and keel of the long-range *fuzhou-* or *fuchuan-*type vessel that dominated the southern coastal areas beginning in the late Tang dynasty (ninth century A.D.). This oceangoing Fujian vessel was distinctly different from shallow water or "sand" ships (*shachuan*), which were built with slightly rounded or flat bottoms and no distinct keels.[43] Though the design of the sand ships may be as old as the Warring States period, the name *shachuan* comes from the Ming dynasty. They were never replaced by the deeper-keeled *fuchuan,* for the keel-less junk was cheaper to build and better suited for operations in shallow waters, such as river-sea deltas and trading areas predominant in the northern China coast.[44] Worcester also makes a division between northern and southern types of junks, and points out that all the more specific local varieties may be placed within this more general outline, though he discusses types representative only of the *shachuan* keel-less design. "The Northern types have bluff bows and flat bottoms, because the ports to which they trade are situated on rivers where grounding is not infrequent. In South China, where deep water prevails, the junks have sharper bows and somewhat deeper draughts."[45] Other scholars take into account western influence in more contemporary designs, particularly in Guangdong and Fujian Provinces, contact zones between Chinese and Indonesian seafaring for a long period prior to the past four hundred years of more recent western intervention. "In general, the more northerly types preserve older and more traditional characteristics, whereas those of the South show many introductions from foreign boat-building techniques. There is a general and transitional change in coastal junks from north to south along the China coast."[46]

In the truly distant past, Chinese civilization began on the northern plains of the Yellow River, and it was only with expansion southward that the ethnic Chinese came into contact with coastal and seafaring people. Some suggest that the use of internal frames, or ribs, alongside and in between the bulkheads was an indication of western influence. Can that be correct? These frames have now been discovered in contexts far earlier than any significant western influence in maritime China, and so should be considered more endemic to the region. Such frames are more frequent in southern China, where the number of bulkheads tends to decline.

The junk keel is a critical component, central to the shape of the hull and the vessel's hydrodynamic characteristics. Hull shape and keel are directly related to deep water capabilities; therefore, it is possible that opinions on whether China was indeed involved overseas might influence the recognition of the junk keel. At the time when the West first made significant contact with maritime China, the imperial government had long been enforcing its own ban on private overseas trade, and coastal shallow water junks predominated. Yet for hundreds of years, the Chinese had built ships both with and without *what the West would recognize as* authentic keels, depending on the ship's usage. This major design distinction has led to a broad association of specific junk types with particular periods of history. *Fuchuan* junks obviously had recognizable keels; *shachuan* junks, a general category that includes more recent junk designs, are not always recognized as having keels.[47] It should be noted that flat-bottomed vessels, while better suited to shallow waters, were not always limited to those areas. The fifteenth-century Bakau Chinese shipwreck in the Karimata Strait of Indonesia, examined by Michael Flecker in 1999, was apparently a flat-bottom, keel-less vessel.[48]

PROPULSION PATTERNS: RIG

The historical evidence of the use of sails is more difficult to assess than the features of the hull, particularly for the underwater archaeologist who rarely encounters the rigging and the lighter structures of the upper works. Due to the wrecking process, physical remains of masts and sails, unlike hull structure, almost never survive the elements of biological and mechanical deterioration in the archaeological context. There is some indication that the Chinese did not begin to use sails for propulsion until the Sui dynasty (eighth century A.D.), though such a delay is hard to imagine given the obvious advantages and early use in all other seafaring cultures.[49] Later, however, Chinese masts and sails clearly underwent technological evolution. By the Song dynasty, masts on inland waterway vessels were stepped in pivoting tabernacles or mast steps on the deck, allowing the rig to be lowered. Maritime transportation upriver necessitated passage under numerous bridges. At least as early as the Ming dynasty and probably much earlier, rigid battens flattened the overall sail shape, making for a very efficient airfoil.[50] Long strips of bamboo were attached horizontally to the sail material itself. Battens allowed the sail to retain its foil shape, maintaining a flatter surface to

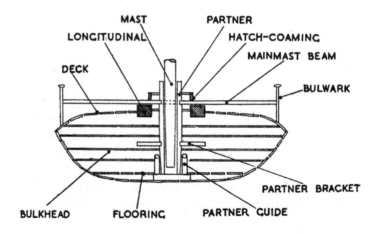

Figure 6. In this detail of the Hangzhou Bay trader, you can see that the mast, located between the partners and directly against the interior bulkhead, does not extend to the bottom of the vessel. (From Waters, "Chinese Junks: The Hangchow Bay Trader and Fisher," by kind permission of the Hon. Editor of the *Mariner's Mirror*)

the wind, even when patches of the actual sail material were torn or missing. This was an advanced and advantageous feature. Batten sails have only recently been adopted by racing yachts and catamarans.

For many, the distinctive feature of Chinese junks is the balanced lugsail rig, a four-sided sail with a gaff or yard at the top. Here again Chinese vessels are distinctly different from western sailing ships. There are three basic differences between Chinese and European sailing rigs (rig being all the gear above decks used for propulsion of the vessel): First, Chinese junks historically had no standing or permanent rigging; second, junk masts were not set solely into the keel of the hull but sandwiched between fixed mast partners adjacent to bulkheads; and third, masts were not necessarily all set along the centerline of the vessel. (Thus, the weight of the mast was carried to the two mast partners, supported by the mast deck beams, bulkhead partner brackets, and carried only *indirectly* to the thwart ship mast step, obviating the need for a single massive keelson.) There were a large variety of sail shapes, most again being classified along the lines of northern and southern types. All, though, were fore-and-aft rigs and, combined with the efficiency of the batten-reinforced airfoil, allowed Chinese vessels to sail close to the wind, an ability that never failed to surprise the western mariners.[51] The windward ability of traditional junks exceeded that of European square-rigged ships.

The final feature of these sails was that they were self-reefing. The heavy fore-and-aft batten lugsail, upon being lowered, tended to fold itself onto the junk. No Chinese sailors had to climb the rigging, or go aloft, in order to reduce sail when the winds increased, as was the case with square-rigged European ships. This obviated the need to maintain a large crew to bring in multiple square sails in a storm, alleviating the danger involved in such an activity, though no doubt raising the heavy sails was quite a chore. On smaller junks the Chinese sail was economical to operate.

From the sample of Song–Ming period shipwreck sites come examples of transverse mast steps, perpendicular to the keel and featuring paired indentations for accepting the mast partners (not the mast). These mast partner steps were located at specific positions along the junk's main axis. The foremast step was usually located 17–22 percent of the overall length aft from the bow, and the mainmast step was generally located 52–57 percent aft from the bow. A third, and lighter, mizzenmast, if in common usage in Song through Ming seagoing junks, does not appear to have been stepped to the keel.[52]

STEERING PATTERNS: RUDDER

Perhaps the most diagnostic feature defining junk sailing vessels, upon close inspection, is the distinct Asian-style rudder. Whereas European rudders progressed from fixed single or double steering oars to fixed and permanent rudders attached directly to a stern post via strong pintle and gudgeon hardware sometime in the thirteenth century, Chinese rudders took shape much as a centerline rudder in roughly the same position, but not attached permanently to the transom at all. Instead, Chinese rudders could often be raised and lowered at will, and were sometimes held in position against the transom with a system of cables and wooden gudgeons or notches. This allowed the rudder to be adjustable, and in fact relatively easy to remove, though large rudders had considerable weight. The Chinese rudder is the earliest example of center or axial rudder designs in the world.[53]

Many different local designs proliferated throughout China, but the rudders of coastal seagoing junks are of particular interest here. These tended to be narrower and capable of extending deeper into the water, well below the bottom of the vessel, thus serving as a stabilizing keel and reducing leeway or leeward drift.[54] Centerboards, or more specifically daggerboards, served the same function of creating a deep keel that could greatly reduce leeward drift and aid the junk in staying on course.

One theory holds that the Chinese rudder developed from the combination of the Chinese steering oar, or *yuloh*, and the high stern sheer of the sampan. The sculling oar, loosely connected at the stern of the boat, evolved into the suspended median rudder.[55] This design has also been termed the vertical axial rudder. The rudder post was set between wooden jaws or notches, which were open, semi-open, or closed. The rudder, if large, was kept in place with the appropriate cable and tackle.[56] The large iron hinges of western designs were absent. The Chinese design featured basic wooden construction, cheaper and perhaps more easily available to local shipwrights.

Archaeological evidence from a late Han dynasty tomb attests to the Chinese use of this kind of rudder approximately one thousand years before such a thing as an axial rudder made its appearance in the West.[57] Worcester speculates that this was due, in part, to the general shape of the Chinese vessel. Median rudders were much more compatible with flat transoms, compared to the early European double-ended designs, which narrowed to a single curving post at the stern.[58] Early European designs, such as Greek round vessels and Viking longships, were double-ended and sailed therefore with steering oars, not rudders. Few rudders from the Song through Ming period have survived in the archaeological context. There are rare examples of the notched wooden gudgeons affixed to the junk transom at the Quanzhou 1 site and the Penglai 1 site, and even indications of the Chinese rudder stock having been slotted between two wooden pillars attached vertically to the aft transom.[59] And of course the large rudder found at the Nanjing imperial shipyard in the 1950s has often been used as an indicator of the great size of Admiral Zheng He's Ming navy ships, but the rudder alone without the ship is only a part of the story.

Chinese rudders, despite their long evolution, are not mentioned in a recent publication claiming comprehensive description of "the rudder."[60] The mechanism for possible transmission to Europe certainly existed in the form of Crusade-era Arab ship captains, and there are some indications that Arab ships, between 1000 and 1200 A.D., featured median rudders, but the question is still open.[61]

For as unwieldy and heavy as these Chinese rudders appeared to be, it should be noted that they were capable of adapting more to the environment—of being manipulated more actively—than the fixed European rudder. Chinese sailors could adjust the depth while at sea. The rudder blade itself could often be enlarged or diminished by adding or removing additional boards using preset holes in the rudder post. Such holes are still in evidence in more modern junks. In short, Chinese rudders contributed to the sailing characteristics of the vessel in several different ways, with a relative amount of flexibility.

Essential to the handling of all large rudders, as well as the hoisting of heavy batten sails and anchors, was the horizontal windlass—the *liao*, or "winders," in Chinese. This is also called the Spanish windlass in Europe. The design of these common labor-saving machines remains fairly constant through time.

The Pattern and Language of Nineteenth-Century Seagoing Junks

Distinctive criteria fall into three broad categories for Chinese junks: hull, rig, and rudder. Here is the generalized pattern language for Chinese ship construction, in some cases drawn more from the archaeological evidence of the Song–Ming period, and in others from earlier or later sources. Specific junks might not reflect these guidelines exactly, but in the general sense these are many of the distinctive elements that appear over and over again in many Chinese junks. Just as categories of ceiling height and wall thickness and southern exposure can be described as components of patterns within regional architectural styles, bulkhead number and rudder design and batten sail style and hull planking arrangement are the maritime counterparts of patterns in Chinese junk design.

Table 3. Basic Junk Construction Patterns

Hull:	1. greatest beam aft of the midship section
	2. transom bow and stern construction
	3. rabbeted planks and angled edge iron nailing
	4. multiple interior transverse bulkheads
	5. seams and holes caulked and filed with *chunam* mixture
	6. half frames adjacent to bulkheads
	7. complex angled keel in multiple sections
	8. use of limber holes
	9. use of iron *gua ju* nails between hull and bulkheads
	10. multiple layers of planking possible
Rig:	1. batten lugsail fore-and-aft designs
	2. regionally distinctive sail shapes
	3. no standing or permanent fixed rigging
	4. masts placed between mast partners
	5. transverse mast steps at specific locations on keel
Rudder:	1. suspended adjustable median design
	2. regionally distinctive rudder shapes
	3. positioned in wooden notches or vertical pillars
	4. relatively narrow, deep forms for oceangoing designs
	5. used in conjunction with horizontal windlass

For the Chinese who built the sailing junks, certain patterns of construction features, proven successful over time, were accepted as the normal definition of a junk. The details of those features, the specific style of stern transom, the placement of masts or angle of keel components within the acceptable range, spoke to the shipwright as well, specifying a particular type of junk, a merchant or fishing vessel, a northern or southern style. With a feeling for the basic patterns of Chinese junk construction as we know them, and an understanding of the possible differences in detail, we are in a better position to describe the characteristics of the ten junks sampled here, and possibly discern variations in Chinese construction patterns due to the introduction of foreign features associated with the dynamic social and economic changes of the nineteenth and early twentieth centuries.

The pattern language approach, as applied by Steven Lubar, helps to illuminate possible connections between technology and society. Lubar's article on objects and the industrial revolution, in *History from Things: Essays on Material Culture,* reveals the material reflection of critical political and social transformations. Within the comparative framework of eastern and western sailing vessels, certain Chinese patterns that feature ease of construction, low cost, and efficiency in operation, such as the sailing rig and the rudder design, seem to reflect the small-scale, village-level, and for lack of a better word "democratic" nature of private junk construction in China. Anthropologist Lewis Mumford bisects technological artifacts into two types of political realities, two different groups of patterns: authoritarian-styled objects, or system-centered, immensely powerful tools; and democratic-styled objects, or man-centered, relatively weak tools that are both efficient and economical.[62] The solid European state-supported armed trade galleons might be seen as falling into the first category, those that are reflective of expansive civilization-building technologies—and the locally built, relatively unarmed local Chinese junks, more along the lines of technologies of the small farmer, falling into the second. After all, on the regional scale of history, China did not use the seas as an arena for state territorial expansion like England and other nations in the West. China was not a "maritime nation" by that standard.

ARMED VERSUS UNARMED TRADE SHIPS

These comparative observations on the technology of ships lead to certain assumptions and related questions. If one accepts that the construction and overall shape of vessels express the nature of the seafaring culture, then in what ways do European vessels manifest the nature of armed trade? How do

Chinese vessels reveal the character of unarmed trade? And if they do, on what basis can comparisons be made between them?

Works describing European ship construction are too numerous to count. Nautical scholars are already well familiar with the thickened oak hulls and closely spaced frames, the large hanging knees and solid deck beams to support the weight of ordnance, and gun ports framed between stout wales, successful ship designs born from a history of armed conflict. All obstructions along the gun decks could be very quickly cleared away, making space for gun crews to efficiently work the cannon. European merchantmen featured many of the same construction patterns. Between the twelfth and sixteenth centuries, the two were often one and the same. Cannon and gun crews and the vessels designed to carry them remained an important part of European commercial ventures in Asia, such as the British East India Company (EIC) and the Dutch Vereenigde Oost-Indische Companie (VOC). These institutions operated as informal navies in their trade to maritime Asia for hundreds of years.

What of the Chinese vessels? If their design truly reflected unarmed trade, then commercial carriers would have been incapable of being turned into an instant navy in the European sense. Supporting timbers would not have been provided to bear the weight of cannon, and material obstructions on deck would have been permanent. Hulls would not be pierced by gun ports, which require more time and material to construct. That seems to be the case. Chinese junk design, centered completely on the transportation of cargo, eliminated these costs, and may have gained an added measure of economic efficiency due to this freedom. Also, the presence of junks did not represent an armed threat to established institutions. Professor Anthony Reid makes the clear case that junk traffic was certainly more welcome in many ports for these exact reasons. The junks sailing to or from China with government approval were often limited in the arms they could carry, to only two cannon and eight rifles, because of fears that they might engage in piracy. Even when Chinese numbers reached dozens of junks and thousands of men in ports such as Bangkok, Hoi An, Pnompenh, Riau, and Sulu, they presented little threat to the local regime, whereas the lesson was not lost of what happened to indigenous rulers in Melaka, Ternate, Jakarta, Makassar, or Banten at European hands.[63]

There are differences in the economic and political costs of armed versus unarmed trade. Equating vessels that originated with the design of floating gun platforms with those of a purely commercial nature seems precarious from several aspects. Kenneth Pomeranz, in *The Great Divergence*, attempts a direct economic comparison of Chinese and European trading vessels. Though he asserts that armed trade granted European nations a decided advantage, Pomeranz states that there is not much difference in long-distance transportation technology in Europe, China, or Japan before the coming of the steamship in the mid-nineteenth century.[64] The only true difference in ship design appears toward the end of his analysis, when "Over time soldiers and sailors became more effective per capita thanks to technological change (e.g. better guns and ships)."[65] This revolution in ordnance and steam propulsion and iron hulls was a major and costly transformation on the maritime scene. But, regarding the sailing vessels, for Pomeranz all European and Chinese designs seem to have existed in an undifferentiated and generalized state of equilibrium, a level playing field. Is this true, or is this an oversimplification?

Carlo M. Cipolla, in *Guns, Sails, and Empires,* places the same faith in the clear advantages of armed trade and European ships over other forms of transportation. "Thanks to the revolutionary characteristics of their man-of-war, it took only a few decades for the Europeans to establish their absolute predominance over the Oceans."[66] But what is predominance? Reid points out that as late as the 1820s, Chinese total shipping tonnage had a carrying capacity of approximately eighty-five thousand tons, still outranking European shipping in the South China Sea.[67] Again, the problem of comparing apples and oranges, or warships and commercial carriers, raises difficulties. There is military dominance and there is economic efficiency, and the two are not always the same.

Is it really possible to separate aspects of armed trade from nautical technology? Armed trade did provide a successful strategy for aggressive and expansive maritime nations, but beyond that, the comparative study of vessels is often glossed over. For some scholars, ships with guns represent the only real measure of any maritime activity. Empires that did not follow this model, as China did not (particularly following the maritime ban in the fifteenth century) are sometimes mistakenly perceived as having abandoned the ocean altogether. Jared Diamond states in *Guns, Germs, and Steel,* "China's abandonment of oceangoing ships (as well as of mechanical clocks and water-driven spinning machines) are well-known historical instances of technological reversals in isolated or semi-isolated societies."[68] China did abandon large and expensive ship construction following the noted Ming dynasty voyages of Zheng He, as well as support for private overseas expansion, but oceangoing ships? This question of armed trade is almost inextricably bound up with nautical technology itself. What are the sea-keeping capabilities of Chinese junks? Taking a closer look at junk design may provide a clearer understanding of the advantages of unarmed trade.

Classification of Selected Vessels

With photographs and sketches from a variety of different sources, we can attempt to interpret the selection of transpacific junks. How well do they reflect the known patterns of Chinese ship construction? What else do they reveal? Chinese junks represent technological artifacts, machines built for efficient and safe transportation. And they represent other aspects of seafaring culture as well, such as floating homes, fishing tools, and even artifacts with mythical significance. In some cases there is a good deal of certainty in the identity of the vessels; in others, especially when there are very few documents and photographs to deal with, the association is less certain. Worcester's *Classification of the Principal Sea-Going Junks* figures heavily in the following analysis due to its unique nature, but this does not imply any real assurance that his terminology, an ethnographic snapshot of junk types in the early twentieth century, was or is the final word in classification.

THE *WHANG HO*: RETIRED FROM THE BEAT

Judging from the rare pictures of the junk *Whang Ho*, and the brief history, the vessel owned by W. M. Milne was a classic example of a large soldier boat (*dabingchuan*).[69] Milne claimed to have obtained the *Whang Ho* in Nanjing. The *Whang Ho* is an exception in this study to Mumford's general "democratic small farmer"–style vessel, for the junk carried cannon and may have played a defined state role. Though there are no references to any one specific locality associated with this military junk, there are certain design elements that associate the vessel with southern Chinese vessel types in Guangdong.

The Milne postcard, a rare image, depicts the rounded stern and large overhanging gallery of southern Chinese origin. The large, three-masted junk also features the high, upturned wings at the bow, and large forward windlass machinery, typical of southern-style trawlers. The junk moves under way despite its fore-and-aft batten sails appearing in tatters, testimony to the Chinese rig design. Foremast and mainmast are stepped far forward, possibly in the specific 20 percent and 55 percent positions aft from the bow. The mizzenmast appears stepped only to the deck. The rounded leech or aft edge of the sail and wide-spaced battens appear southern in design. The shrouds, permanent standing rigging running from the masts to the sides of the hull, seem to be evidence of European influence, suggesting greater

Figure 7. The junk *Whang Ho*, a Guangchuan southern coastal vessel, under way circa 1908. (Courtesy of the San Francisco Maritime National Historic Park, H7.21)

foreign contact among the southern-style junks in Guangdong Province.[70] Unfortunately, from this stern angle, many features, such as gun ports, are not visible.

Worcester's *Junks and Sampans of the Yangtze River* includes drawings of a typical oceangoing war junk from the mid-nineteenth century, showing the same rounded stern arrangement and overhanging gallery. The masts and sails in these drawings appear quite similar to those of the *Whang Ho*, as do the high wings or upward projections of the bulwarks (sides) at the bow. A square fenestrated Guangdong rudder, regionally distinctive, is also visible beneath the stern. Small lookout houses appear on deck, as mentioned in nineteenth-century western accounts, which generally found war junks to be large and cumbersome masses of timber. Observers also noted the considerable sheer of the hull, the large quarter galleries, and the wide variety of both foreign and domestic guns of different caliber mounted on wooden carriages.

Firsthand western estimates place the size of the larger war junks in the neighborhood of 800 tons. The crew for such a vessel is estimated to have been from forty to sixty men.[71] This may have included soldiers tasked with boarding, capturing, and sailing confiscated vessels back to port. An estimate of the average size of war junks in the early nineteenth century was between 250 and 300 tons, a little over 100 feet in length.[72] Smaller war junks, possessing six cannon (three per side) may have ranged around 150 tons.[73] Judging solely from the number of cannon carried on board, this particular *dabingchuan* seems, then, to be in the larger class. There are not enough details available to be able to assess how being outfitted with cannon may have affected the design elements of the junk's deck and hull construction.

These are the types of junks that met the British naval expeditionary forces in what we refer to as the Opium Wars. Fleets of war junks in the Chinese army had previously been composed of inner and outer "water squadrons" and had traditionally been used in anti-pirate operations, as well as in patrols to prevent uncontrolled immigration.[74] In the nineteenth century these war junks were mainly used in coastal patrols—they did not have long-range missions familiar to western navies. Most of the Chinese fleet was actually part of the Green Banner land force, established by the Manchu rulers as a kind of provincial constabulary.[75]

Junks like the *dabingchuan* were not, of course, the only type of Chinese war vessels prevalent. Water forces were divided into different categories. Other designs, known as Chasers (*cang cang chuan*), Flat Bottomed (*shachuan*), Quick Leaping (*kuai duan*), and Fast Horse (*kuai ma*) were used when appropriate. Suppression of salt smuggling and protection of small fishing vessels were also tasks for military junks. The *dabingchuan,* though, most closely resembles the transpacific junk *Whang Ho,* and if Milne's junk was truly more than one hundred years old in 1908, it must have been one of the luckiest of war junks, having survived the wars with foreigners and various actions against pirates of all sorts.

Besides cannon, Chinese crews had access to weapons such as spears, pikes, matchlock muskets, and larger gingalls, which were mounted on the bulwarks. Closely woven and relatively elastic large rattan shields, some two to three feet in diameter, were mounted on the upper gunwales. These offered effective protection not only against swords, but against long-range musket shot as well.[76]

The trend for war junks over time, particularly in response to the lack of effectiveness against British ships during the first Opium War in 1839–1842, was for vessels to become larger and mount more guns. Some authorities record ordnance the size of the western thirty-two-pounder cannon on Chinese war junks.[77] The use of gun ports increased. The new naval force was placed under an admiral of the Yangzi, whose jurisdiction extended over five provinces. "The fleet was more in the nature of a large constabulary force and was highly organized and efficiently run, with a strict code of honour and regulations for all contingencies."[78]

Four cannon can clearly be seen in another Milne postcard of the *Whang Ho*, as the gun crews stand at the ready. With at least eight guns on the main deck, this junk may be a slightly smaller version than the Paris sketch from 1842 (figure 9). The cannon appear to be late eighteenth or early nineteenth century Armstrong pattern British pieces, of eighteen- or twenty-four-pounder size. The breach rings at the rear of each gun just above the knobs, or cascabels, identify the pieces as post-1780 designs.[79] Also visible is the elevated port wing at the bow (upper right in figure). Cannon continued to be used on junks up to at least 1946. These old cannon were not just for display, but continued to be used, firing almost anything that could produce damage, from broken ceramics to scraps of iron and nails. It was not enough; even local authorities noted their antiquated nature. "The bow and spear, small guns, and native-made cannon which have hitherto been used by China cannot resist their [European] rifles, which have their bullets fed from the rear opening. . . .Therefore, we are controlled by the Westerners."[80] Robert Cardwell, traveling in China in 1946, reported seeing several "ancient muzzle-loading cannon of our great-grandfather's day. Although

Figure 8. The deck of the war junk *Whang Ho*, circa 1908, looking toward the bow. (Courtesy of the San Francisco Maritime National Historic Park, H9.21)

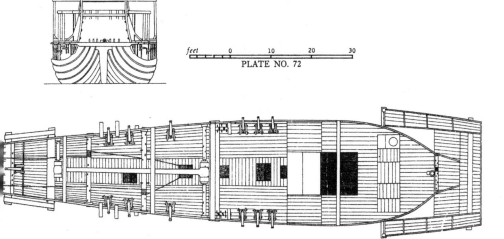

PLATE NO. 72

Figure 9. An 1842 plan view sketch of a *dabingchuan,* or large soldier boat. (From Worcester, *The Junks and Sampans of the Yangtze,* courtesy of the Naval Institute Press)

some of the guns were of Chinese manufacture, many of them—to judge by their markings—were survivals of the armaments of long bygone and now almost forgotten warships."[81]

Lieutenant Paris's 1842 plan view shows the layout of the main deck of a *dabingchuan.* Dark rectangles mark the hatches leading into the lower holds, and the large outboard quarter galleries at the stern to the right-hand side of the figure are immediately apparent. As in many Chinese vessel designs, the maximum width, or beam, of the vessel is aft, rather than forward. Transom bow and stern, and offset horizontal windlass on the starboard side, appear as well. Unfortunately details such as fastenings, bulkheads, mast partners, keel, and other hull features are not mentioned.

The *Whang Ho,* then, appears to have been a real and considerably aged war junk from the China coast showing traditional patterns of Chinese junk construction mixed with some foreign influence, consistent with the basic features of a nineteenth-century large soldier boat. Its significance is tied to the historic prevalence of piracy in Asian waters, battles fought during the Taiping Rebellion, and possibly even a lucky engagement with western forces. China's first serious encounter with elements of a more modern navy occurred during the Opium Wars. At that point it became obvious that wooden war junks no longer controlled the seas. Such was the era of the *dabingchuan.* The establishment of the modern naval arsenals and shipyards, and the adoption of steel and steam technology, and particularly the purchase of a flotilla of modern western-style, iron-hulled gunboats in 1880, would render these older wooden sailing war junks quickly obsolete.

The fact that western-style cannon were carried on the upper deck of the Chinese war junk adds a touch of irony to the phenomenon of technological assimilation on the Chinese coast. This does not, however, invalidate the long history of the junk war fleets, nor dampen interest in what was, for so long, the Chinese imperial order at sea. Chinese war junks, with their large crews and incendiary weapons, operated under their own paradigm, and only suffered in comparison to non-Asian technologies at the very end of a very long reign.

THE *NING PO*: PONDEROUS, MAGNIFICENT BUTTOCKS

All available source images identify the junk *Ning Po* as representative of the Fuzhou pole junk category of China's southern coast. Worcester assigns the name *hua pigu,* translating this as flowery buttocks, without explanation. Possibly this is an allusion to the decorated stern transom. According to Paul Chow, navigator of the junk *Free China, hua pigu* is not odd at all for the name of a style of junk. The *pigu,* the buttocks or stern of the vessel, was adorned with an abundance of flowery designs. And furthermore the opening for the "head," or toilet, on Chinese junks was at the stern. "From a certain angle, you can look in and see a real *pigu!*"[82]

This particular type of vessel has received a greater amount of attention than others. Pole junks, so named due to their massive cargoes of logs or poles hauled up and down the China coast, were some of the largest and most conspicuous vessels in Asian waters. They were truly massive and heavily built for their rough trade. Rafts of lumber, especially Fujian pine (*Pinus massoniana*) used for furniture-making and junk construction, were often floated down the Min River of Fujian Province. Upon arrival at Fuzhou, the rafts would be disassembled and the logs stacked to await shipment by sailing junk to Shanghai and other parts of China.[83] These would be loaded both on deck and outboard of the pole junk attached by cables and overhanging beams. These junks generally made five or six trips per year in this fashion, between June and September, taking advantage of the monsoon winds.[84] The large vessel itself would almost disappear behind its enormous cargo.

Chinese sailing ships such as pole junks usually were constructed of three different types of wood: the Fujian pine mentioned above, known to the Chinese as *maweisong;* fir (*Cunninghamia lanceolata*), known as *shan;* and camphor (*Cinnamomum camphora*), or *xiangzhang.*[85] Typically camphor wood would be used for structural members, such as frames, as well as windlasses.

Figure 10. The *Ning Po* on display at Catalina, as she slowly settles into the mud at Ballast Point. ("Ning" is misspelled in the photo.) Note the rounded wales evident on the mid hull. (Courtesy of the San Francisco Maritime National Historic Park, George M. Beard Collection D8.30)

Fir would be employed as hull strakes and bulkheads; and pine used for the keel. Pole junks sometimes carried the very material of their own construction, distributing their timber along the Chinese coast.

The *Ning Po*, 138 feet in length and 31 feet in beam, was a medium-sized (300 ton), three-masted, Fujian-style oceangoing trade ship. Pole junks ranged between 120 and 180 feet long, and between 200 and 400 tons. (These outer dimensions encompass the size of another famous Chinese junk, the *Keying*, which arrived in London in 1848.) The normal complement for Fujian vessels of this size was some twenty-five or thirty crewmen.[86] Fifteen internal bulkheads (incidentally, the same number as the *Titanic*), and over thirty frames or ribs arranged between these divisions, gave the craft great strength. The use of a higher number of frames may indicate a greater foreign influence in comparison to junks further north.[87] Frames are drawn adjacent to the multiple interior transverse bulkheads (figure 11). These pole junks are alternately described as having no keel, or having a very shallow keel. In all instances, though, their hull shape is rounded and generally flat-bottomed.

The division of the interior of junks into so many compartments not only served to protect the vessel from sinking (in case one of the sections was flooded or compromised in some way), but also functioned as a convenient

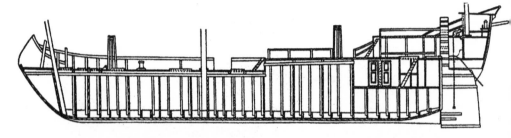

Figure 11. An idealized elevation sketch of a Chinese pole junk, with the very large rudder raised within the transom and the large number of bulkheads and frames clearly visible. (From Worcester, *The Junks and Sampans of the Yangtze*, courtesy of the Naval Institute Press)

device to manage the use of space on board the craft. The master of the junk could lease each compartment individually to merchants, rather than divide shares by tonnage in the European fashion.[88] Kenneth Pomeranz examined the nature of the monsoon trading pattern in relation to this compartmentalized design. He found watertight bulkhead compartments for the cargo of individual merchants to be an appropriate system for the slower-paced monsoon trading pattern in Southeast Asia. This is in comparison to the different system of European trade in the Atlantic.[89]

Besides frames, there are other possible influences on the design of the *hua pigu*; namely, upright rather than horizontal capstans, a western invention, were documented on pole junks in the nineteenth century. Large capstans and winches dominated the working deck for hoisting heavy sails, mooring cables, and cargo. Labor-saving devices were essential. Very large and heavy adjustable rudders could weigh several tons on the big Fujian coastal traders. These, too, were raised and lowered by hand with winches. Several thick, rounded wales stretched along each side of the hull, giving the vessel longitudinal rigidity, the hull appearing carvel-built with no indication of multiple layers of planking. The sizeable dimension of all scantlings (all structural ship timbers) was the primary reason for the longevity of these big junks. They were simply heavily overbuilt for their cumbersome trade. Worcester records several examples as being more than 150 years old.[90]

Though Chinese pole junks constructed in Fujian Province were made of local fir and more resinous pine, the *Ning Po* was slightly different. The junk's upper works were teak, with teak and camphor wood used throughout interior bulkheads and hull planks. Interestingly, the size, time period built, and use of teak on the *Ning Po* are all indicators suggesting that this vessel may have been built in Siam (Thailand), Chinese ship construction being fairly common there at the time due to cheap labor and higher quality materials.[91] Siam possessed a major overseas Chinese merchant community engaged in maritime trade. Deforestation on the Chinese mainland made sources of lumber from overseas more and more significant. Such deforestation also drove up the price of ship construction in China. Average costs rose some 700 percent between 1550 and 1820.[92]

The bow and stern transoms and copious decorations were among the distinguishable features of these craft. The ornately carved oval stern, complete with yan or swallow bird motif, images of the immortals, and serpent depictions on the quarters, was typically Fujianese in character. Such stylized decorations were long established and very standardized. Only minor variations have ever been encountered.[93] They appear here similar to examples from the preceding centuries (figure 12).

Figure 12. The *Ning Po* aground at Dead Man's Island. The rudder trunk and false transom are visible, as well as decorative motifs of the yan bird and the eight immortals on the oval stern. (Courtesy of the San Francisco Maritime National Historic Park, D3.20)

As the stern transom itself is pierced to receive the adjustable median rudder, the entire compartment is not watertight. Thus, the stern transom is often called the false transom, the real transom of the vessel being the first watertight bulkhead forward of the rudder post. Such an arrangement served to offer a measure of protection to the rudder. The mizzenmast can be seen stepped high on the transom stern. The foremast appears in the photographs close to its expected position, roughly 17–22 percent. The mainmast, however, appears forward of the 52–57 percent position. Unfortunately Worcester's sketch (figure 11) does not reveal details of the mast step or partners.

Though the aging wooden *Ning Po* was aground at Dead Man's Island for days, the massively built vessel was patched and refloated following the storm. The visible shrouds supporting the masts suggest a western addition to the Chinese vessel. The *Ning Po,* before completing the Pacific crossing to California, was re-rigged with western gaff-style sails.

A spacious cabin was built on the quarter or aft deck of the larger vessels, though smaller pole junks had no stern accommodations or raised quarter deck. Such raised quarters at the stern of large vessels invariably recall, for western observers, the towering galleries of medieval craft. The owner or captain of the vessel, the *laoda,* had his quarters at the stern, and the shrine to Tianfei or Guanyin or both was located far aft as well.

The wide and high wings at the bow (figure 10), allegedly built to give the junk its fish-like appearance, also served to divert quartering waves, and also usually supported the horizontal windlass used to lower and raise the large anchor, or to haul the foresail.[94] The adoption of western capstans on the foredeck did away with the horizontal windlass forward, but the flaring wings to port and starboard remained. Often the Chinese windlass, located elsewhere on the deck, remained side by side with the newer western labor-saving device. The use of the newer technology became part of the language of the pole junk pattern.

Transom bows, sometimes cumbersome to western eyes, functioned quite well for Chinese junks. In order to reduce the vessel's pitching motion, frequently the first previously watertight compartment forward would have holes drilled through the hull, below the waterline, allowing water to enter when the vessel dipped its head under the ocean surface, and then drain when the bow rode free above the waves.[95] The first interior bulkhead forward, then, was the true watertight transom. The bow also may have featured another odd element of East/West hybridity. "The stem head is invariably a solid piece of wood covered with an iron plate. On this iron plate will more often than not be seen a familiar home advertisement such as Fry's

Figure 13. One of if not the last of the large coastal traders, the *Ning Po* resting quietly at Catalina Island. The topsides were later destroyed by fire, and today little remains above the mud line. (Courtesy of Catalina Island Museum)

Cocoa, or Colman's Mustard."[96] Old iron scrap had been imported from the United Kingdom into China.

Like the *Whang Ho,* the *Ning Po* reveals certain established patterns of construction, namely: transom bow and stern, multiple bulkheads with adjacent frames, and suspended median rudder. Sparse documentation again leaves specific internal details out of the picture. The critical details of archaeological interest from excavated wreck sites, such as fastener patterns, rabbets, and limber holes, are not apparent. The *Ning Po* also introduces a pattern that does not emerge clearly from the archaeological or documentary record, the large rounded wales in the hull. Do these appear in other examples of Pacific junks?

Large Fuzhou pole junks no longer exist. Their demise was recorded by Worcester himself, during his duty in China in the 1920s. For ponderous dignity the Fujian pole junks were unsurpassed, yet their maneuverability was such that they needed no outside assistance when entering and leaving Shanghai. Chinese inventiveness and originality seemed to have reached their highest point in these larger types, which, unhappily, rapidly vanished from the maritime scene. At one time there were hundreds of pole junks operating all along the coasts of China. At upward of 180 feet long, these were some of the largest Chinese junks built in the late nineteenth century.

Northern vessels such as *shachuan,* or sand boats (meaning flat-bottomed boats), were of similar dimensions, and shared many of the same design features.[97] The general *shachuan* vessel design represents one of the important major classifications of Chinese junks.[98] Though the *Ning Po* shows specific elements altered by outside influence, the junk captures patterns from an earlier age. Maritime archaeologists are currently looking at the possibility of test excavations on the mud-covered remains of the *Ning Po* at Ballast Point, as there could be much learned from a detailed examination of the junk's lower hull.

THE *AMOY*: THE UNSINKABLE VESSEL SUNK

Unlike the government war junk and the large ubiquitous Fujian coastal traders, the smaller Amoy junk designs reflected an even more specialized and regionally endemic fishing and local trade craft, vessels completely devoted to the small-time ocean "farmer." Local Amoy fishing boats were seldom seen north of Shanghai or south of Swatow.[99] The area around what is known today as Xiamen has been known historically for the rough weather of the stormy Formosa channel between Taiwan and the Chinese mainland. Junks from Amoy were famous for their sea-keeping abilities in all such weather, and have therefore been the subject of some research into their design. Amoy, or Xiamen, is a port with a long history of activity, known for its communication with coastal and overseas trade. To be a Chinese sailor from Amoy might be somewhat analogous to being a British sailor from Liverpool, or a Yankee from Nantucket.

These small but handy Amoy fishing junks varied in size from fifty-five to seventy feet in length, and from seventeen to twenty feet in beam, with a depth of five or six feet. They were handy, well-balanced, and comparatively fast craft that were once quite numerous, bobbing about like corks without shipping any water over the sides. There were several reasons why they kept the sea so well. Their small size relative to the ocean swells allowed them to ride over each wave and not plunge into the surface; the construction features of their adjustable rudder and high transom bow added to their stability; and the unique Chinese sail rig, and particularly the forward rake of the foremast, served to help lift the craft out of the waves.

Amoy trade junks, at seventy feet in length and sixteen feet in beam, were at the larger end of the scale for local designs, being longer and narrower than many fishing vessels.[100] But the graceful curves and prominent sheer lines of the two types, the fishing junk and local trading junk of Amoy, seem quite similar. The trade junks traditionally operated between Amoy and Fuzhou. The transpacific junk *Amoy,* a twenty-three-ton, three-masted,

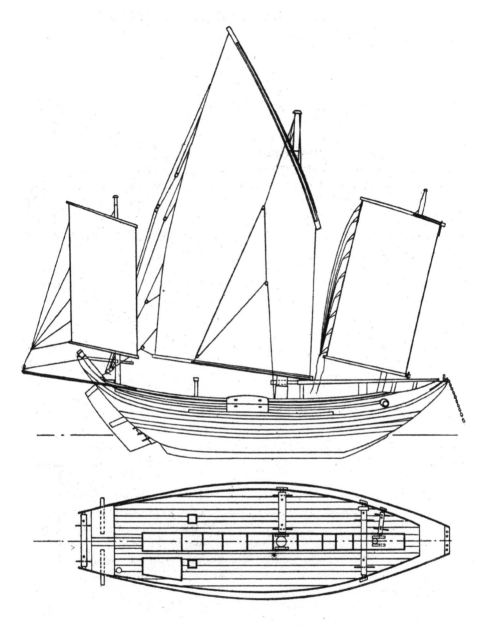

Figure 14. An elevation and sail plan for a small Amoy fishing junk. Note the raised rudder and the lack of standing rigging. (From Worcester, "The Amoy Fishing Boat," by kind permission of the Hon. Editor of the *Mariner's Mirror*)

sixty-five-foot vessel built in 1921, most closely resembles an Amoy trading junk.

The sweeping sheer, or curve of the deck from fore and aft, as well as the considerable forward rake of the foremast (set between partners affixed to the forward bulkhead), are apparent in figure 14. The acute angle and large overhang of the transom bow is also notable. Several "winders," or wind-lasses, are shown on deck, two on the port side and one crossing the bow completely. The forward horizontal windlass can be seen between the fore and main masts in the plan view perspective. The elevation drawing depicts the fore, mid, and aft keel segments, scarfed or joined at angles, reminiscent of multiple examples of Song dynasty junk hull construction.[101] The Quanzhou 1 wreck fore keel was elevated roughly 25 degrees from the main or mid keel, and stern only 10 degrees from the mid keel.

The deep, narrow, suspended adjustable median rudder of the Amoy junk, though completely hidden in the photograph of the junk at Eureka, appears plainly in figure 16. This was characteristic of many similar designs. One cable attached to the shoulder or upper portion of the rudder blade

Figure 15. The junk *Amoy* and numerous passengers during its West Coast tour, at Eureka, California, in 1922. Note the rounded leech and battens of a southern rig design. (Courtesy of the San Francisco Maritime National Historic Park, Wallace Martin Collection K7.22)

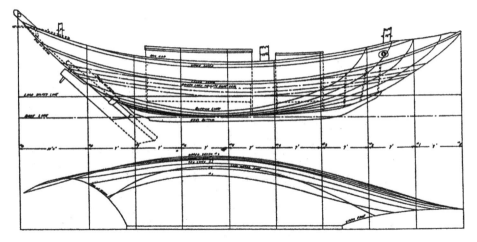

Figure 16. Elevation and waterlines of the *Amoy*. Note the range of rudder adjustment, marked by the dashed lines. (From Gould and Foster, *Junks— Construction and Regional Characteristics*)

to raise and lower the rudder, and one or two cables attached to the heel or lower portion of the rudder blade to pull the rudder forward against the stern of the junk, holding it in place against the flow of the water. Thus, the suspended median rudder was held flexibly, without fixed attachments such as iron pintles and gudgeons, but positioned between vertical pillars. The rudder post usually rode in a wooden groove or loose socket. P. Du Halde, in the eighteenth century, noted the arrangement of cables that operated the Chinese rudder. One set raised and lowered the rudder blade from a windlass mounted above the transom; the other set ran forward beneath the vessel's hull, from the bottom of the rudder to the forepart of the prow, where they were tightened by the deck windlass. The arrangement led to some unforeseen obstacles. Cables underwater gave rise to vibrations, "the continual yawing that gives it a trembling motion without ceasing, from whence arises another inconvenience, which is that there is all the difficulty in the world to keep a vessel steady on the same rumb."[102] The type of junk that Du Halde journeyed on remains unclear.

Nonetheless, there is much testimony to the handiness and maneuverability of Chinese junks revealed in other sources. Observers commented positively on Amoy junk designs, which seemed to handle well, having been designed for the open ocean and bad weather. "Groups of them may be seen occasionally standing out boldly to sea in the northern end of the Formosa Channel, when a moderate gale is blowing and a high, steep sea is running, tending their anchored fishing-lines and showing their fine weatherly and maneuvering qualities, and rarely shipping any water."[103]

Gould and Foster's document on junk construction from the U.S. Naval Ordnance Test Station at China Lake, *Junks—Construction and Regional Characteristics,* gives the actual hull lines for the junk *Amoy* (as well as pointers on how to sink the craft and which areas were vulnerable to attack during the Southeast Asian conflict). The document reveals the junk's flat bottom shape, thick hull wales, and multiple interior bulkheads that define cargo spaces, set adjacent to fore and main masts. Again, the light mizzenmast is stepped high on the stern transom. It appears that support for the foremast must be borne by the mast partners and distributed through the bulkhead, for the foot of the mast barely intersects with the very end of the fore keel or "stem" itself. In this case the transom bow extends beneath the waterline. This facilitates sea-keeping qualities. As with other junk examples, the maximum width of the *Amoy* is aft of midships. Frames do not appear to be drawn into this plan—the bulkheads themselves assume this function in smaller vessels. The foremast seems to correspond to the expected pattern in comparison to the archaeological sample, but again the mainmast is forward of its predicted location at 52–57 percent aft of the bow in terms of (estimated) overall vessel length.[104]

The deep, adjustable, narrow rudder was characteristic of Chinese seagoing junks. Perhaps it was not the maneuverability that was the weak point of the suspended median rudder, but the vulnerability to damage. The transpacific junk *Amoy* was disabled several times by storms and rudder damage during its Pacific crossing. This may have not been the rudder design of choice for deep ocean crossings, but one more suited to coastal trade and fishing.

Figure 17 gives some idea of the steering arrangements of the *Amoy.* The large vertical timbers that bracket the adjustable rudder post, the "hard muscles" in Chinese, are integral to the stern transom.[105] The windlass for raising and lowering the rudder is the topmost timber on the transom. A *yuloh,* or feathered sculling oar, can be seen resting along the port quarter. Many small junks such as these Amoy vessels could be propelled in and out of the harbor by hand-power alone.

As noted previously, the deep rudder, besides steering the junk, operated as an additional keel, reducing drift to leeward and stabilizing the vessel in rough seas. The shape of the bow, as well, kept the junk dry in rough seas. As with the pole junks, bow compartments in many Amoy junks were frequently free flooding, allowing greater stability. And the flat surface of the sharply overhanging transom bow itself, when thrust into an oncoming

Figure 17. The *Amoy*'s rudder post head is barely visible behind the steering tackle in the transom slot. The uppermost crosspiece is the horizontal windlass for adjusting the rudder, and is integral to the transom's design. (Courtesy of the British Columbia Archives)

Figure 18. The *Amoy* enters Victoria Harbor in 1922 following its Pacific crossing. (Courtesy of the San Francisco Maritime National Historic Park, Hatch Scrapbook G7.19)

swell, served to provide lift to the vessel and keep the junk from burying its head. This surface is plain in figure 18, as are the rounded and partially finished wales or hull planks. The oculus, or eye, as befitting merchant vessels, peers straight ahead (the eyes of fishing junks look down).[106] The former scans for dangerous rocks and shoals, the latter for schools of fish.

The sail rig of Amoy junks also added to their seaworthiness. The particular manner in which the bamboo batten sails are rigged, or attached, to the masts provides lift during gusts or high seas. "The only means by which the sail is stopped from riding up the mast is by the fore topping lift and the panels [upper rigging and sails]. In smaller junks and sampans the sail can be seen sliding up the mast in hard puffs. It is precisely this effect which gives such great lifting power to the sail."[107] No individual rigging held the bottom of the sail down on Chinese junks. This was in distinct opposition to the western tradition. It was one of those surprising secrets within Chinese ship design, responsible for the almost universal observation of this type of vessel remaining "as dry as on the day of her launching, with not a drop of water in her."[108] It has been a given, in the western historical experience, that all vessels work, or flex, in a seaway—that all wooden vessels leak. Near Amoy, junk construction was such that "a well or two made in the bottom of the hold of the vessel is sufficient to keep it dry; hitherto they have had no knowledge of a pump."[109]

Amoy is a region with long ties to the sea. The area's geographical situation along with coastal Fujian Province, with its steep mountains adjacent to an extensive and indented coastline, points toward a natural reliance on marine resources. It is only fitting that some of the best examples of the Chinese shipwright's skill and art, the efficient and seaworthy fishing and trading junks, come from Amoy. Records of the *Amoy,* which crossed the Pacific in 1922, reveal specific patterns not seen in the first two examples. The keel design closely mirrors Song–Ming period vessels, as do the hull shape and transom construction. There are multiple bulkheads, but only seven, and these not evenly spaced but placed as needed to delineate below-deck storage on the small craft, as well as to lend support to fore and main masts. Rounded wales appear again in a carvel hull, rather than multiple clinker/carvel layers of planking. Both rig and rudder reflect regional styles and established construction patterns. These elements make the *Amoy* technically fascinating. The fact that the *Amoy* was also a graceful and elegant object, something seemingly almost alive, seems like icing on the cake.

Figure 19. Junk *Amoy* in the quiet confines of Victoria's inner harbor. (Courtesy of the British Columbia Archives)

THE *FOU PO II*: BUT LOST IN AN INSTANT

It is indeed unfortunate that the junk *Fou Po II*, while its crew lay convalescing at the hospital in Kalaupapa, was swept onto the rocks and totally demolished. All plans and documents, all papers and photographs of the junk and the three-year voyage were lost in that wreck. A single photograph of the junk, and of very poor quality, exists at the local newspaper archive. The vessel most closely resembles an Amoy trader, the same type as the junk *Amoy*. The three-masted design with exaggerated sheer, the acute overhanging transom bow, the raked forward mast, and the fact that the vessel was built at Amoy serve to help identify the junk. All previous remarks might apply to this case.

The junk's maritime ethnographer captain, Eric De Bisschop, having spent years sailing around Ningbo and Amoy, was aware of the many qualities of the junk design, and the Amoy type in particular. He touted the vessel's seaworthiness and reputation for rising over the waves, shipping no water. De Bisschop found the junk an embodiment of the knowledge of the ages: "roomy, easy to handle, and inexpensive to build. . . . With her hull painted in red and gold Chinese designs from her bows to her overhanging stern, with two big eyes like Spanish onions on her square bow, she was reminiscent of the Middle Ages."[110]

Kalaupapa, on the north shore of the island of Moloka'i, is exposed to the storms and swells of the wide fetch of the North Pacific Ocean. There may be very little left, if anything at all, of the remains of the *Fou Po II* today.

THE *HUMMEL HUMMEL*: A SMALL PIECE OF VARIOUS REGIONS

Though Dr. E. Allen Petersen, who purchased the *Hummel Hummel* in China in the 1930s, reported that the small junk was a Ningbo-style fishing vessel, the junk does not fit well with Worcester's classifications of vessels in that area. The *Hummel Hummel* had only two masts, and stern quarters and lines that are foreign to all documented description for that area. Given the variety of different designs, and the capacity to build variations on any of them, this is not too surprising. The junk was possibly a variation on the local Ningbo styles. All classifications, as Worcester himself has noted, are approximations. Worcester's *Lu Meimao*, or green eyebrow junk, is closest to the image of the *Hummel Hummel*. These junks operated chiefly in the Shanghai, Dinghai, and Ningbo areas, as small fishing and trading vessels. The name came from a patch of green color behind the oculus, or eye, of the junk. Typically, these types were approximately sixty-six feet in length and thirteen feet in beam, much larger than the tiny thirty-six-foot (nine-

Figure 20. Junk *Hummel Hummel* under way, minus a small mizzenmast at the stern. (From Petersen, *Hummel Hummel*)

foot beam) vessel that Dr. Petersen brought across the Pacific. Petersen does not record the specific type of junk, but since it was built in Ningbo, it was a Ningpo junk. By comparison, Worcester divides the Ningbo and Chusan area coastal junks into seventeen different styles in his *Classification.*

The small, eight-ton, camphor wood craft *Hummel Hummel* was used locally mainly for fishing and as a cargo carrier to Shanghai. The mainmast was of iron wood, while the foremast was a flexible bamboo pole. Both fore and main masts appear very far forward of their predicted positions. Rounded wales are evident in the hull, and no standing rigging is visible. The bow featured the narrow transom style, which tended to prevent seas from breaking over the forward deck and cabin.[111] Much like the Amoy-style junks, the *Hummel Hummel* remained dry in the roughest of seas, but the motion was not at all a pleasant one for its sometimes unhappy occupants. Passing gales rolled the small boat mercilessly. "The old *Hummel Hummel* bobbed, pitched, and rolled and went through motions you wouldn't believe a boat could go through. But no waves broke over her. Huge white crested devils rushed at us from the darkness, but none could catch her unaware."[112]

Compared to the more enclosed stern transoms of the Amoy junks to the south, the *Hummel Hummel* had a stern representative of what Worcester has termed the semi-closed variety, representative of Zhejiang junks further to the north. This was part of the general southern-northern transition from rounded and oval shapes to square sterns, itself a reflection of the deep water to shallow water design transition.[113] The bow of the *Hummel Hummel,* on the other hand, appears to have been modeled on classic Fujian Province design lines. This small junk may have been, then, somewhat of a regional hybrid, an example of the shipwright's ability to mix and match stylistic variations for a new pattern.

The small *Hummel Hummel,* while obviously not representative of large, long-distance coastal carriers of China's seafaring history and less revealing of established traditions, still maintains some of the expected constructional features of Chinese junks. The multiple thick and rounded wales in a carvel hull, interior bulkheads, *chunam* caulking (replaced by the new owners with zinc strips while in Yokohama), typical rudder, and batten lugsail without shrouds or standing rigging combined to form a simple yet seaworthy vessel. The interesting combination of bow and stern designs representative of different regions highlights the innovative ability of junk masters. Are smaller, more endemic craft more susceptible to variation than larger, more standardized designs?

THE *SEA DRAGON*: "AND NEITHER THE TWAIN SHALL MEET"

Richard Halliburton, after an extensive search, finally claimed to have located a skilled shipwright who subsequently built a Wenzhou-style oceangoing junk in a shipyard in Kowloon. By all accounts, the vessel that was built was an untested hybrid design, not a combination of Chinese coastal styles but a mix of eastern and western technologies. From the Chinese perspective, both the *Sea Dragon*'s symbolic and physical integrity had been seriously breached by incorporating an engine and propeller shaft, the inclusion of which necessitated the removal of watertight bulkheads and a redesign of the hull and stern area. From the western perspective, the exceedingly lofty design appeared top-heavy and unstable, liable to capsize at the first strong gust of wind.

Worcester describes six coastal junks of the Wenzhou region, but, perhaps not surprisingly, none of his examples truly coincide with the appearance of the *Sea Dragon.* The only three-masted Wenzhou junks that were of comparable size and vaguely resembled the East/West hybrid were the *wusha chuan,* or black sand junks.[114] These craft were typically sixty-seven feet in length and seventeen feet in beam. They were strongly built seagoing traders with square bows and transom sterns. Worcester made no mention of any special decorative motifs, though another Wenzhou junk known

Figure 21. Halliburton's *Sea Dragon* under sail. The square objects attached to the side of the hull are unknown additions. (From Halliburton, *Richard Halliburton*)

as the *shan chuan,* or eel boat, featured enough of the typical Fujian stern decoration that Fujian junkmen had their own name for the style, *malan,* or blue horse junks.[115] Here again the overlap between regional styles seems apparent from the scattered documents. Precedence existed for the mixing of Zhejiang and Fujian junk styles. Halliburton and his *Sea Dragon* would take this combination one step further, boldly introducing a western engine into a construction so long influenced by *and designed for* sail alone. Would it work? Not in this case.

The general geographical pattern associated with regional sail shapes assigns the more flat-headed and rectangular sails to the north and the more hump-backed leech or curved scalloped-edged sails to the south in general and Guangdong in particular.[116] The number of battens within the sail also provides clues to the regional identification of junk construction. More battens per sail represent northern designs, while rigs with between four and six battens per sail are characteristic of Guangdong in the south.[117] The transom bow and stern, position of fore and main masts, mizzen stepped high on the stern, and use of rounded wales in the hull of the *Sea Dragon* are familiar from the preceding examples.

Figure 22. The decorative and incredibly lofty transom of the *Sea Dragon* offers no sign of the rudder trunk, or "false" transom. (From Halliburton, *Richard Halliburton*)

The exceedingly tall stern of Halliburton's junk would appear to be homage of sorts to the very standardized forms of decorative motifs from Fujian Province. Was it an intentional exaggeration on the part of its builders? The inscribed characters announce the junk's name and home port. This was something not always carried by Chinese junks, which traditionally relied on masthead devices and paint schemes for identification, and sometimes did not possess individual names. There are no images of the junk's hull below the waterline, but the lack of any rudder trunk or false transom, so obvious in Chinese junks with adjustable suspended median rudders, denotes a radical design change, meaning a western-style rudder blade, firmly affixed with steel hardware aft of the submerged propeller. This also suggests an extension of the main or mid keel aft, no angled stern keel section, a vertical stern post—in short, a very different design for the whole stern of the vessel.

The most significant changes in its construction do not appear in the photographs. Placing a heavy engine in a wooden sailing junk demanded a large amount of redesign. Chinese bulkheads and structural timbers had to be moved or eliminated, and large supporting beams and blocks added to serve as the engine bed. The keel had to be redesigned. The loads and stresses on the entire wooden structure were very different from those of purely sail-driven craft. Not only did the weight of the engine need to be considered, but the transfer of thrust to the entire structure along a single axis, something previously unknown, had to be taken into account. There was no keelson to transmit this thrust, as that was not a necessary part of the evolution of junk construction. This was not a problem in details only, but a basic mismatch between the machine and the design of the sailing junk, between two differing technologies.

> One of the more serious problems facing the junk builder today, and one for which no precedence exists to guide him, is the seating and support for motors. The engine bed in the Hong Kong junk . . . illustrates the problem. The propeller shaft, and consequently the engine bed, dips downward aft while the bottom planking drops away forward. The engine beds are so deeply notched over the last frame that their [*sic*] cross sectional area is reduced to almost nothing. For all practical purposes, the bed does not bear on this frame. The bed is notched adequately into the second frame, rests on top of the third frame, and is blocked up on the forth and forward frames. Sway braces are two-by-six inch timbers raised on blocks on each side of the bed. The length of the engine bed is little more than that of the engine itself. It extends between the two bulkheads, which delimit the engine-

room, and this compartment is no longer than is needed to house the engine itself. The junk builders admit to worry over the adequacy of engine support. In the absence of other information, they provide a bed that experience indicates would be adequate to support a load of this magnitude. No consideration is given to the distribution of thrust strains. Perhaps the clearest indication of a failure to appreciate the consequences of their actions is seen in the cutting of the aft frame to provide clearance for the shaft. This frame, virtually the only place where the notched engine bed permits some transfer of thrust to the hull, is not even fastened to the keel.[118]

As western ship architects were well aware, the amount of vibration involved in powered propulsion literally could shake apart wooden vessels. Thrust needed to be transferred at points along the propeller shaft to strongly supported thrust-blocks kept perfectly in line with the rigid machinery, not placed solely on an inadequate engine bed. Such a situation could lead to leaks anywhere along the shaft fittings and an engine that literally pushes itself out of the engine room.

From a broader perspective, the true revolution in propulsion only came about in conjunction with a change in hull technology, with the combination of steam engines and iron hulls, not just with the addition of the marine power plant alone. Wooden vessels of many cultures, made up of hundreds if not thousands of individual components, are flexible craft, ill-suited to the more demanding tolerances and stresses of the large power plant. Ships are carefully designed, complex artifacts. The development of the marine power plant was really tied to the much larger economic advancement of foundries, iron plate rollers, coal and other fuel sources, etc. And to fully adopt the one component was to really initiate a change for the associated technologies. (This was the lesson that the Chinese government learned with the creation of the modern Fuzhou shipyard in the nineteenth century. Steam technology and iron ship construction necessitated western mathematics and engineering classes and instruction in French language and much more. The experiment was complex and slow to take root, but may have had a chance, had the French not bombarded the facility to bits during the Sino-French War.) Only with great difficulty were engines adapted to wooden sailing junk designs. In general, the resulting product was very unlike the original form. Halliburton wanted both the engine and the original form.

Engine technology was not the only area influencing design changes in junks. As western contact increased dramatically during the late nineteenth and early twentieth centuries, some junk builders added other alterations.

Junk construction in Hong Kong selectively adopted western techniques, using more numerous frames and thinner, lighter materials. There was a general trend of lightening the whole vessel, perhaps indicative of changes in other ports where western influence was also able to penetrate. The results could be design failures, adopting piecemeal certain elements did not insure the advantages to the whole. Chinese carpenters saw no reason to create matching bearing surfaces where parts of a frame were joined—stresses were transmitted from one part of the frame to another not through structural timbers but through the planking. Without an entire restructuring of the junk, these western additions made the design worse rather than better.

Combining design elements from at least three regions on the Chinese coast (Guangzhou, Fujian, and Zhejiang), along with drastic structural changes in the adaptation of western propulsion, the *Sea Dragon* was indeed an uncharacteristic and dangerously hybridized vessel, mixing technologies that were compatible only with the greatest care and attention. Certain patterns were carried through, such as transom bow and stern, position of masts, decoration, etc. But essential patterns of bulkheads, keel construction, and rudder were altered. The design did not translate into a decipherable language, any known configuration. It was an unhappy marriage of East and West and, although there is no certainty that such a dubious combination led directly to the demise of the junk and its crew, vanishing in the mid-Pacific cannot instill a great deal of confidence in this experiment. The final significance of the *Sea Dragon* stems less from any elements of recognizable language in regional sailing junk design and more from the category of whatnot-to-do in the conversion of modern junks.

THE *MON LEI*: AN ORPHAN OF UNCERTAIN ORIGIN

Borden, in *Sea Quest,* refers to the junk *Mon Lei* as a fifty-foot, Swatow-type, carvel-hull, short-keeled junk, believed to have been built somewhere in central China in 1850.[119] Again, though Worcester in his *Classification* identifies ten different oceangoing junks in the Swatow area, associating a single type with the images of the *Mon Lei* proves difficult. The most likely model in this case is the *hengtuo*, a flat haul junk trawler.[120] The continuous smooth sheer lines, prominent wales, and vertical parallel masts are all similar. The overall size of the *hengtuo* is slightly larger than the reported size of the *Mon Lei*, but variations at this point are almost to be expected. The rudderpost and tiller of the established Chinese pattern can be seen emerging just above the sweep of the stern gunwale in Worcester's sketch of the *hengtuo*, figure 23.

Figure 23. The *hengtuo,*
a flat haul Chinese
trawler from Swatow.
(From Worcester,
Classification)

The rounded leech of a southern junk sail appears both in the sketch and in a rare photo of the *Mon Lei* arriving in New York on August 8, 1947 (figure 24). The *Mon Lei*'s sails seem even more southern, with comparatively fewer battens in evidence. Transom bow and stern, masts in familiar forward positions, and carvel hull with rounded wales depict the familiar nineteenth-century patterns.

Later images of the *Mon Lei* record a small wheelhouse constructed on the stern deck, and the absence of sails. Apparently the junk had been modified to carry a small engine, with all the attendant problems previously mentioned. Exactly how this was done remains unknown. And where there is a wheelhouse, there can be no free-swinging tiller, as is apparent in Worcester's drawing, meaning no characteristic Chinese suspended adjustable rudder. Unfortunately, no dates are associated with these images, but it is most likely at least a decade later than the junk's East Coast arrival.

The major difference between Worcester's idealized design and the *Mon Lei* is in the critical rudder arrangement. Although Worcester reports that Swatow junks had nonhoisting rudders, their angled position relative to the transom still appears typically Chinese. He does note that, when not in use, the rudders were "streamed," detached and floating astern.[121] This eliminated the wear and tear of the rudder knocking about as the vessel worked at her moorings. Fittings, then, would therefore most likely have included the Chinese loose wooden gudgeon mount with cables holding the rudders in place, and/or the vertical pillars creating the rudder slot. Images of the stern of the *Mon Lei* do not depict anything like that, but rather what seems to be a much more westernized rudder. Such a feature is reminiscent of a lorcha, a hybrid

Figure 24. The *Mon Lei* under way in the late 1940s. (Courtesy of Mystic Seaport, Mystic, Conn.)

Euro-Asian vessel combining a western hull with a Chinese sailing rig. Lorchas were first built in the sixteenth century in the Portuguese colonies of East Asia, and featured decks laid out in typical European fashion, with stern and forecastles, deck houses, and bowsprits, as well as fixed rudders.

Even more perplexing, an image of the *Mon Lei* in San Francisco shows the stern rudder trunk and the rudder post high in the air, minus the detachable tiller, in an apparently hoisted position. There is no evidence of a wheelhouse, nor could there be for this type of rudder to operate. For half of the ten junks that Worcester lists in the Swatow area, and this includes all of the examples bearing any resemblance to the *Mon Lei*, the rudder is listed as the nonhoisting type. It is unclear, though, from these few images if this is a further example of adaptation to western technology, or simply an example of different and unrecorded traditions in junk construction. There is always the possibility that these images are the sporadic record of changes made to the style of rudder, alteration being possible anywhere. Perhaps upon arrival on the West Coast, the *Mon Lei*, with its adjustable Chinese rudder, was converted to a motorized vessel with a modern wheel and a fixed rudder.

Figure 25. The *Mon Lei* of Aberdeen on a stopover at San Francisco before proceeding to the East Coast. Note the carvel hull with rounded wales and the hoisted Chinese rudder. (Courtesy of the San Francisco Maritime National Historic Park, A1.20)

Figure 26. A 1957 watercolor of the *Mon Lei* hauled out on the marine railway in New York. Note the addition of the large triangular deadwood section. (Courtesy of Mystic Seaport, Mystic, Conn.)

The vessel then continued on to the East Coast for a gala arrival under the *Ripley's Believe It or Not!* flag in New York in 1947. Figures 25 and 26 also record alterations to the home port and Chinese characters on the junk's transom. The watercolor image might not capture the entire minutia of the photograph, but it does include obvious changes in the junk's rig. The mizzenmast is gone, and what appears to be a foresail furled around the stay (a stay on a Chinese junk?) rises from the bow. Jib-type foresails, attached to mast stays, are not typical Chinese features.

The question of the changing rudder, the changes in the sail rig, the loss of the third mast, the wheelhouse, and the incomplete association with the *Hengtuo* design—these things speak of an original Swatow junk being altered during its voyage to New York, altered to nearly (or beyond) the point of clear identification. Perhaps the ultimate loss or change of historically established patterns, in junks and other vessels, was simply inevitable. Even if an effort had been made to preserve specific types of sailing vessels, they might only remain preserved as static displays in museums, their language or the meaning of their patterns slowly becoming incomprehensible over time. Junks get used.

THE *CHENG HO*: CHRISTOPHER COLUMBUS'S CANAL BARGE

There has been much speculation over the descriptions of the large treasure junks, the *baochuan,* which carried Ming dynasty Admiral Zheng He and his comrades overseas in such regal splendor in the early fifteenth century. Models based on certain historical texts have been built in China, and these are our closest estimates to understanding the *baochuan,* but there is very little archaeological evidence to support them. The historical descriptions are not detailed, they are not plans. For numerous reasons, including the power struggle between Confucian bureaucrats and imperial eunuchs, as well as the landward orientation of the entrenched government, all detailed knowledge of the *baochuan* designs has been lost. Were they really large enough to carry hundreds of Chinese marines in each ship on journeys lasting more than two years across the Indian Ocean? Could wooden sailing ships over four hundred feet long (as recorded in the dynastic histories) successfully negotiate the marine environment? Do we really know what they looked like? And the question of their design does not even address the recent speculation that portions of Zheng He's fleet circumnavigated the globe, a proposition based on even shakier foundations. At least one fact though, among this sea of speculation, remains perfectly clear: Zheng He's *baochuan* did *not* have twin 110-horsepower diesel engines.

The junk *Cheng Ho* did, as well as air conditioning and a host of other concessions to comfort. Although the vessel, which might more properly be called a junk yacht due to its origins as a specially built scientific cruising craft, was said to represent the junks of the early Ming navy, such a claim could not have been taken very seriously. What kind of junk was it then? Certainly it was another hybrid, combining different technologies usually at odds with each other. The lines, though, were reportedly taken from a one-hundred-year-old salt junk.[122]

Salt junks, or *yan chuan,* occupied a critical position in the transportation of one of China's major domestic commodities. Illustrations of *yan chuan* exclusively feature river craft. The bulk of the trade was between the major resource producing areas at the coasts and the interior, particularly the Yangzi River valley. As a measure of the size and importance of this business, in 1867 alone the Yangzi River salt trade employed approximately eighteen hundred junks and thirty thousand sailors.[123] Associated almost exclusively with the vitally important commodity, salt junks reflect some of the oldest designs of Chinese vessels. Such craft would, in theory, be candidates for any proposed replicas seeking to re-create centuries-old designs. This is true at least for those seeking to replicate salt junks. Unfortunately, by the early twentieth century when Worcester conducted his research on Chinese junks, many large salt junks were becoming a thing of the past. Steamships were slowly taking over the trade. Most illustrations of the remaining examples typically display the strong, low, straight, box-like lines and balanced rudder designs of Chinese river junks. They do not appear at first to resemble the images of the *Cheng Ho*. Closer inspection of the junk yacht, disregarding additional superstructure, reveals the straight sheer lines of the *yan chuan*. It does seem possible that someone took the lines of the salt junk and built a yacht, claiming somewhat inexplicably that the vessel represented an early Ming seagoing *baochuan*. This single association between river salt junks and the *Cheng Ho* is very basic, and fails to convey a great amount of information on possible regional influences. It does not apply to other design features. Simply because something is old does not mean that Zheng He sailed on it.

The oculi, additional hull strakes, and the forward wings so familiar to certain coastal trade vessels have been added on top of this salt junk box-like hull. In other words, oceangoing patterns unassociated with river junks have been placed, almost in a random fashion, on top of an unsuitable foundation. The three-masted rig and transom bow and stern construction are familiar, though the single narrow wale, more akin to a deck-level rub rail, is too high up on the carvel hull to recall other nineteenth- and early twentieth-century designs. Furthermore, European-style shrouds and stays support the three masts, and European davits hold a small shore boat outboard the stern quarter. Such changes supposedly adapted the river hull to the open ocean environment. Herein lies a problem with the claim to oceangoing representation, not to mention the Zheng He and Ming dynasty pedigree.

While the large *baochuan* are not well understood, enough has been recorded and discovered about a variety of other historic designs to be reasonably sure that oceangoing junks in the Ming dynasty were purposefully built for the open ocean. This includes basic patterns such as the exaggerated upward curve or sheer of high bows and sterns, as seen and commented on so often by European observers in Southeast Asia. Making river junks into units of the huge Ming navy by the practice of tacking on added lumber in a kind of afterthought is a questionable proposal at best. Besides pursuing the alleged antiquity of certain hull designs, it seems silly to think that salt junks could have been the model for the huge *baochuan* built by expert junk masters at the government shipyards in Nanjing. One might as well add some makeshift structures to a Thames River barge and claim to be crossing the Atlantic on a replica of one of Columbus's caravels. Many of the elements of the *Cheng Ho* appear to be Chinese, but were juxtaposed with no apparent thought to regional compatibility, or even the very basic difference between river and ocean vessels. The *Cheng Ho*'s language is indecipherable.

And this is not to mention the electric lighting and air conditioning and diesel engines placed on board. The junk had refrigeration and adequate fans. Ratlines, rope ladders for climbing the shrouds, appear above the decks, a European innovation. The overall effect is one of which Walt Disney could have been proud. Essentially the *Cheng Ho*, named after the famous admiral, was a luxury vessel for adventurous scientists, complete with a self-contained botany lab, built under the direction of an American architect, and not copied from junks used during the fifteenth century. The real origins of the *Cheng Ho* lie in Hong Kong, where the vessel was built, and not in the early Ming period. Like many Hong Kong junks, the scientific yacht featured a very square stern shape, maximizing interior cabin space. Boxy Hong Kong junks have proved very popular with the overseas yachting society as a design that provides ample interior space for living on board.

What the junk *Cheng Ho* really signifies on a symbolic level, besides another hybridized bastard vessel, is the strong and continuing fascination with the voyages of Zheng He of the fifteenth century. This fascination easily incorporates romantic images of grand junks anchored at exotic locations, and with certain concessions to comfort and science, the traveling scientists on the *Cheng Ho* in Southeast Asia did experience exactly that. They were, after all, sailing in their junk some of the very same waters as the famous Ming admiral. Mere curiosity and romanticism, though, did not drive the search for any reasonable facsimile of an early Ming dynasty vessel very far, nor can they supplant research and evidence. The *Cheng Ho* is in the class of the *Sea Dragon*, a junk artificially created, for which there is no category in the Chinese tradition.

THE *FREE CHINA*: THE CURE WORSE THAN THE DISEASE

The junk *Free China* provides, fortunately, an excellent opportunity to return to the study of historically established patterns of Chinese sailing vessels. The *Free China* was built neither to satisfy a roaming scientist's romantic visions, nor to make money at a world's fair—and more importantly, the vessel is still around today. The crew members that brought the junk across the Pacific are still available for interview. Their stories, along with photographs and film footage, are firsthand resources and contributed greatly to this study. The story of the junk that crossed the Pacific was a well-known feature news item in 1955, particularly in Taiwan and San Francisco. Several decades later, though, it has almost vanished from popular memory.

Figure 27. The *malan,* or blue horse junk, representative of an idealized *Free China* design. (From Worcester, *Classification*)

In many ways the *Free China* resembles nothing so much as a smaller version of the Fujian-style coastal merchant, the pole junk. The distinctive features of junks from that region, the high oval stern and long sheer lines with prominent wales, are consistent among Fujian vessels. The patterns are similar. This general type can be broken down into specific variations. Worcester provides a descriptive variation of the Fujian junks known as the *malan,* or blue horse junk. These vessels operated most frequently between Fuzhou, Ningbo, Taiwan, and Shanghai.[124] With fine, graceful lines, profuse decorations on a square bow and an oval stern, a well-raked foremast, and a deck cabin, the *malan* is a very close model for the *Free China*. Figure 27 displays the conspicuous gallows frame (for sail support) on the foredeck and the *malan*-style seven-batten mainsail.

The junk's Chinese crew recognized the type of vessel as a flat head junk. A number of other designs have names such as "square head" and "flat head," so the designation was not uncommon. The junk type was also referred to locally as a *danjiqi,* a "single tiny body."[125] Whether known as a *hua pigu* or

Figure 28. The junk *Free China* coming in under a low fog bank at San Francisco's Golden Gate Bridge in 1955. The vessel lines, battens, stern motifs, deck windlass, and cabin all recall the *malan* design, but the mizzenmast has been removed. (Courtesy of the Reno Chen collection)

a *ping tou* or a *malan* or a *danjiqi*, the junk's features speak for themselves. These variations in names highlight the many challenges to classifying junks and forming appropriate terminology.

The *Free China*, when she first arrived in California, was in close to original condition. No engine, no shrouds or stays, no modern rudder had been fitted on board. No air conditioning cooled visiting scientists; no wheelhouse emerged from the stern deck. After purchasing the craft from the previous owner, Paul Chow and his crew worked with a traditional Chinese shipwright to make repairs and ready the vessel for sea. Sails were mended, paint applied, and spares located, but no extreme design changes were made. The only concession to modernization, in terms of safety, came with the addition of a five-horsepower winch to assist the small crew in handling the heavy sails. The junk sailed with only one-third the normal complement on

Figure 29. Harry Dring and associates on board the *Free China* at Alameda in the 1950s. Note the square bow, deck windlass, gallows frame, and raised rudder. (Courtesy of the San Francisco Maritime National Historic Park, A5.17)

Figure 30. *Free China* runs broad downwind across the Pacific. (Courtesy of the Paul Chow collection)

board. Junks of this design traditionally had around fifteen crewmen. The *Free China* crossed the Pacific with six. A curved steel tube gallows frame, manufactured in Japan, was also added for the heavy mainsail to assist in sail handling.

Though not large enough to carry huge poles up and down the Chinese coast, the *ping tou* or *malan* junk served as a general cargo carrier. At the time the *Free China* was purchased, the vessel was in the business of ferrying loads of salted ribbon fish back and forth between the islands of Matsu and Taiwan. The junk had allegedly been caught smuggling contraband more than a few times in past years, and so speed was an important criterion for the previous owner. Though any amount of speed under sail would probably have been ineffective against modern patrol vessels, the ability to make fast passages would have minimized the time the contraband was in transit, thus reducing the risk of being apprehended.

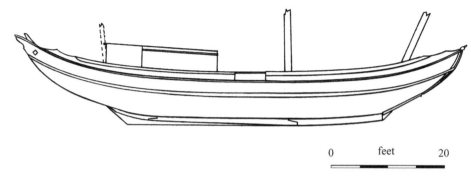

0   feet   20

Figure 31. This elevation drawing of the *Free China* shows the triple-segmented, horizontally scarfed keel, plus perhaps an additional keel extension aft. (Drawing by Henry Rusk, courtesy of the Al Dring collection)

The eighty-foot vessel featured ten interior watertight bulkheads, and ten interior watertight compartments. The forward compartment, with two holes drilled through the submerged hull planks, served as the free-flooding anti-pitching compartment, common to Fujian junk types.[126] The keel built into the junk is quite apparent in figure 31, even though some made mention that the *Free China* did not have a keel. Perhaps this discrepancy is due to several definitions of keel, for the *Free China* was a flat bottom vessel with no keelson. The plans originally drawn by illustrator Henry Rusk (figures 31 and 35) show a distinct keel. Furthermore, other Fuzhou pole junks, described by several sources as being flat-bottomed and keel-less, appear in Worcester's drawings to have the same structural timber extending well below the center line garboard strakes.

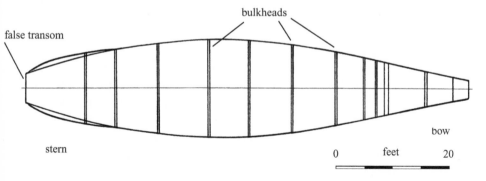

bulkheads

false transom

stern

bow

0   feet   20

Figure 32. This plan view sketch features the bulkhead positions and graceful lines of the *Free China* design. (Drawing by Henry Rusk, courtesy of the Al Dring collection)

Figure 33. The keel of the *Free China*, up on blocks at a boat yard in the Sacramento Delta. Had there been a keel addition by this point? (Author's photo)

Was the *Free China*'s keel added at a later date? Not all of Worcester's drawings show the keel timber, and the *Free China*, according to several sources, had a keel extension applied later, during the many years spent sailing around the San Francisco Bay area.[127] Exactly when this keel extension was added, and when Henry Rusk's plans were produced, is not clear. Photographs of the *Free China* as the junk exists today show what may be an original shallow keel, with the much deeper keel extension attached (plus a propeller).

The images and plans of the *Free China* make clear a number of Chinese construction patterns well established by historical and documentary records. These include bow and stern transom build, multiple interior bulkheads with mast partners affixed, masts in now familiar forward positions (mainmast forward of the 52 percent aft spot, an alteration from Song–Ming design), greatest beam aft of midships, complex "short" keel (but without angled fore keel or stem), batten lug rig, masts with no standing rigging, medial suspended rudder with vertical pillars and horizontal winch, appropriate decorations, etc.

The turret-built hull design, readily seen in the sketch of the *Free China*'s cross sections, is another pattern of Chinese ship construction. For many junk designs, access to the watertight holds exists only through relatively narrow hatches in the center of the deck. The hull strakes literally curve over the gunwale or tops of the holds, the upper strakes then readily shedding any water that might break over the decks. The raised hatches appear somewhat like turrets. Often an additional level platform that serves as the "false" deck is built above the topside hull strakes. The flat-bottomed Jiangsu traders are Worcester's best examples of the classic turret-built Chinese vessel.[128] The particular design feature here seems to date far back in time, and can be

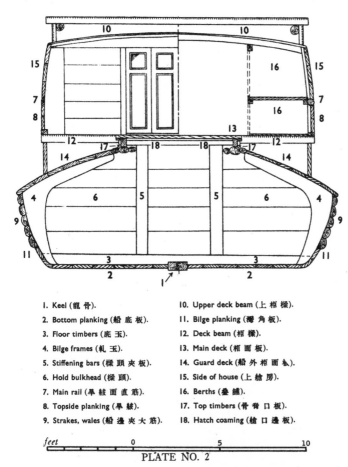

1. Keel (龍 骨).
2. Bottom planking (船 底 板).
3. Floor timbers (底 玉).
4. Bilge frames (軋 玉).
5. Stiffening bars (樑 頭 夾 板).
6. Hold bulkhead (樑 頭).
7. Main rail (旱 皷 面 直 筋).
8. Topside planking (旱 皷).
9. Strakes, wales (船 邊 夾 大 筋).
10. Upper deck beam (上 柤 樑).
11. Bilge planking (灣 角 板).
12. Deck beam (柤 樑).
13. Main deck (柤 面 板).
14. Guard deck (船 外 柤 面 木).
15. Side of house (上 艙 房).
16. Berths (叠 舖).
17. Top timbers (骨 脅 口 板).
18. Hatch coaming (艙 口 邊 板).

feet 0   5   10

PLATE NO. 2

Figure 34. A turret-built Jiangsu trader, with a false deck placed on top of the upper hull structure. The hatch, feature 18 in the image, is in the center, with hull planking extending continuously from the hatch coaming downward. Note the flat-bottomed shallow keel. (From Worcester, *The Junks and Sampans of the Yangtze,* courtesy of the Naval Institute Press)

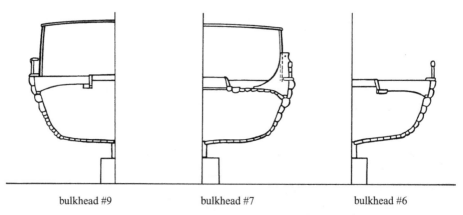

bulkhead #9   bulkhead #7   bulkhead #6

Figure 35. Sketches of the *Free China*'s cross section at three selected stations. Its keel and turret-style construction are most obvious here. (Drawings by Henry Rusk, courtesy of the Al Dring collection)

found on many other designs, such as the Hangzhou Bay trader detailed in D. W. Waters's article "Chinese Junks: The Hangchow Bay Trader and Fisher."[129] Some believed that the Jiangsu-style ships originally traded to the Red Sea and East African ports before the Middle Ages. The turret-type construction led to great strength in the hull, and the protected compartments, especially where they curved inward to meet the narrower bow and stern, were "masterpieces of ship construction."[130]

Figure 36. The *Free China*'s helmsmen standing watch at sea. (Courtesy of the Reno Chen collection)

Figure 37. The *Free China's* rudder released from the transom while in dry dock for maintenance. The oval shape of the stern is reminiscent of the junk *Amoy* from the same vicinity. (Courtesy of the Paul Chow collection)

The rudder was, of course, the typical Chinese deep oceangoing rudder, suspended by a windlass high on the oval stern, and held in place by cables running underwater to another winder on the bow. Though the tillers that attached to the rudder post were broken when the crew failed to reduce sail in strong weather, the *Free China's* rudder itself suffered no mishaps. The tremendous weather helm, though, is indicative of an unbalanced rig. The rudder post, slotted between two massive vertical timbers in the stern transom, the "hard muscles," is reminiscent of the Amoy junk designs.

Figure 38. Painting the foot of the *Free China*'s hoisted rudder. The rudder cable, or *dule*, running forward beneath the hull to the bow holds the post against the transom. (Courtesy of the Paul Chow collection)

Though the *Free China* was quite representative of Chinese working vessels when she arrived in San Francisco, she has not remained that way. There have been drastic alterations to almost every aspect of the Chinese junk. The interior bulkheads have been removed; the high oval stern chopped off, the foremast cut down, rigging added to the mainmast, a diesel engine installed, and a western-style steel rudder attached. Only the distinctive bow and overall lines of the remaining portion of the hull are left. These changes, despite efforts to preserve the junk in close to its original pattern, came as quite a shock to the crew members, who saw them for the first time at their fifty-year reunion in 1995.

It is unfortunate that the junk was so radically altered, but there is no legal protection for historic objects such as these in private ownership. Though

Harry Dring installed the diesel engine, he did keep the junk sailing on the Bay for years in close to its original form. Govinda Dalton, who purchased the junk in 1989, did the most to alter the vessel's shape when he removed the entire stern compartment. Parts of the junk are scattered around California. The original rudder, cut in half and headed for the dumpster, was saved by John Muir of the San Francisco Maritime National Historic Park. The heavy ironwood foremast resides in the park's warehouse as well.

Though the methods were drastic, the unfortunate destruction of the *Free China*'s Fujian stern does give a clear picture of the hull profile, including the individual planks and wales and turret build of the original junk. The strong longitudinal deck members above and the relatively thin hull planks at the bottom give an accurate illustration of the way the junk structure is hung downward from its deck rather than built up from the keel. The remains of the cut down vertical pillars indicate the position of the original rudder slot. A frameset appears on the aft side of the transom/bulkhead, but there is no indication of L-bracket *gua ju* stiffeners between bulkhead and hull. The hull is carvel built with rounded wales.

Electrical wiring, bilge pumps, a bathtub, and numerous clotheslines have so altered the original vessel that its current significance comes not from the many features that it still might have displayed, but from the mere fact

Figure 39. The *Free China*'s cross section and interior bulkhead (now the stern transom) were revealed when some ten to thirteen feet of the junk's original traditional stern was cut away with a chainsaw. (Author's photo)

Figure 40. The much altered *Free China* today, on blocks at a boat yard near Sacramento. It was saved from the firewood pile, but at what a cost. (Author's photo)

that it has, even in this altered form, survived. Most technical details of Chinese ship construction exist as rare photographs and a few drawings. The *Free China*, albeit altered, is an historic survivor. The author has questioned numerous nautical historians and archaeologists both in the West and in China, and has yet to find evidence of any older Chinese wooden sailing vessel tenuously hanging on in operating condition. One hundred years, if that indeed is the age of the ex-smuggling junk *Free China*, is a very long life span for a wooden vessel of any type, let alone one that has not yet received preservation status.

THE BEIHAI JUNK: HIDDEN TREASURE FROM THE *SHUISHANGREN*

In this last example of Chinese nautical technology, the junk in question was neither used in a traditional setting, nor built by enterprising westerners, nor ever even sailed across or in the Pacific. The nameless Beihai junk is the only known example of a Chinese vessel hand-built by Chinese shipwrights for preservation in a western institution. Its construction was a deliberate attempt to capture all the authentic details of a single design. Guy Lasalle, on assignment for a Portland museum, had great difficulty locating two shipwrights in China. They built the junk from memory only, specifically for the American museum.

There is no real representation in Worcester's *Classification of the Principal Sea-Going Junks* that resembles the vessel built in 1989. Only models with the most general similarities, such as relative position of the mast and daggerboard and windlass, exist. The general patterns are there, but not the language specific to this particular Beihai junk. Worcester's closest model approximating the design of this small, two-masted fishing junk is the *gaode chuan,* named after the construction location in Guangxi Province on the Gulf of Tonkin. Cabin, mast, daggerboard, and windlass are depicted in equivalent positions, and the size is approximately the same, though the bulwarks at the stern are considerably simplified compared to the vessel in question. The forward adjustable drop keel, or daggerboard, set vertically in a watertight trunk, appears in thirteen of Worcester's case studies for the area, and the sharply pointed (not transom) bow is noted in sixteen of the eighteen documented examples.[131] The sailing rig of the Beihai junk, however, most closely resembles the two-masted *danzhou chuan,* including a forestay, shrouds, and a small jib sail. It is possible that the rig is a western adaptation. These were the most common type of fishing boats in the Guangxi district, their slight drafts allowing them to cross the shallow waters of the bay.

It should not be surprising that, while certain elements remain recognizable in the seven or eight decades since Worcester collected information on junk designs in Guangxi Province, some features have drastically changed. Also, the Chinese workers who built the junk had resided in Vietnam for a considerable length of time. Though most features of the Beihai craft appear common to the Chinese junks of the area, the very long overhanging bulwarks at the stern do not appear with frequency on Chinese vessels. They are more indicative of Vietnamese junks, as recorded in silhouette by J. B. Pietri in *Voiliers D'Indochine.* Such features seem to have been common diagnostic indicators for junks of the extreme southern waters.

The elevation and plan view drawings show the trunk for the daggerboard on the foredeck, as well as the starboard location of the horizontal windlass and an extended tabernacle just forward of the low cabin. The Beihai junk features a pivoting mast, the lower portion adjacent to a bulkhead and set into a short board running fore-and-aft on top of the floors. This timber is notched vertically at the top to accept the pivoting foot of the mast. The lower portion, or tabernacle, does not make contact with the keel. No fewer than eleven separate hatches give access to the interior holds. The companionway hatch leading into the living area rests in the center of the cabin roof. A box for privacy surrounds the toilet, or marine head, on the starboard stern overhang. The open overhang and long strakes extending aft are not

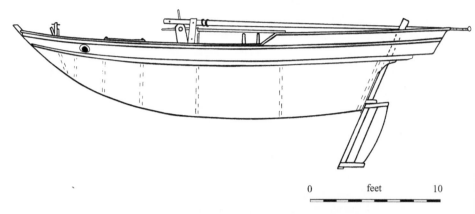

0   feet   10

Figure 41. An elevation plan of the Beihai junk in Portland, Oregon, including depictions of the interior bulkhead positions. (Author's sketch)

typical of any of the other Chinese designs, but the same type of feature can be seen in images of the Vietnamese *ghe manh du song ca* and the *jonque de pakhoi* in Pietri's *Voiliers D'Indochine*.

Daggerboards, and related leeboards, have been in use in China for a very long time, and most believe that they were originally developed there. These vertical boards, either through the hull or fixed over both port and starboard sides, proved handy in stabilizing relatively flat-bottomed vessels and

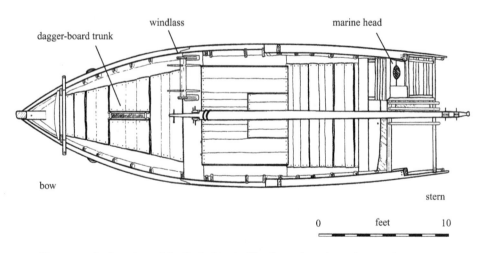

0   feet   10

Figure 42. A plan view of the Beihai junk. The daggerboard trunk is on the foredeck, and the mast is lowered. (Author's sketch)

Figure 43. The Beihai junk, a sharp-bowed fishing junk common to the *shui-shangren*, in the Portland Urban Forestry storage yard today. The safety railing was added by museum staff prior to its display. (Author's photo)

preventing leeward drift. Certainly they were common in the late Ming era. Called "broad water boards" (*pian pi shui ban*) or "waist rudders" (*yao tuo*), references to them appear from the sixteenth century onward, particularly in southern China and Annam.[132]

Similar in many ways to the most common sailing junks that once inhabited the Gulf of Tonkin, the Beihai craft is an accurate representation of a vanished art. In addition to being a document of Guangxi and Vietnamese vessels, it also encapsulates many of the more general Chinese junk construction patterns, complete with all accessories. A bamboo skiff, the rudder, a two-piece *yuloh* sculling oar, and the daggerboard, along with dirt and debris, have been cleaned off the decks of the junk in figure 43. The vessel sits amid broken roof tiles and cement blocks. Rigging and batten sails and tiller, as well as cooking utensils, storage jars, and a selection of personal effects, are all in storage at the Children's Museum in Portland. The junk and its artifact assembly are complete.

The stern transom features wooden gudgeons for the large, twelve-foot rudder. Watertight bulkheads separate storage holds. Adjacent to and interspersed between the bulkheads are regularly spaced sets of light frames, attached to a relatively light floor timber at the turn of the bilge. There is no keelson. As with other junks, a series of flush level hatches give access to the

Figure 44. A bowshot of the Beihai junk. Note the shallow keel on a rounded hull and the prominent stem. (Author's photo)

storage holds and, when closed, constitute the major portion of the deck. Raised hatch coamings keep most of the water on deck from entering the hold. The thirty-three-foot junk contains seven watertight compartments, dividing the hull of the vessel at convenient intervals into storage and living spaces. The hull is carvel built, planks through-fastened at bulkhead stations and edge-joined at an angle, holes being filled with *chunam* caulking.

A shallow keel runs the full length of the hull, curving smoothly from stem to transom stern, the keel timber being 50 percent thicker than hull planks. The sharp bow is most obvious, as well as the downward-looking eyes that typify Chinese fishing vessels. The bow crosspiece, which extends beyond the sides of the vessel, though, is not a feature usually found on Chinese junks. Lines were typically secured over the forward rail of the transom bow, something that is impractical with a sharp stem post. The crosspiece here is another Vietnamese feature, known as an "anchor tumbler," or *nga*.[133] The stern resembles a semi-open rounded style, but one that is entirely open above the deck line. The rudder post drops into a curved notch on the deck level transom, and another wooden gudgeon is placed further down. The daggerboard, or *zhongcha ban*, trunk is set in the middle of the forward hatches. The daggerboard trunk extends straight through the vessel. A simple peg or bolt through holes in the daggerboard allows it to be set to various depths.

All construction details are similar to established local Chinese patterns. *Chunam* caulking material fills all the seams and fastener holes. Triangular notches were chiseled into all surfaces where boards were edge-joined, and these indentations were then filled. Tung oil was applied to all surfaces, though after fifteen years of being unprotected from the weather, the protective coating has worn from exposed wood. Some of the seams have opened, as the wooden planks, after being out of the water for such an extended period of time, have shrunk. Dry rot has begun in a few spots, but in general the hardwood used to build the junk has held up very well over the years. Fortunately, Guy Lasalle purchased the junk back from the museum in 2006 and reportedly has plans to restore the rare craft.

Certainly the Beihai junk, a wonderful representation of Gulf of Tonkin styles, is a rare glimpse of East Asian construction techniques. This small, one-family fishing vessel, however, has important social significance as well. Guy Lasalle was commissioned to find a junk representative of the types used by families as permanent homes. The exhibit at the Portland Children's Museum, "Homes On the Go," introduced the history of the *tanjia,* or "egg families" (perhaps due to using eggs as payment), also known as *shuishangren,* or "people on the water," the minority group of boat inhabitants once prevalent in unknown numbers along the Guangdong and Guanxi coastlines

Figure 45. The Beihai junk's watertight holds, or *shuimi cecang,* with the forward hatches closed. (Author's photo)

in China, a phenomenon reflective of widespread waterborne coastal groups in Southeast Asia and the South China Sea.

Documentation of the Chinese *shuishangren*, like the many other maritime subgroups scattered throughout the area, has been difficult. Often these groups have been nomadic, transient, illiterate, and determined to avoid the many regulatory institutions of the state. History, as we know, is biased toward settled and fixed cultures. Ocean nomads make it a point to avoid ports and remain as distant and independent as possible.[134] Nonetheless, several excellent anthropological studies exist of the sea nomads of Southeast Asia, such as the Bajau Laut of Sabah, the Selungs of the Mergui Archipelago, the Moken of the Andaman Sea, the Orang Laut of the Riau Islands, and others. Scattered groups with similar heritage are known by different names, and even discerning the identity boundaries of the above groups proves problematic. Also, there is no simple division between land farmers and nomadic boat people, but a wide continuum of lifestyles ranging from itinerant farmers with coastal villages who migrate regularly by sea, to the much more nomadic sea raiders. In many cases the peripheral boat life necessitated a symbiotic relationship with coastal villages, trading fish protein for rice and other goods.[135] And for seafarers who rely so heavily on their vessels, the boat can be much more than just a means of transport and accommodation. For the Moken of Southeast Asia, the boat "is undeniably the fixed and stable element in which the nuclear family is able to blossom . . . the boat is responsible for Moken social and physical mobility."[136] Is this always the case? Generalizing about the adaptable maritime lifestyle may be hazardous, except to emphasize the diversity of coastal lifestyles that can blur the distinction between sea and shore, and the great mobility based on maritime transport.

In China there is an historical record of discrimination against this roving, mobile group of local maritime laborers and fishermen. Owners of such vessels and their families were traditionally labeled *danhu*, or "ship households," and systematically discriminated against by the government. These ship dwellers, or *danmin*, were often not allowed to own or to reside on land.[137] Scholars like Ho Ke-en trace references to boat people under various names through two thousand years of history, seeking the origins of the water people and offering a survey of Chinese primary sources.[138] An oppressed pariah people without social status, they are seen by some as aboriginal southern "barbarians," related to the Yue people who once populated Guangdong and Guangxi provinces, who sought refuge from the northern Han Chinese by leaving the land entirely. Others have linked them to prominent clans from central China, who chose their maritime existence to escape the ravages of war and persecution. Robert Antony identifies the *danhu* boat people as Cantonese speakers engaged in fishing, ferry services, and general coast and river transport.

> Treated like outcasts by those on land, they lived their entire lives on the water. By the eighteenth century they were concentrated in the Canton delta and around Chaozhou, though they were also found on the Fujian coast. So dense were their anchorages that the land dwellers described them as "floating villages." The Hokkien and Dan, as well as other people who made their livings as common sailors and fishermen, were generally all lumped together, quite derogatorily, as "water people" (*shuishangren*) by the rest of society. Discernable by their shared poverty and discrimination, and despised by their neighbors on land, seafarers occupied a marginal existence on the fringes of respectable society. It was not uncommon for water people to fluctuate between legitimate pursuits and piracy.[139]

Eugene N. Anderson emphasizes the legitimate economic niche of suppliers of high-grade protein for land dwellers. Traditional pursuits included fishing and preparing salted fish, oyster farming, pearl diving, and transporting local goods and passengers. Many boat dwellers have spent most of their generations avoiding those who made the distinct effort to record their own history.

For the Chinese boat people, South China and particularly Hong Kong were important centers. Hiroaki Kani focuses on this critical location, providing a brief history of the people, religion, and vessels of the floating population. In Hong Kong alone there were 136,000 boat people as of 1961. And that even takes into account a long process of incorporation into the Hong Kong land population, for the boat people were not exclusively limited to harbor craft. Firsthand observations confirmed the *tanjia* occupying the harbor of Hong Kong from the moment of the settling of the colony, and then moving ashore with time. Those who moved ashore tended to disavow their *tanjia* lineage in order to mix on more equal terms with the community.[140]

Some groups, such as the Moken of Southeast Asia, were never systematically incorporated into any pre-colonial or colonial state. Others, such as the Orang Laut, abandoned their sea nomadism at the end of the nineteenth century.[141] European missionaries who had contact with Chinese sailors and boat dwellers seemed to enter a different world, and failed to record very much about the maritime lifestyle. Missionary intentions were to change the culture, not to save it. However, these efforts produced very mixed results. "What little record there is left of the Chinese reaction to this activity is mainly in the expressed hopes of the foreigners for converts. The boat people were naturally not interested in the cultural or missionary efforts of their passengers."[142]

Only in the twentieth century did large numbers of boat-dwelling families begin to vanish. They were the target of dedicated government campaigns to settle junk dwellers ashore and provide hospital and educational facilities (and by the way collect revenue). An economic niche was vanishing as well. With the coming of steam power and industry and then containerization, visiting ships grew enormous in size and no longer required a host of harbor craft peddling wares, providing coal heavers, laborers, etc. There was no longer the chance of human contact between vessels, only a vertical steel wall. Settled modern society no longer had a place for floating and transient boat populations, those who have no permanent address beyond the location of their own boat.

Today the transition in the lives of the former boat people in China is a matter of national pride, and Chinese tour guides gladly point out the new schools and housing developments that have brought the boat people permanently ashore in places like Hong Kong and Aberdeen and finally given them a place to call their own. With a sentimental glance over the shoulder, though, motorized harbor junks take tourists to a protected bay, where they may see the last of the *shuishangren* still residing on board a relatively small population of wooden fishing trawlers.

The Beihai junk, from the same region as many of the historic Chinese boat dwellers, is a rare record of this past lifestyle, exhibiting an advanced functionality in a simple form. Its design is a departure from the familiar patterns of many of the other junks from regions further north, but it still exhibits specific Chinese characteristics. The Beihai junk, except for a few iron hoops, spikes, and bolts, was built completely from wood by hand in just a few months.[143] Its separate holds provide structural integrity and storage for fish or cargo. Its small size means that it can be handled easily by one person. If the wind drops, it can be propelled by the sculling oar. It is well suited to provide shelter and a means of sustenance for one family, a very handy vessel. This is the junk pattern language of the *shuishangren*. The design seems perfectly adapted to its maritime environment. In Mumford's terms, here is the "democratic small farmer" durability and economy of the Chinese water world. For years the story had been relegated, through want of preservation efforts, to the blackberry bushes of Oregon. Hopefully, that has changed now for this small gem.

Significance of Selected Junks

Having classified these junks as representing a variety of types and multiple aspects of Chinese vessel construction, the issue of this group's significance and the prevalence of certain recurring construction features can be revisited. These vessels contribute in a concrete manner to our understanding of seagoing junks. Not every craft is an ideal example of Chinese working sailing vessels, but after all, the ideal is itself an abstraction. All contribute to our understanding, but obviously some more so than others. From this level of analysis, these vessels fall into three different categories: first, junks that connect in some way to patterns that recall general Chinese characteristics, such as the *Whang Ho, Ning Po, Amoy, Fou Po II, Free China,* and the Beihai junk; second, junks that are local designs more representative of endemic variation than general patterns, such as the *Hummel Hummel* and the *Mon Lei*; and third, junks that are deliberate foreign hybrid creations, so changed from their patterns of origin as to be almost unidentifiable, such as the *Cheng Ho* and the *Sea Dragon.* The six junks of the first type, and particularly the *Ning Po*, the *Amoy*, the *Free China*, and the Beihai junk, emerge as the most useful examples for understanding patterns of Chinese construction. All four of these junks, as intact or broken as their remains may be, have been located, and therefore more intensive examination is an exciting possibility.

How did the initial list of general junk construction patterns fare when applied to the specific transpacific samples? Though documentation of the ten junks was uneven, and many of their features remain hidden from view, several of the basic patterns in hull shape and components, masts and rigging, and rudder assemblies can be seen recurring throughout most of the sample. Some of the patterns from the Song–Ming archaeological sample are borne out, such as fastening patterns, median rudders, bulkheads (but not necessarily their spacing), maximum hull width being aft of midships, etc. The earlier practice of rabbeting planks and layering strakes (clinker/carvel) seems to vanish, though, and the nineteenth- and twentieth-century junks feature keels on rounded hulls and flat bottoms, not V-shaped profiles. In addition, certain newer patterns have been brought to light by the transpacific junks, and some additions to the pattern list might be made. Carvel-built hulls with multiple (often three) rounded wales running above the turn of the bilge is a common design element unseen in the initial list. Also, the turret construction of Fujian junks is apparent, and details of mast and step (mast not touching the keel) are revealing, though absent so far from the archaeological record.

These junks are significant in their own right as examples of Chinese nautical technology. But what really lends certain junks like the *Ning Po* and the *Free China* additional historical significance is the fact that they clearly represent design patterns of a much earlier period, a time when sailing junks in East and Southeast Asia played a larger economic and social role. For hundreds of years, such vessels carried cargo and people overseas, to and from the Chinese mainland. These transpacific junks represent the last of the vessels from the historic junk trade. There are two reasons for this statement: first, comparison of the selected vessels with historic images of junk trade ships, and second, the premise that junk design did not change significantly during the several hundred years in which the junk trade dominated commercial activities in Southeast Asia (see chapter 6).

The larger cargo vessels, such as the *Ning Po* and the *Free China*, deserve close attention. These vessels are portrayed as the epitome of Chinese ingenuity in ship design by Worcester. They are examples of Fujian three-masted coastal traders that correspond in interesting ways to the general descriptions of junks in the Southeast Asia market.[144] J. C. van Leur estimates the size of Chinese ships trading to Southeast Asia in the fifteenth and sixteenth centuries at between 200 and 400 tons.[145] John Crawfurd, the British diplomat, found the average size of vessels of the early nineteenth century to be a little smaller, in the 150- to 200-ton range.[146] Herold Wiens estimates that, for the 1920s, the average capacity of coastal trading junks at a selection of thirty-one coastal ports had fallen to around 60 tons, and that encounters with junks with a carrying capacity of more than 100 tons had become very rare.[147] The volume of old-style native shipping, if not totally eliminated, had been much reduced in many areas, often being relegated to carrying small cargoes between ports that were beyond the seasonal routes of the steam launches. These size estimates overlap with the range of the more contemporary vessels, from the 700-ton junk *Keying* (chapter 5) to the 300-ton *Ning Po* to the 50-ton *Free China*. The trend, if there is one, seems to have been decreasing size over time, but the sample is too small to make such an estimate with confidence.

Information from the *Ning Po* and the *Free China* must be compared to historic documents. Yoneo Ishii, in *The Junk Trade from Southeast Asia*, makes use of Japanese silk scrolls from the seventeenth and eighteenth century that depict Chinese vessel designs. The Tokugawa Shogunate, wary of any foreign vessels, whether they were Dutch or Chinese or otherwise, kept careful records of all such visits at Nagasaki. Short-range and smaller Chinese vessels, known as *kuchi-bune* by the Japanese, came to Japan from the nearest Chinese provinces of Jiangsu and Zhejiang. *Naka-bune,* or

Figure 46. A *tosen*, or Japanese depiction of a Chinese junk, from an eighteenth-century Japanese scroll. (From Yoneo, *The Junk Trade,* by kind permission of Dr. Yoneo Ishii)

middle-distance ships, came from Fujian and Guangdong provinces. And the larger, long-distance Chinese junks, the *okubune*, originated from places in Southeast Asia such as Champa, Tonkin, Malacca, and Batavia.[148] Images were included with the written reports, and these show the overall shape and construction features, and even the decorative motifs at the stern transom, to be very similar in style to the transpacific *Ning Po,* indeed similar to several Fujian Province designs. High wings at the bow, horizontal windlasses, stepped quarter decks at the stern, heavy wales, large oval transoms complete with standardized motifs of the yan bird and immortals—all are similar to the last of the pole junks in the early twentieth century. Such a comparison is strong testimony to the existence of a stable and well-known design tradition, an established pattern. It really would appear that certain Chinese junks, which have only very recently vanished from existence, were representative physical artifacts of hundreds of years of maritime history and nautical construction.

The same style of vessels appears recorded in the vicinity of the foreign factories at Canton over an equally long period of time. The collection of paintings at the Greenwich Maritime Museum features these similar styles of vessels, the familiar patterns of Chinese overseas trade junks. The Fujian trade junk depicted in figure 47 clearly shows the median rudder, wales, windlass, and transom bow and stern patterns, as well as similar decorative schemes (chapter 4).

Figure 47. A nineteenth-century Fuchuan trading junk, representative of the many junks on the sea routes to Southeast Asia. (Drawing by Captain J. H. Drummond, © National Maritime Museum, London)

Figure 48. One of the best junk technical drawings, a Qing dynasty seagoing vessel, attributed to a 1757 account of the Liu Qiu Islands. (From Ronan, *The Shorter Science and Civilization in China,* courtesy of Cambridge University Press)

These same design elements can be seen repeated in a Qing dynasty sketch of a seagoing junk, from the *Liu Qiu Guo Zhi Lue,* an account of the Liu Qiu islands from 1757 A.D.[149] Though in this depiction the sailing rig is shown with numerous alterations, which may be due to the western influence of spritsails and topsails, the construction features are typical of the large Fujian coastal traders. High wings at the transom bow, in this case spanned by a decorative cross piece, the cabin and raised deck at the stern, several horizontal windlasses that cross the deck, and even the cables that serve to restrain the adjustable rudder of this three-masted vessel are clearly visible, running underneath the hull toward the bow. It is very similar in form and equipment to the Fujian junks and serves to anchor these vessels to patterns of construction features several centuries old, making the strong connection between certain of the transpacific junks and the vessels of the historic junk trade to Southeast Asia.

It is surprising, then, that what once were such recognized and well-used craft should have dwindled to near nonexistence in the last century. Over time certain minor elements were changed. Some technologies were introduced from the West, particularly the labor-saving device of the capstan and specific sail rig arrangements. The basic elements, though, meaning the hull and rudder and overall shape along with certain cultural/decorative features, remained consistent until the design disappeared. Maritime historian William Still, former director of East Carolina University's Program in Maritime Studies, has remarked on the tendency of shipwrights of all cultures to act conservatively in regard to radical design changes. Certain alterations can only be approached very carefully, given the dire consequences for the failure of experimental designs. This may indeed be true for certain patterns, though elements do obviously evolve within this context.

Wooden Chinese sailing craft carried a large percentage of trade goods and passengers to and from many of the ports in the Asian world over a period of many hundreds of years. The significance of the vessels representative of this trade goes beyond physical design alone. The functions of these junks, their seaworthiness and sailing abilities, made that trade possible. And the East and Southeast Asian trade, especially for the expansive period from 1450 to 1650, played a central role in the regional, and some would say world, economy.[150] The domination of these monsoon trade routes by Chinese-built junks continued into the nineteenth century. The bulk of the carrying capacity did not fully shift to foreign vessels until sometime around 1820.[151] Cargoes of spices and scented woods, rice and sugar, metal ores and silk, cotton and ceramics, and many more things than can be named here cannot be passed off as mere luxury items, but must be evaluated, as Jennifer Cushman has shown, as staple products.[152] Chinese merchants and their ships, particularly during the Song and Yuan dynasties, became one of the dominant foreign mercantile groups operating east of the Strait of Malacca.[153] Given some of the new directions in the field of world history, referring to investigations of regional economies before 1500 A.D. by such scholars as Andre Gunder Frank, Janet Abu-Lughod, Christopher Chase-Dunn, and Thomas Hall, it would be hard to overestimate the significance of Asian maritime trade routes. These junks, what little we know of them, represent the tools of the trade, the units by which those merchants conducted their operations.

FUCHUAN AND SHACHUAN

Stepping back further in time, the significance of the nautical innovations that produced both the *fuchuan* and the *shachuan* junk patterns can and should be set in the context of the larger scale operations. Tang dynasty records indicate that Chinese junks ventured as far as the Euphrates River. *Fuchuan* junk styles, dominant between the Tang and the Song dynasties, have also been associated with the large overseas expeditions of Zheng He in the early Ming period, fleets traveling as far as East Africa. The large *bao-chuan*, or treasure galleons, though, have been referred to as *shachuan*, flat-bottomed vessels. The rise in popularity of the more economical *shachuan* junk styles coincides with the technical innovations and period of economic prosperity of the Song dynasty. During that period, as evidenced in Marco Polo's travels, Chinese junks voyaged to the west coast of India. Fujian ships were considered unsuitable for the shallow waters of the Arabian coastline. *Fuchuan* and *shachuan* vessels, in other words, functioned through and far beyond the Southeast Asian junk trade. From this perspective of world history, Janet Abu-Lughod, in *Before European Hegemony*, describes major re-lated and interlocked subsystems of the thirteenth-century world economy. In one of these, the Indian Ocean–East Asian subsystem connecting India and Southeast Asia and China, Chinese junks often played a crucial role.

The initial differences between the *shachuan* and the *fuchuan* styles of junks are fairly clear. Ultimately, it seems that both contributed to the form of nineteenth-century examples seen here. Gang Deng indicates that the *fu-zhou* ship became the functional prototype of all seagoing vessels sometime after the tenth century. But following that development, it seems that com-ponents of these designs shifted, that certain elements of the *fuchuan* were carried into the *shachuan* pattern. "The shallow water ship was designed for both river and sea traffic. It retained some features of the fuzhou ship such as multi-holds, multi-sails, stern rudder, and a low deck length-beam ratio. The main change was the disuse of a keel and thus the ship bottom became U-shaped."[154] (The reference to the disuse of a keel refers more perhaps to the classic Chinese V-shaped hull design?) The merging of designs perhaps produced an economical coastal vessel capable of transiting between shal-low rivers and the open ocean. This contributed to the mistaken impression in the West that all Chinese vessels were, and always had been, shallow water ships.

The chronological transition from one type to another is only an approxi-mation reflecting the popularity of different styles. The origins of V-shaped and flat-bottomed vessels are murky, and both seem to have been in ex-istence at least as early as the late Tang period.[155] The archaeological evi-dence is clear on the existence and popularity of vessels with multi-section keels and V-shaped hulls of the *fuchuan* style.[156] But, notably, the evidence includes an apparently flat bottom Chinese junk in the *overseas* trade, the Bakau wreck dated to the early fifteenth century.[157]

While it is clear that there are at least two early general vessel designs, the *shachuan* and the *fuchuan*, it is not as well understood how certain elements of these two designs may have merged over time, as suggested by some of the ten transpacific junks. There are external shaping influences that have in the past changed the predominance of one design over the other, such as imperial decrees in the fifteenth century, or the changing economic viability in Southeast Asian trade. Gang Deng's assessment might help to shed light on the historic sample, that junks like the *Ning Po* and *Free China* and others are the design descendants of this *shachuan* tradition, showing certain elements of the *fuchuan* pattern. Sean McGrail has investigated the similarities and differences between *fuchuan* and *shachuan* and seeks critical evidence of this division in earlier periods. Here are traces of these types of design changes in the nineteenth and twentieth centuries.

PEACEFUL PATTERNS?

Almost without exception, these Chinese junks represent designs associated with peaceful operations. Except for the *Whang Ho*, there are no traces of cannon or other ordnance in real use on the junks. Bulkheads interrupt the interior decks, longitudinal hull planks remain free of gun ports, and cargo or living spaces or provisions occupy the entire form of the vessel. Unfortunately, existing records lack the kind of detail that would allow for an analysis of the scantlings, the sizes of the structural timbers, which might suggest the past potential for conversion to military use. The fact remains that in the seventeenth century Zheng Chenggong did defeat the Dutch naval forces at Taiwan, and Pomeranz maintains that this reveals the potential China possessed for the same type of armed trade carried out by Europeans. Perhaps, but is the establishment of several decades of maritime operations between Southeast Asia and the South China coast by a local "navy" and local sailors really the same as the Dutch extending themselves from Europe to the Moluccas, or the Portuguese Estate of the Indies controlling distant Melaka? Is the Chinese defeat of Zeelandia in 1661 really comparable to the capabilities of the European East India companies?

Obviously, Chinese junks were capable of fulfilling a role in the Imperial Navy, and of carrying weapons. Ming dynasty military vessels possessed an array of weaponry. A military treatise of 1576 states that each Ming combat vessel, as of 1393, was required to carry four guns with bores the size of rice bowls, twenty guns of smaller character, ten bombs, twenty rockets, and a thousand rounds of shot.[158] The Qing emperor Qianlong, in 1721, clearly stated his position on the necessity of Chinese merchant junks maintaining some kind of arsenal at sea.

When Our trading vessels go abroad they have to carry cannon to defend themselves from the pirates—not only would We have difficulty in prohibiting the merchant ships of various nations trading at Kwangtung from carrying cannon, but also We would have difficulty in prohibiting merchant ships of Our interior from doing likewise. If We prohibit them from carrying arms absolutely, then if they met pirates on the high seas, they would have difficulty in resisting the pirates. How can We drive them into such a helpless condition? Moreover, it perhaps may be that not only the pirates of the interior engage in piracy, but also bandits of various other nations carry cannon and guns on the high seas in order to plunder passengers and merchants. If the oceangoing ships of the interior are not permitted to carry cannon for their protection—then even though they might take the risk of being unable to protect their goods, their lives surely deserve to be safeguarded and protected! If We strictly prohibit them from carrying cannon, how can Our merchants and passengers protect themselves from the plundering of the pirates? . . . In short, if We are afraid of having sore throats when We swallow food, We might as well not eat at all.[159]

Nonetheless, all the documents related to nine of the ten junks in this study remain void of any evidence of weapons. Even though rare diagrams of dynastic-era junks depict gun ports cut into the hulls of vessels, or perhaps merely painted on the sides of vessels, no such features are in evidence in this sample. The Qianlong emperor did not specify how many of what type of cannon were to be allowed on board, or where they were to be placed. In the nineteenth century, the armament for junks on the South China Sea was strictly regulated. Port officials allowed no more than two cannon, eight fowling pieces, ten swords, ten sets of bows and arrows, and thirty catties of gunpowder to be carried on board merchant junks.[160]

Cannon, as had been developed in China before the Jesuit introduction of European innovations in ordnance, were not equal in effectiveness to the long-barreled, solid-shot weapons as we know them today. Qing emperors were, no doubt, familiar with European cannon, but the effectiveness of local versions of these weapons, as well as the often questionable nature of the gun powder provided to ships (despite the fact that the Chinese invented the powder), raises serious doubts as to how well armed this armed trade may have been. In short, allowing merchants to carry unspecified cannon in defense from regional pirates is not the same as adopting the technologies and methods of organized and effective armed trade, far from it. But did the absence of powerful weapons detract from the technical oceangoing capabilities of Chinese vessels? If anything, the lack of arms made them more economically efficient.

The real differences in costs between armed and unarmed trade may be more reflective of the human resource rather than the presence of naval ordnance. The super-abundance of crew on European warships and privateers immediately stands out in comparison to Chinese vessels. English diplomat John Crawfurd notes that junks in the nineteenth century seemed to have more crew than comparable European vessels, but he was comparing unarmed merchantmen on both sides. The evaluation of the differences between armed and unarmed trade is much more difficult. Whereas a large Fujian pole junk might have possessed a crew of thirty sailors, armed merchant ships such as privateers went to sea with 120 or more on board. The American schooner *George Washington,* less than one hundred feet long and carrying only three cannon, went to sea with eighty men.[161] And what better example is there of the operations of armed trade than the practice of privateering and "Guerre de Course," the semi-formal war on commerce? Additional crewmen were needed for boarding captured commercial vessels, the prizes, and sailing them home.

The problems of recruitment and manning, of providing additional provisions for the voyage and additional wages for the crew, the reduction of cargo space, and the need to remain on station are only some of the additional costs of maritime aggression. Cipolla and others have highlighted the technical advantages in European vessels, but the true basis for comparison between modes of maritime trade may lie elsewhere.

Though the details may not be completely worked out, it is clear that several specific junk styles in this transpacific sample can be associated with the historic junk trade as well as with earlier and wider trade patterns. Elements of these broad design classifications of *fuchuan* and *shachuan* were photographed and captured in time, before they vanished from the maritime scene. The reflection of these historic elements is the technical aspect of this work. Many of these features are known now only as occasional models in the few maritime museums that maintain them. Six decades ago the beginning of the end for all such vessels was already in sight, an unfortunate byproduct of the Pacific war in the 1930s and 1940s. World War II, modernization, and cultural exchange doomed the large fleets of sailing junks. Those who noticed their passing also noted with regret the lack of recorded plans and specifications.

The great war junks used by the Chinese in former days, resplendent in scarlet paint and golden decoration, have all disappeared, giving way to steel-built cruisers and gunboats of European design; so, too, have gone the magnificent merchant junks that voyaged to India and the Persian Gulf in Marco Polo's day and long before, vessels that boasted even then many of the features that, re-invented, characterize quite modern European ship design. . . . But though these finely built junks have accompanied the European built tea-clipper to the lumber room of Ocean, Chinese sailing craft of the present day, dingy and roughly built as they often are, conserve the essential features of the type.[162]

The few roughly built junks today, in some cases represented only by a handful of photographs, possess vessel design patterns literally centuries old. In geographical terms, they are a sample that stretches from the coast-lines of Ningbo in the north to Beihai on the Gulf of Tonkin. In maritime terms, these junks, from the small Beihai fishing vessel to the large Fujian pole junk, range among the maritime zones of the inner rivers and coastal strip, or *neihe*, to the inner sea, or *neihai*, to the outer ocean, or *waihai*.[163] In chronological terms, certain elements stretch back to the creation of the *fuchuan* and *shachuan* design patterns, with roots set at least as early as the Tang dynasty, ninth century A.D. Joseph Needham was clear in his praise of the technological achievements of the Chinese and other Asian shipwrights and his appreciation of their long seagoing traditions. "The conclusion that this indicates a clear technical superiority of Chinese seamanship seems almost unavoidable. . . . European seamanship probably owes far more than has been generally supposed to the contributions of the seagoing peoples of East and Southeast Asia."[164] Given these Chinese junks that crossed the Pacific in the early twentieth century, and given the advancements in their designs over time, one can only interpret statements such as "China gave up oceangoing vessels hundreds of years ago" as unintentional but misleading simplifications meant only to address certain aspects of official maritime policy.[165]

chapter 4

The Living Culture of Chinese Vessels

Beyond being mere tools dedicated to the economically efficient transportation of persons and cargo from point A to point B, junks sailed within wider social, political, and even religious realms as well. This chapter extends the physical analysis of the junks into the realms of maritime folklore and religious beliefs, the borders of the supernatural. While the economic and political aspects of the sailing vessel fit better into an historical context, the social, cultural, and religious aspects are steeped in elements of folklore and symbolism. The machine of the sailing junk cannot ever be truly separated from the larger social and cultural context, for these very things give the junk its full meaning.[1] This is true not only for Chinese junks, but for the broader category of historical sailing vessels of many different cultures. For example, the traditional boats of the Moken sea nomads in Southeast Asia played a role far more complex than just fishing, navigation, and habitation. Moken boats were also sanctuaries for guardian spirits, their construction based on the symbolic representation of the human body. The launching of a Moken boat involved placing food in the boat's "mouth," and certain items like cigarettes in the hold, its "belly."[2]

Junks were adorned or constructed with features that had no other apparent functions than to assuage the crew of their natural fears at sea, or to comply with certain established observances of the coastal seafaring culture. Many of these cultural features, though not part of the physical operation of the craft, fulfilled very real social functions, types of risk management. As part of this risk management, wooden sailing vessels took on living qualities. Junks, with their ornate carvings and decorations, were treated as living entities, much like many of the seafaring craft of other cultures. In fact, during the seventeenth century, regulations were passed in England to reduce the amount of costly and purely decorative carvings that proliferated all over navy vessels.[3]

Certain trends in maritime folklore seem universal, particularly where smaller, hand-built, wooden sailing vessels are concerned. The reverence that most mariners feel toward the creaking, groaning wooden vessels that literally cradle them in warmth and safety as they travel through a cold and hostile ocean is commonly noted in the maritime world. Folklorist Horace Beck notes the central position played by the environment in the maritime realm, stating that "Few areas of the world are better suited to the preservation and creation of folklore than the sea."[4] Given the often dangerous nature of work and life at sea, it is not difficult to understand the metaphor of the ship as a living being, being referred to by Europeans in the female gender. Vessels lend themselves in many ways to symbolic interpretations that cross the line from physical to cultural signs, taking on meanings that go far beyond technical analysis.

As complex cultural artifacts, junks and other vessels are expressions of a general seafaring culture. Myths, legends, celebrations, ceremonies, decorations, charms, and all sorts of customs and social routines make up a part of the meaning of junks. This has not always been explicitly acknowledged by those in the maritime professions, though it may be intuitively clear. Often, maritime archaeologists are more concerned with only the technical aspects of physical construction, but ethnographers recognize a symbolic reality as well. Dr. Fred McGhee recently stated that ships, often technological marvels, "are primarily cultural and political entities and ought to be thought of and investigated as such."[5] Political entities as well? Certainly the Chinese officials who objected to a war junk like the *Whang Ho* becoming the property of westerners felt the social and political inappropriateness of such an act. As a symbol of the dynasty, an official bearer of the flag so to speak, it could not be released to any foreign power. In a sense, the vessel itself was a representative of fading imperial culture.

Other junks in the sample reflect a more commercial and nonofficial side of society, associated with the culture of merchant sailors. Richard Gould applies a broad anthropological perspective in order to find social meaning behind vessels. Gould finds the construction features themselves are the archaeological remnants of a cultural system as it existed when the inhabitants (sailors) were alive and functioning as a society.[6] Maritime ethnographers have recognized this for decades. Christiaan Nooteboom in 1952 held that boats were, without a doubt, "the most living cultural object known . . . the ship serves as the central element in many cultures and that some of them will remain incomprehensible without a relatively deep understanding of their vessels."[7]

The assumption here is that crews of wooden sailing vessels formed a society or subset of society that was somehow different and sometimes completely separate from the normal population. Sociologists who specialize in seafaring cultures refer to the seagoing society as "a total institution, comparable in significant respects to the hospital, the army camp, the prison, the cloister, and the boarding school."[8] Maritime society often featured a distinctly different view of the world. Nautical charts, nautical language, unique rituals, ceremonies, and stages of naval advancement, unique punishments—all indicate a reality strikingly different from that of land society.

Others highlight some of this separate nature by emphasizing a number of distinctive maritime traits: nautical similes, boat symbols, proverbs, ship models, votive offerings, myths, etc. All of these things make up parts of a "maritime cultural landscape," anthropologist Christer Westerdahl's term signifying a broader "human utilization (economy) of maritime space by . . . settlement, fishing, hunting, shipping, and its attendant subcultures, such as pilotage, lighthouse, and sea park maintenance."[9] The traces of Westerdahl's maritime society extend both on the sea and along the coasts. The seashore itself is not necessarily the clear dividing line between maritime and terrestrial cultures.

Authors like Greg Dening shed light on the separate society of sailors as well. Dening, in *Mr. Bligh's Bad Language*, uses the structure of the ship itself to enhance his self-conscious theatrical metaphor, and for the most part finds the ship a microcosm of society as a whole. The ship is a stage upon which the rituals of social power, in this case the hierarchical command of the Royal Navy, are played out. Its very construction reflects the prevailing social order. Yet Captain Bligh's problem, according to Dening, is that Bligh, an officer, did not fully understand the nature of the common maritime society in which he found himself. He did not understand the rituals and ceremonies observed only at sea. Bligh, the landsman, was therefore inadequate as the "lead role." By forbidding the crew to engage in ceremonies endemic to the maritime world, such as hazing rituals associated with crossing the line or equator, Bligh violated the rules of the uniquely maritime society. Remaining unaware of the difference between terrestrial and maritime societies led to one of the most famous mutinies in European maritime history. These things have little to do with the actual technology or operations of making the craft move through the water.

Just as the West has a rich heritage of ceremonies, traditions, and objects, its figureheads and coins beneath the mast step, its Poseidon and Davy Jones, China has the oculi, coins, inscriptions, carvings, gods, and much more. The eyes portrayed on the bows of Chinese junks are perhaps the most striking, for they play off the universal anthropomorphic assumption of ships as living beings, imbued with very humanlike characteristics. There is no concise reference on the plethora of ceremonies and superstitions, on the number and types of gods considered sacred to seagoing Chinese sailors. There is only the scattering of partial descriptions and the images of the vessels themselves.

Observances popular among the working-class sailors would, in all likelihood, not reflect any strictly official elite dogma of the more defined Chinese practices, such as Daoism and Confucianism and Buddhism. More likely, transient coastal populations on working junks practiced what is loosely called popular religion, a dynamic mixture of multiple beliefs and traditions. Historians Patricia Ebrey and Peter Gregory highlight the expansion and role of popular beliefs originating from the transition period between the Tang and Song dynasties. If the three great institutions of Buddhism, Daoism, and Confucianism can be represented by the peaks of three adjacent triangles, then popular beliefs are represented by the overlapping bases of those same structures.[10] This makes up a fourth religion, yet one particularly difficult to define. Though this mountain peak model of the total four strains of Chinese religions may reveal flaws upon close examination, it does serve to emphasize the hybrid nature of common beliefs among the masses. Unfortunately, it proves quite difficult for historians to unveil the complex domain of these popular beliefs. There is less and sometimes no documentation left behind by lay and common practitioners of the popular realm. Practices combine an eclectic mixture of systems into a plethora of cults and symbols. There is no single maritime practice.

Regrettably, in the many selections of essays assembled by Ebrey and Gregory, as well as in other sources, scholars have often skipped over the specific topic of seagoing popular beliefs. The most important exception is attention paid to one particular goddess, Mazu, as well as some scattered information on the beliefs of coastal fishing populations. There is little doubt that the Chinese deep water sailing world featured many more. James Fenimore Cooper stated that "superstition is a quality that seems indigenous to the ocean."[11] But how do we get at these hidden beliefs? There is no text that specifically addresses this task, but an attempt will be made here to partially lift the veil surrounding portions of the popular religion by analyzing a portion of the many significant symbols built on and into Chinese junks.

How are the seafaring cultural beliefs and practices recorded by the physical form of the junk itself? Do such depictions really represent a maritime
culture, or simply the general culture of Southern China? Given the nature
of the ocean environment, are there similarities between Chinese and European maritime folklore? These are not easy questions, for Chinese nautical
beliefs fall into an obscure corner of an already difficult topic. Though not
many of the practices described in the following pages were conducted by
the western crews that brought some of the ten junks across the Pacific, the
vessels themselves had been constructed with all or many of the appropriate
features of the Chinese maritime world. The junks reveal traces of Chinese
maritime popular beliefs. The following headings are arranged to roughly
reflect an idealized voyage of a "living" vessel, rather than the surgical division of the ship into its inanimate portions. This is anthropomorphism, and
animism, the imbuing of natural objects with living souls and even supernatural powers.

A Ship's Birth and Leaving or Making Port

The ceremonies that accompanied the actual departure of Chinese junks
went well beyond mere recognition of ritual decoration on the ship. Junk
launchings were important social occasions marked with religious significance. Worcester's record of a launching ceremony describes a temporary
altar constructed of anchor chain, onto which is placed cups of wine and joss
or incense sticks. Holding a live chicken, the shipwright performs the kow-
tow in the direction of the junk's bow, as well as to the port and starboard
sides, pouring the wine on deck as he does so. Blood from the sacrificed
bird is then sprinkled on the bow and daubed at all important locations on
the vessel.[12] Ship launching, though, is only one of many activities involving
the supernatural. A more detailed portrait of the permeating influence of
religious traditions in the selection of auspicious dates and times for setting
out on a voyage features heavily in China traveler John Gray's nineteenth-
century description.

> At the commencement and termination of each voyage, the goddess
> Tien-how receives a special homage. When a junk is ready for sea, a
> number of Taoist priests are invited to go on board for the purpose
> of chanting prayers and offering sacrifices to Tien-how. But should a
> violent storm arise after all these religious observances and threaten
> the safety of the vessel, there is an all-prevailing opinion amongst Chi-

nese sailors that it is owing to the anger of the gods against some sin-
ful person, or persons, on board. A similar notion prevailed amongst
[European] mariners in ancient times. . . .

The departure of a vessel from port takes place on a lucky day, selected by Taoist priests, or, in their absence, by astrologers. The day
generally selected is either the first or fifteenth of each lunar month, at
the new or full moon. As a junk is leaving port, other crews which hail
from the same port mount the poops of their junks with the view of
propitiating the wind and waves in favour of the departing vessel, some
of them energetically beating gongs and tom-toms, whilst others, to
dispel all evil influences, increase the din by discharging popguns and
fire-crackers. When the vessel reaches the port, religious ceremonies
are again observed in honour of Tien-how. The services on such occasions are not usually held on board the junk, but in a temple in honour
of the goddess. They consist of thanks giving, prayers, and offerings
of boiled fowl and pork, or small portions of the merchandise which
the junk has brought to port. In 1864 I entered a temple dedicated to
Tien-how on Fishers' island, one of the Pescadore group. . . . In the
same temple there was a large model of a Chinese junk, which I was informed it is the custom of the islanders to carry in procession through
the streets of their villages when celebrating the natal anniversary of
Tien-how.[13]

Mazu, also known as the Queen Empress of Heaven or Heavenly Consort,
Tianfei or Tianhou (Tinhau in Hong Kong), was and is one of the most
important goddesses for Chinese sailors as well as overseas communities.
Temples to Mazu were found all along the southern Chinese coast, as well
as overseas. She was one of the few minor historical figures who, after becoming a local deity worshiped by coastal people in Fujian, developed into a
massively popular goddess in South China during the late Song period.

According to most accounts, Mazu's real name was Lin Moniang, a
daughter of a Song dynasty bureaucrat (960–987 A.D.). Reportedly, in one
version of the story, a young girl named Lin fell into a deep, three-day trance
at the same time as her brothers were encountering a storm at sea. Her image appearing before them, she led them to safety and became venerated by
local fishermen. The goddess of the sailors was later elevated by imperial
recognition to the status of official godhead, receiving a title appropriate to
her rank.[14] The cult of Mazu fell under the direction of the Imperial Board
of Rites. Not much is recorded concerning how Mazu died and passed into

heaven, and there are a number of alternate versions of similar myths as well. For instance, Mazu is also remembered in Taiwanese oral traditions as having been the daughter of a poor peasant fisherman in Taiwan.[15]

The Mazu cult provides an example of the widely dispersed nature of maritime beliefs and popular gods. Mazu's local fame quickly pervaded the South China coast at a time when certain state-sanctioned cults successfully challenged previously established doctrine. Later, none other than Ming admiral Zheng He, Mazu's most famous supporter, dedicated his voyages to her by erecting a stone tablet in 1431.

> We have traversed more than one hundred thousand *li* of water spaces and have beheld in the ocean huge waves like mountains rising sky high, and we have set eyes on barbarian regions far away hidden in a blue transparency of light vapors, while our sails loftily unfurled like clouds day and night continued their course (rapid like that) of a star, traversing those savage waves as if we were treading a public thoroughfare. Truly this was due to the majesty and the good fortune of the Court and moreover we owe it to the protecting virtue of the divine Celestial Spouse.
>
> The power of the goddess having indeed been manifested in previous times has been abundantly revealed in the present generation. In the midst of the rushing waters it happened that, when there was a hurricane, suddenly there was a divine lantern shining in the mast, and as soon as this miraculous light appeared the danger was appeased, so that even in the danger of capsizing one felt reassured that there was no cause for fear. When we arrived in the distant countries we captured alive those of the native kings who were not respectful and exterminated those barbarian robbers who were engaged in piracy, so that consequently the sea route was cleansed and pacified and the natives put their trust in it. All this is due to the favors of the goddess ... the miraculous power of the goddess resides wherever one goes.[16]

Mazu's popularity continues in certain locales today. She is usually prominently featured in Chinese New Year's parades among overseas Chinese communities, and she is particularly popular in San Francisco. Original overseas Chinese communities were offshoots of maritime merchant activity, and thus the goddess of the sailors remained well suited for distant settlers. Contemporary oral accounts attribute the successful defense of Taiwan against Communist mainland attack to the goddess, her arms catching some of the bombs midair and preventing explosions by causing the bombs to be duds.[17] Today there are literally dozens of temples to Mazu in the vicinity of

Figure 49. An effigy of the seafaring goddess Tinhau (Mazu), accompanied by her celestial attendants, at a temple in Hong Kong in 2002. (Author's photo)

Hong Kong, where the goddess is worshiped not as an historical symbol, but as an immediate and living being.

Judging from the distribution of her cult alone, it is clear that Mazu was a goddess important to both sailors on seagoing vessels and the coastal maritime population in general. The image of Mazu was usually found on board vessels flanked by her attendants Qianli Yan ("Thousand Mile Eyes"), and Shunfeng Er ("Fair Wind Ears"), supernaturals credited with the possession of abnormally sensitive ocular and auricular perception. Mazu reportedly captured both of these on Peach-Blossom Mountain, and they assisted her in rescuing sailors in distress.[18] Offerings of chicken and roast pork, accompanied by incense and candles, and prayers for protection while on the deep sea, were always made on the twenty-third day of the third lunar month.[19]

Statues of Guandi, the popular god of war, and Guanyin, the Chinese Buddhist goddess of mercy, also could appear on board seagoing vessels. These portable images must have functioned in a similar fashion to their land-based counterparts, hearing the supplications of the crew, particularly in times of duress. Guandi, or Guanyu, it was said, had begun as a seller of bean curd before becoming a famous general. Could this have resonated with the large number of river junks involved in transporting bean curd? According to one story, Guanyin, the daughter of a northern king during the Zhou dynasty, had lived for nine years on an island near Ningbo, healing the diseased and saving sailors from shipwrecks.[20] On the southern China coast, Guanyin, who is often depicted as seated upon the shoreline deep in meditation, has often been identified with Mazu herself, the two images sometimes merging into one entity.[21] Many other gods associated with the sea, such as Yen Gong, the god of the sailors, Long Wang, or the Sea Dragon King, and Fengbo, the Earl of the Winds, are described in E.T.C. Werner's *A Dictionary of Chinese Mythology*. As might be imagined, the mythical realm of Chinese sailors included the highly bureaucratized *Shui Fu*, or "Treasury of the Waters," where many divisions and subdivisions of ministries and councils, led by spirits and dragons and gods, replicated the bureaucratic and social structure of Chinese society for the maritime mythical realm. Werner in *A Dictionary of Chinese Mythology*, Clarence Burton Day in *Chinese Peasant Cults*, and Robert Antony in *Like Froth Floating on the Sea* capture a portion of the plethora of Chinese maritime spirits, showing the great diversity of the popular beliefs of sailors.

The more familiar European ceremonies required upon vessels being launched or departing from ports need not be examined in too much detail here. The social and political and even economic importance of new vessels beginning their life on the sea manifested in large celebrations and sometimes informal holidays for the local region. Vessel launchings are still occasions for celebrations, speechmaking, and consecration by the smashing of champagne bottles against the prow. In the past such events involved direct blood sacrifice of animals, and occasionally humans, as in the Viking ritual of "roller reddening" by tying slaves beneath the ship's timbers. Poseidon and Neptune fulfilled specific nautical roles for European sailors. Saint Elmo, patron of the sea, and Saint Christopher, patron of all travelers, also garnered particular favor among the sailing population.

Housing the Gods and Goddesses

Some of the many gods and goddesses associated with the oceangoing junks have been mentioned above, but others of the inland lakes and rivers of China existed as well. How were they cared for on board junks? Boats, as complex cultural objects, possessed the need for sacred as well as secular spaces. The Lepa boats of the Bajau sea nomads in Southeast Asia featured a symbolic orientation of sacred space similar to the layout of their owners'

Table 4. Summary of Maritime Mythology

Name	Brief description	Reference
Jinghaishen	God who quells the sea	Antony 153
Fengyi	A god of waters, deified as *shuishen.*	Werner 126
Fengbo	Wind Uncle, a stellar divinity directing the winds; also said to be a dragon.	Werner 126–27
Guanyin	Goddess of Mercy, especially popular with merchants.	Werner 225–27
Guandi	Chinese god of war.	Werner 227
Long Wang or Si Hai Long Wang	Sea Dragon King, the "Neptune" of the Chinese, with palaces at the bottom of the sea. Although found on earth, the proper element for dragons is the water. Such powerful creatures could be protectors of sailors and grant safe navigation to trade vessels.	Werner 285–93; Day 74; Antony 153
Shuishu Huangdi	Emperor of the waters	Antony 153
Beidou; Beidi	Spirits of the stars of the Northern Dipper; god of the north.	Werner 369; Antony 153
Jumu	Gale Mother (Hainan Island)	Antony 153
Hongsheng	Ocean deity, Canton area	Antony 153
Tangong	Ocean deity, Canton area	Antony 153
Yang Si Laoye	One of the gods of sailors, often depicted as a youth dressed in white, carrying an axe and grasping a dragon (control over the dragon king). Worshiped by all who dwell in boats or are associated with the sea.	Werner 398
Mazu	Also known as Tianfei, Tianhou, Tianhou Niangniang; heavenly concubine, goddess of sailors.	Werner 503
Yang Si Jiangjun	Worshiped by boatmen, wood merchants, managers of rafts . . . holds axe and dragon, identical to Yang Si Laoye. Axe is the symbol of workers of wood.	Werner 585
Yen Gong	God of sailors, said to have lived during the Song or Yuan dynasty, a native of Fuzhou. Responsible for saving an emperor's life. Capable of calming storms at sea.	Werner 590–91
Lu Ban	Patron of carpenters, credited with invention of paddles, oars, and boats as well. Patron of ship builders.	Day 109
Shen Feng Da Ji	God of the favorable winds, also known as a boatman's patron.	Day 163
Yu Hua Wu Sheng	Fisherman's patron	Day 213
Longmu	Dragon Mother	Antony 153
Sanshanshen	God of the Three Mountains	Antony 153

stilt houses, an entrance for guardian spirits as well as cooking and sleeping space at the bow and refuse/defecation opposite at the stern.[22]

On Chinese junks sacred space and housing for the appropriate idols was typically located in a special section or altar in the stern cabin, as with the Fujian pole junk, or in a separate compartment built on deck between the stern cabin and the mainmast, as with the northern style Antung trader.[23] Incense was burned before the images in the joss house, offerings were made, and often the compass was housed in the same sacred vicinity. Some of the transpacific junk voyages reveal participation in these traditions.

Of course, many of these traditional beliefs have been altered or suppressed in more modern societies. Sometimes mariners, still familiar with the old gods, conspicuously adopted more modern ways in the name of progress. Navigator Paul Chow describes the launching event of the junk *Free China* as marking a small break with the past. "America has her young Washington chopping down the cherry tree. China has her young Sun Yat-sen knocking down the idols made of mud in the temples. Claiming ourselves to be intellectuals, we would not think of calling upon the Tian-Hou Niangniang's blessing. Firecrackers were the only thing allowed."[24] Firecrackers never seem to lose their social acceptability. A great deal of noise in general upon launching and setting out from port seems the general rule. The description of the noisy send-off in John Gray's nineteenth-century excerpt above seems very similar to European practices, where ships arriving and departing were saluted by cannon fire as well as the organized cheers of the vessels' crews.

The mention of sacrifices, or *ji*, in the Gray excerpt and the selection of the lucky day for departure indicate that the event was firmly grounded in popular traditions, rather than more institutionalized practices. (Europeans were also quite superstitious about the timing of voyages, and it was only relatively recently that insurance agencies stopped charging official penalties for vessels leaving port on Fridays, or on the thirteenth of any month. In general, Wednesday, originally sacred to Woden, proved a more prudent choice.[25]) Daoists did not generally encourage sacrifice, for their pure immortals did not need to eat or drink. Certain observers found the notion of sacrifice distasteful. Karl Gutzlaff, a missionary who traveled along the China coast in the early nineteenth century, kept a keen eye out for the more common traditions. Such maritime superstitions, for Gutzlaff, were a mark of base ignorance. He describes the image or model of a vessel, one about to make a voyage, being taken in procession to the goddess's temple, where a banquet is laid out. There are rounds of prayers and prostrations, and the captain appears in full regalia. The statue of Mazu is then carried to the junk amid much music and procession, while "the jolly sailors anxiously strive to seize whatever may happen to remain of her banquet."[26]

Several of the transpacific junks, such as the *Sea Dragon* and the *Free China*, are known to have had some sort of celebration along these lines, usually incorporating elements of western launchings as well. The *Free China*'s launch was accompanied by speeches, banquets, fire crackers, and gifts, but not the parade to the temple of the sea goddess.

Several other transpacific junks also featured the traditional idols as passengers across the ocean. The scientific junk yacht *Cheng Ho*'s image of Mazu had to be housed, due to space restrictions, in the botanical library, where the Chinese crew made offerings amid the scientific volumes. A small, red altar, once tacked to the forward bulkhead of the living compartment in the Beihai junk in Portland, now only contains a candle, the image of the god or goddess long absent. And from the junk *Ning Po*, a statue eventually surfaced, causing a small mystery in the maritime circles of Southern California. A figurine initially identified by Dr. Michael Saso as the temple guardian Wang Lingguan, a figure not usually associated with ships, originally arrived with the *Ning Po* and was only recently returned to the museum on Catalina Island. What this statue was doing on the junk is puzzling. It turns out that the wide-eyed bearded figure is an image of the *Wangye* cult, "a spirit cast out to sea in the *Da Wangye* (exorcising the demons of pestilence, pirates, maritime patrol, etc.), all along the coast of SE China, Chekiang, Jiangsu, Fukien, Kwangtung, even to Vietnam and Okinawa."[27] Dr. Saso suggested that when the vessel was sold, the Mazu statue may have been taken out and the *Wangye* image put in its place, thus the *Ning Po* carried the spirit of pestilence and demons away from the Chinese villages and far overseas.

Worcester notes that the figure of *Wangye*, the River Guardian King, was quite well known among sailors. Apparently the Guardian King's profession was somewhat like that of a pirate in the twelfth century, including a stronghold on Tungting Lake. So secure was this fortress that he arrogantly challenged the imperial forces, only to be defeated by General Yo Fei. In his despair, he cast himself into the lake. "Nearly every junk has a model of him. The figure is often handed down from father to son and may serve in several junks."[28]

European vessels were also not without their symbolic statues. Statues of Catholic saints were placed within special niches built into the ship, the saint often being of the same name as the particular vessel. Votive candles, prayers, and even offerings of food and libations might prove effective during times of duress. If not, captains could berate the statue, sometimes even tying a line to the powerless saint and tossing the idol overboard to be towed astern. If the storm were particularly powerful, the captain might cut the line.[29]

Construction of Successful Voyaging

Many features on Chinese junks were deemed important to its safe passage over the seas. Possibly junks featured as many, if not more, cultural affectations as any other seafaring vessels. The physical nature of the ship itself reflected an intense concern with proper religious observation. Written characters in well-known phrases, *chengyu*, adorned appropriate features of the vessel, while other religiously significant artifacts were built directly into the hull, keel, mast, and beams. John Gray's nineteenth-century observations recorded these auspicious carvings and other important decorations. He described strips of red paper pasted on the mizzen, main, and fore masts, upon which were written, "The mast is as the general commanding ten thousand soldiers; From every side of the compass may fair winds blow; May this mast scorn tempests, from whatever quarter of the heavens they may come."[30] On the new moon, and again on the full moon, the taffrail (uppermost rail around the stern of the vessel) was dressed with triangular banners, while red, white, or black flags adorned the main top. This particular practice of placing significant ritual phrases at certain locations on the vessel does not seem to have any familiar western counterpart, unless the western ship's name serves a similar role.

Chinese characters were often carved onto the stern transoms as well, though these did not always necessarily signify the name of the vessel.[31] This could cause a certain amount of confusion for western travelers, and often these particular phrases, or *chengyu*, were interpreted as vessel names. The *Ning Po*, before her renaming by Gordon, was referred to as the *Jin Tai Feng*, or *Kin Tai Fong* in many western sources, as if the auspicious characters represented the actual name of the vessel. Such characters might readily have been found on numerous merchant junks, but were possibly supplications to the fates rather than identity labels. "Whenever people put money together to open a shop or build a ship, they attach the name 'Chin' [as a prefix to the name of their partnership]. The character 'chin' [gold] symbolizes cooperation."[32] Needless to say, it also symbolizes cold hard cash. Other *chengyu*, or *duizi*, on the transom reflect poetry, such as "water that sleeps in the moonlight," or "white robe crumpled by the son of heaven," or "pale cheek touched by the rainbow," and so on.[33] There seems to be no limit to the number of different phrases meant to flatter the gods and bring good luck:

Figure 50. The *chengyu* on the rudderpost of the junk *Free China* read "*wan jun zhu shuai*" (general commanding ten thousand troops), a fitting statement for the helm position. (Courtesy of the Reno Chen collection)

"be invincible in all directions! . . . may there be abundant fish! . . . may there be seasonable weather."[34]

The matter of ship names in the European world occupies an interesting ethnographic niche. Vessel names combined a variety of factors, such as the type of trade carried out, nation of origin, type of vessel, etc. Types of ship names change with time as well. Names carried with them an element of luck, as well as the negative stigma of supernatural influences; what ship has been named *Titanic* since 1912? Basically, European vessel names were expected to protect the ships from harm from either natural or supernatural forces, and also to promote the ships' commercial ventures. These are the same things accomplished by the Chinese *chengyu,* so the important functions of the vessels' names still seem to be accounted for, even though the actual name of the Chinese ship may simply reflect the identity of the owner and today perhaps only an unembellished number.

The oculi, or the eyes of the ship, have for a long time been associated with Chinese vessels, the portal "by which the sailors imagine that the vessel can espy sunken rocks, shoals, and other dangers of the deep."[35] These eyes often gave the bow of the ship the appearance of a fish or sea monster. The eyes of fishing vessels appeared to be looking downward, while those on commercial vessels gazed straight ahead.

Actually, the oculus typically associated with Chinese ships is one of those truly universal maritime customs stretching back into the past beyond documented reference. Oculi have been found throughout the entire width of the Old World, from the Mediterranean to the China Sea, with the singular and unexplained exception of the west coast of India.[36] It is possible that the custom in southern Europe originated in Egypt, for the painting of the Horus eye is depicted on the bows of funeral boats. The function of the eyes at the bow of Chinese ships was partially mirrored perhaps by the presence of figureheads on western craft. The origin of the oculus for the West extends at least to Greek times, when many ships were depicted with such eyes. Some western figureheads feature large, bulging eyes, more reminiscent of the traditional oculi of ancient Mediterranean vessels. Nothing seems to capture the animism that permeates the reverence of the wooden sailing vessel better than the practice of adorning it with figureheads or eyes.

The suspected origins of the oculi in China, though, have not been thoroughly investigated. Horace Beck speculates that the animistic eyes painted on the bows of ships, such a widespread feature, were originally transmitted both eastward to East Asia and westward to the Mediterranean by Arab sailors.[37] The passage of time allowed the Chinese practice to develop multiple styles. The three distinct types were the dragon, the phoenix, and the tadpole stylized oculi.[38] Dragon eyes—large, rounded forms usually painted on separate wooden pieces and nailed to the hull—were found in the Chusan Archipelago and Fujian. These rounded eyes were also found in Hong Kong, but there, as elsewhere in Guangdong, they were elongated into a stretched oval form in imitation of more southern Annam styles.[39] Most of the transpacific junks featured dragon-style eyes at the bow. These are clearly evident in the numerous drawings and photographs throughout this study.

Rolls of coins and ceremonial mirrors were sometimes buried within the joints of the keel of the ship itself, placed in holes drilled within the scarf. These holes were known as *baoshougong*, or "longevity holes." The thirteenth-century wreck at Quanzhou provides one of the earliest examples of this. Placed in patterns resembling specific constellations, in this case Ursa Major, known in the West as the Big Dipper or The Plough, and in China as the Great Bear or Northern Dipper (*bei dou*), this unique construction feature goes back at least to the Song dynasty and reportedly was still in practice in 1949.[40] Nails at this late date took the place of rolls of coins, and a single coin replaced the mirror.[41]

The constellation pattern of the seven stars, *qi xing*, and the mirror representing the moon, have significant connotations. The seventh day of the seventh month marks a major celebration in the Chinese calendar, and the *qi xing* were frequently represented in Daoist ritual. According to legend, it was the Northern Dipper constellation as the Great Bear who decided the time of death for humans. Chinese astronomers felt the shafts of the constellation held influence over the change of seasons. Furthermore, in Taiwan, the seven constellation holes are drilled into the board upon which the human body is placed in the coffin. Exactly what this says about the nautical application of these longevity holes remains difficult to determine. The bright mirror, or *jing*, was also carved into the scarf deep within the keel. This is a good omen, serving to make spirits visible to themselves.[42] Perhaps evil sea spirits would then take flight at their own countenance? A rare, mid-nineteenth-century document on the navy of Fujian refers to this physical feature as the "seven stars wood," placing this significant timber across the interior stern transom, instead of in the keel scarf of the ship.[43]

This does not seem too unlike European sailors' placing coins beneath the mast steps of their vessels, always face up. The coins under the mast step were, perhaps, a prepaid toll to Charon, the ferryman of Hades.[44] Silver coins have long been placed beneath the mast steps of sailing ships. Furthermore, Scottish shipwrights often hide a gold coin "for luck" somewhere within the splice of the main keel, and sometimes fix a gold sovereign to the main deck beam for similar reasons. Modern sailing yachts continue to place coins beneath the mast step. In motorized vessels, silver coins were sometimes used to shim or adjust the engine bed.

The extensive decorations on both stern and bow transoms have been noted throughout the previous chapter. Significant depictions of the *taiqi yin* and *yang* image, one of the most powerful metaphysical symbols, were usually placed high on the stern and often on the bow transom as well. This was a strong indication of the animistic concept being applied to the Chinese junk. Occasionally the eight trigrams would be seen surrounding the *taiqi* symbol. Perhaps this related to the directions of the wind, for the Chinese wind rose was represented by a fan with eight radial sections.[45]

Legendary immortal figures from Chinese history, often with the stunning yan bird arising from the stormy sea, decorate the graceful stern transoms of Fujian vessels. Worcester refers to this creature as the *yan niao*, a type of swallow known for swift flight, unperturbed by the stormy ocean as it perches on a rock amid the crashing waves.[46] The bird then imparts its qualities onto the vessel itself. The serpent painted on the stern quarter of large coastal trading junks is likewise a common feature frequently seen on vessels from Fujian Province.

Not only was the swallow in China a sign of spring and fecundity, it had a specific maritime connotation. According to legend, every winter the swallow returned safely from the bottom of the sea, where it had spent its time inside the shell of the mussel, a bivalve.[47] Junks, too, would hopefully always return to land. From the economic perspective, the regurgitated nests of certain swallows in Southeast Asia and the Indian Ocean were (and are) a major import item and, when added to soup, a renowned delicacy in China. The reported benefits of this dish included, among other things, the power to increase sexual potency. Many merchants and sailors made a good living carrying the expensive nests of the swallow across the South China Sea, borne away in ships with the very same *yan niao* on the stern.

The maritime significance of birds is, of course, not limited to Chinese sailors, but common to all observant seafarers. Europeans held the petrel and the albatross in particular reverence, assuming that these seabirds were restless forms of their dead comrades. Other birds, in general, represented good omens. Pacific Islanders also relied on birds, particularly for their navigational abilities, returning to unseen islands at sunset over the horizon. One canoe prow ornament from Micronesia features "two sea swallows who appear to be facing each other—swallows who might act as guides in a dangerous storm."[48] Birds, then, are commonly incorporated into the maritime world as protective devices or symbols.

The swallow on the stern of Fujian junks was typically depicted as perched on a rock emerging from the stylized, wave-tossed sea. In Chinese art, pictures of rocks jutting out of the sea are common representations of the Daoist paradise in the eastern ocean.[49] These same islands were the legendary targets of ancient Chinese Pacific maritime expeditions, as emperors sent adventurers in search of longevity drugs from the tree of long life, along with the jade fountain from which flowed the elixir of life. Traditional

Chinese gardens often include jutting stones representing these islands of the blessed.[50] The islands, commonly identified as Fangzhang, Penglai, and Yingzhou, lie somewhere in the Pacific off the Chinese coast. Some scholars suggest that the Penghu islands, off the southwest corner of Taiwan, are the same as the mythical home of the Eight Immortals, while others suggest the islands of the blessed used to exist immediately offshore of Qingdao and Shanghai, but have since been joined to the mainland.[51] (Interestingly, the Penghu islands lie astride historic sailing trade routes for Chinese mariners. Local sailors would have been very familiar with the navigational hazards of these hundreds of rocks, shoals, and reefs. In 1983, researchers from Taiwan's Ministry of Education located over one hundred historic shipwrecks among the Penghu islands, stretching back in time to the Song dynasty.)

Other cultures share similar images of immortal and mythical landfalls. The island of Dilmun in the Sumerian Gilgamesh epic has been tentatively identified as corresponding with the Bahrain islands of the Persian Gulf. Plutarch made the pseudo-geographical identification of Roman Elysium with the Canary Islands. Celtic myths allude to paradises in the western sea, somewhere in the Atlantic.[52] Atlantis itself is island mythology. The connection between sacred locations and customary shipboard decorations may not be too hard to imagine, particularly as boats have played a role in sacred journeys into the spiritual world from at least as early as the time of the Greeks.

Besides birds and islands, other images of myth and legend found their place on sailing junks. Stories from the Three Kingdoms period (third century A.D.), painted in bright colors with scenes of heroic exploits by great generals or statesmen, and depictions of the Eight Immortals, or *ba xian*, appear in the records. The Eight Immortals, featured so often in Daoist iconography, were reportedly the inhabitants of those elusive islands of the blessed. Their travels across the South China Sea to attend the feast hosted by the Queen Mother of the West, Xi Wangmu, would seem to have been a natural subject for junk ornamentation.

The serpent, which appears so often on the stern quarter images of Fujian junks, carries more ambiguity than symbols such as the Eight Immortals. As one of the five noxious animals, the snake could represent an evil and treacherous creature; yet serpents could make gifts of great wealth, and snake meat was allegedly good for the eyes. Did such images on the stern quarter assist the junk's eyesight? Or were these images variations of the powerful dragon symbol, including the legendary Sea Dragon King, which lived in a palace at the bottom of the sea? Such water snakes, or *shuishe*, had the power to calm

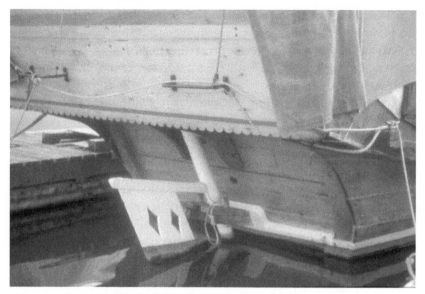

Figure 51. Traditional features persist today, such as the diamond-shaped fenestrations on a modern junk in Pt. Richmond, California. (Author's photo)

the waves.[53] Serpents, as well, often corresponded to types of river gods. River gods, among other spirits (*shen*), needed to be appeased, for they could be hungry for human sacrifice.

Occasionally cultural features serve dual purposes. The conspicuous diamond-shaped fenestrations, or holes, cut into the large, square rudder blades of southern Chinese junks have been commented on in a number of different sources. While the popular explanation holds that fenestrations are cut in rudder blades and even cut through keels in order to free the junk from possible entanglements with evil marine spirits, hydrodynamic tests in towing tanks reveal that the rudder with holes cut in the blade performs more effectively at low speeds.[54] This phenomenon depends on the localized turbulence of water passing through an opening actually increasing the effective surface area of the rudder blade. Anecdotally, sailors held that cutting these holes in the rudder blade made it that much easier to maneuver, or "put over," for the pressure acting against the rudder blade would be partially relieved. The practice still persists in modern wooden examples and even present-day mass-produced steel rudders on junks in China.[55]

There are other similar examples of specific construction features that serve both a symbolic and a physical function. The semicircular notches at both the prow and stern of Moken boats, symbolic of the boat's mouth and anus, also serve naturally as steps into the boat from the water or the beach. The mythic history of the Moken, captured in the epic poem of Gaman, reveals that the prow and stern notches are permanent marks of the judgment of Queen Sibian, who condemned the Moken to a life of wandering.[56]

Like the *chengyu*, or ritual phrases mentioned above, fenestrations below the waterline on Chinese rudders did not appear on European ships, at least not until they were adopted for experimentation purposes on the rudders of high-speed torpedo boats.

Death at Sea, or Shipwreck

All this attention to the maritime spirits was of vital importance in the Chinese view, for the gods or fates could grant or obstruct financial success to the voyage and ensure a safe and fast passage. The Chinese, like sailors all around the world, maintained a special aversion to death by drowning. For a Chinese mariner to lose his life at sea meant that there would be no body to bury, hence no grave to be cleaned, so no ancestor to be revered. It was to be forever separated from family, and thus to be avoided. And in the Chinese tradition, dead ancestors who did not receive proper sacrifices of wine and food became hungry ghosts, or *egui*. Those who drowned at sea became water ghosts, *shuigui*, and their spirits hungrily sought out living victims to take their place.[57] For this reason, Chinese mariners never buried their dead at sea, a ritual some other mariners practiced without hesitation. If the *shuigui* could not find a proxy, then they were doomed to never achieve rebirth. This was such a noted phenomenon that several observers reported incidents of Chinese sailors refusing to give aid to victims struggling in the water, or refusing to assist vessels that had capsized and were in the process of sinking.[58] Water ghosts were also believed to be able to move inland and visit villages. Occasionally, dozens of these malevolent spirits were said to join together and attempt to drown *en masse* all who ventured on the waters.[59]

The nautical dead represent a topic regarded with special potency by many maritime cultures. European sailors who died at sea, particularly during accidents that denied them the appropriate funerary rites, were understood as having the ability to return to the area of their death and haunt other passing vessels. Vessels that experienced tragic or multiple losses of life were sometimes even abandoned at the dock, their crews refusing to sail on them again.[60] European sailors, unlike the Chinese, could be given proper rites and buried at sea, while the bodies of Chinese sailors were, wherever possible, returned to their village.

Sacrifice and blood donation played a role on junks as well. The Chinese crew of the *Cheng Ho*, following an unfortunate fire on board the vessel in the South Pacific, performed certain purification rites, sacrificing a chicken and sprinkling the blood about the decks before offering the cooked remains to Mazu. Blood was thought to cleanse all sins and exorcise evil spirits. Chicken sacrifice often accompanied births or deaths on board junks. "The ceremony of blood donation is one of the important rituals that must be observed. . . . Many of these offerings are made, of course, in the shrine of Tin Hau, the patron saint of the boat people."[61]

European vessels, nearing completion of their construction and prior to launching, would also sometimes be blessed with animal sacrifice, the blood of goats and sheep, as well as chickens, being sprinkled on the decks and into the adjoining water. European blood rituals involved a substance of unfaltering vitality. In Chinese culture, blood consecration had the power to animate all sorts of statues and images. Pictures of gods and goddesses gained souls by having their eyes painted over with blood.[62] Blood consecration was a direct method of animating the sailing vessel, of purifying its soul. Were the oculi on Chinese vessels painted at the same time? The junks were animated, but were not, after all, representations of gods and goddesses themselves.

If the junks were thought to have the power of sight, then one might have to be careful to protect them from gazing at scenes that could damage their souls. Like European vessels, Chinese ships were regarded as living beings, capable of possessing or suddenly acquiring good or bad luck. Robert Fortune observed this hazard firsthand in the mid-nineteenth century.

In going up one of the rivers at this time I observed the effect of a curious superstition which both amused and surprised me at the time. Every one knows that nearly all the junks and boats of China have eyes carved or painted in the bows. I had observed them on all parts of the coast, and had often heard the reason said to be given by the Cantonese, namely, "Suppose no got eye, how can see?" But I did not imagine that any one was so superstitious or ignorant as to fancy that these junks or boats really could see with the eyes which had been given to them. It seemed, however, that I was mistaken. As I was sailing slowly onwards one of my boatmen seized his broad hat, and, rushing past me to the bows of the boat, placed it over one of the eyes. Several other boats in company were also blinded in the same way; some with hats, others with coats, cloaks, or anything that came readiest to hand. I did not understand this proceeding at first, but soon found out the cause. A dead body was floating up the stream with the tide, and if the boat is allowed to see an object of this kind some evil is sure to happen to the passengers or crew before the voyage is over. Such is one of the superstitions of the Chinese, and hence the reason for covering up the eyes of the boats in order that they might not see.[63]

One junk, after having capsized, was salvaged, repaired, and put back on the market. Though practically brand new, no buyer could be found. Sailors would have nothing more to do with the vessel.[64] The same sorts of incidents have been recorded for European ships and their crews, who sometimes cut up unlucky vessels or burned them to get the bad luck out. On occasion Moken boats in Southeast Asia would be abandoned following the death of the owner, in order to discourage the specter of death from prowling too closely to the vessel.[65]

Many aspects of seafaring superstitions can be seen as risk avoidance—taking care not to do the wrong thing and so offend the fates or gods—rather than taking positive action. When eating broiled fish, the *shuishangren*, boat people of Hong Kong, were careful not to break off any of the bones, nor turn the fish over. Both were actions that symbolized damage to the boat, imitating wrecking or capsizing. When they drank, they did not toast "bottoms up" for the same reason.[66]

European sailors also possessed a host of behavioral modifications, such as never whistling on board a ship (unless in a dead calm) or scratching the mast for a breeze.[67] Many fishermen in the Pacific refuse to sail with bananas on board. Mariners today are sometimes reluctant to engage in certain taboo subjects. Only a few years ago, officers on board a modern containership in port at Honolulu confessed to feeling uneasy discussing shipwrecks in the Hawaiian Islands. They finally informed the students that this particular topic was not really appropriate for shipboard discussion. Even in the world of steel containers and modern shipping, certain specifically maritime traditions continue. Not much can be said against all due respect for the power of the ocean.

A Living Nautical Terminology: Animal Symbolism

Shipwrights and sailors, no matter which culture they are from, need, use, and modify when necessary a distinctive terminology suited for their very specialized environment. This has led to the creation of separate maritime or nautical dictionaries in a number of different languages, including Chinese and Japanese. The single drawback of most of the available East Asian references is that they reflect the modern industrial maritime world, applicable to motorized vessels, whether propelled by coal-fired boilers, diesel engines, or even nuclear reactors. They do not often recall the maritime reality of sail prior to these radical changes.

Western sources celebrate the pre-industrial sail era. Even landlubbers use nautical jargon from the distant past. Frustrated with repetitive failure, we often find ourselves "flogging a dead horse," driving us to become "three sheets to the wind," especially if it is cold enough to "freeze the balls off a brass monkey." (An effigy of a horse was flogged and hoisted aloft, marking the end of working off advanced wages and the beginning of making real pay; general drunkenness could send men reeling down the street, flapping like loose halyards in a stiff breeze; iron cannon balls stacked on brass holders would, if the weather were cold enough, go rolling across the deck due to the differing rates of shrinkage in dissimilar metals.) Nautical language captures much of the romantic culture of the sailing past, and was often the mark of Jack Tar on shore, a nickname for the generic sailor.

Nautical terminology often reveals the animistic tendency, for much of this language reflected animal names and animal parts. Donkey engines (auxiliary boilers) and horse latitudes (zones north and south of the equator) and the dreaded cat-o'-nine-tails (the lash) spiced the sailor's world. Dogs proved particularly popular. Sailors not "dogging it" (working) might be ordered to take the "dog iron" (pry bar) and "dog down" (secure) the hatches against their "dogs" (clamps), all this during the "dog watch" (split watch between 4:00 p.m. and 8:00 p.m.).[68] Specific language such as this is unique and inseparable from maritime culture. Nautical language reflects the special attitudes held toward sailing vessels, the living creature aspect of ships. The animism that surrounds sailors of different cultures reflects a common inclination to anthropomorphize the inanimate object amid a dynamic environment.

Fortunately, one document captures some of this language for Chinese mariners and sailing vessels. A shipbuilding manual for the Fujian navy, written by a naval functionary around 1850 A.D., has been saved in the Hirth collection of the Royal Library in Berlin.[69] In technical details it does not go beyond the single image of the Qing dynasty vessel from the *Liu Qiu Guo Zhi Lue*. It does, however, list the local terms for a variety of ship parts, allowing a glimpse of the specialized nineteenth-century language of regional Fujian junk builders.

The bow transom, or "wave pressure board" (19), is capped by the bow rail, or "hare's ears" (18), which are used as fairleads or guides for lines and cables. The "sparrow's tongue board" (6) here features a carving of a lion's head. A "deer's saddle" (23), or hardwood board, reinforces the bow transom,

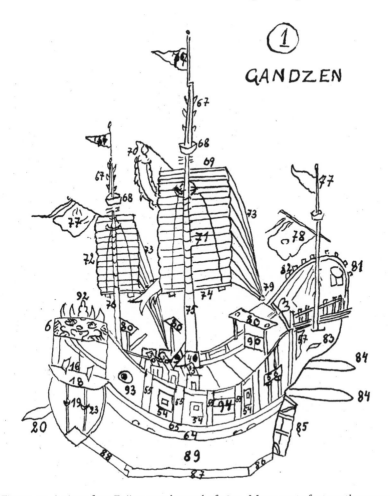

Figure 52. A sixty-foot Fujian naval vessel of 1850. Many parts feature the names of various land and sea animals. (From Moll and Laughton, "The Navy of the Province of Fukien," by kind permission of the Hon. Editor of the *Mariner's Mirror*)

and has holes cut for the underwater cables. Sculling oars or sweeps (20 and 84) extend beyond the vessel's hull. The "dragon's head bone" (88), or forward keel, is attached to the "dragon's middle bone" (87) and the "dragon's tail bone" (86). The "dragon eye" (93) is just forward of the gunwale supports, or "wave protection boards" (55), which are pierced by "gun eyes" (54) of varying number. These are above the series of rounded wales, the "water snake" (65) above the "running horse" (64). On deck, the windlasses (30) are fixed and strong "winch-oxen," and the "peace-oxen" (33) near the mast, provides

Figure 53. A water serpent motif decorating the stern quarter of a fishing junk in Hong Kong's Aberdeen Bay in 2002. (Author's photo)

tie-downs for halyards. Three "sail support boards" (80), or gallows frames, take the weight of the rig when lowered. Wind vanes (77) flutter above the "flag for the god of the sea" (78). This is also called the Mazu banner.[70] The standard decoration of the Fujian serpent, the "tail of the harvest fish" (83), can be seen on the stern quarter. Truly, this singular document provides an amazing glimpse into the nineteenth-century junk master's art.

Superstitious Mariners Everywhere

How much more can be inferred about Chinese maritime ethnology from the examination of the junks themselves remains an open question. A handful of photographs and a couple aging examples like the Beihai junk and the *Free China* provide wonderful but rare evidence. It is obvious, though, that the physical form of the junks themselves does reflect the social setting, the religious beliefs, and the cultural folklore of Chinese seafarers, and that these junks occupy the same special niche reserved by sailors of many other cultures for their vessels. The decorative Fujian-style sterns of the *Ning Po* and *Free China,* the decorative serpents and the images of sacred islands—

Table 5. Comparison of Maritime Cultural Phenomena

Chinese Attributes	Euro/American Attributes
Auspicious launch/departure dates	Lucky/unlucky days of the week/month
Firecrackers	Cannon fire
Prayers at Temple	Prayers at church
Mazu	St. Elmo, Poseidon/Neptune, etc.
Idols carried on board	Saints carried on board
Oculi	Figureheads
Chengyu	—
—	Ship name
—	Ship gender (female)
Coins hidden in construction	Coins hidden in construction
Longevity holes	—
Mirror hidden in construction	—
Fenestrations	—
Reverence for birds	Reverence for birds
Reference to mythical islands	Reference to mythical islands
Eight Immortals decoration	Poseidon, Saints, etc.
Serpent/dragon	Numerous monsters, Kraken
Belief in water ghosts, *shuigui*	Belief in water ghosts
Use of blood consecration (chicken)	Use of blood consecration (champagne bottle)
Numerous behavioral modifications	Numerous behavioral modifications
Animal symbolism	Animal symbolism

these things did not exist as random elements, but instead reveal a consistent maritime culture, a familiar Chinese context.

Though Chinese maritime folklore and vessel construction may seem sometimes quite different from western traditions, different particularly from the Celtic origins of British nautical traditions and the predominantly English-Scottish-Irish folklore of New World maritime beliefs, there are certain similarities between them. Risk abatement, the physical, emotional, and even spiritual search for protection from a potentially dangerous environment, exists as a common theme among seafaring societies. The firsthand observations of maritime rituals in China, the sometimes thinly veiled surprise recorded by clergymen and diplomats, do not necessarily represent a sailor's appreciation of familiar ceremonies.

There has not been much written on the commonalities of the transnational maritime society beyond a few certain articles on the "total institution" of the ship, mentioned above. And from the technical standpoint, the many specific differences between European and Chinese wooden sailing vessels do not speak of a common heritage or shared traditions. But it is in the realm of human seafaring behavior, the many ways in which sailors in the past have attempted to cope with their environment, where the argument of a common maritime realm might be further advanced.

Do these seagoing practices and artifacts represent a separate maritime culture? Or are such things only the selective borrowing of already familiar symbols? This is a complex question, but from the small sample of evidence available, the maritime practices and artifacts do appear to be unique to the maritime world most of the time. The individual gods or goddesses are often specific to the sailor's experience. Where they are not, as for example with Guanyin, they may tend to merge with specifically maritime images, Mazu. Specific saints and gods were granted responsibility for the European sailing world as well. Yet, certainly, praying in churches or temples is a generalized behavior. Celebrations with firecrackers, twenty-one-gun salutes, etc., are all well-known expressions everywhere.

Constructional features, the many things like oculi and figureheads and longevity holes and rudder fenestrations, these things obviously have no counterpart in the terrestrial experience. That is only to be expected, though, as the wooden sailing vessel is a very specialized and dynamic form itself. Belief systems, expressed in ship names and gender, and in *chengyu* and the many unique behavioral modifications of sailors everywhere, seem extremely limited to the nautical realm. Water ghosts and sea serpents and Davy Jones and the Flying Dutchman, these things exist only for the maritime culture. Yet certain elements, such as blood sacrifice, are more general manifestations. In short, from this brief examination, the maritime cultural world partakes in some similar elements of the terrestrial world, yet adds on to that many more variations, as well as endemic features, which only make sense to the sailing world. Such particular practices are important elements of seafaring cultures, indicative of a separate and specialized social group.

These ten junks that crossed the Pacific provide an opportunity to glimpse the maritime realm of Chinese beliefs and behavior, in spite of the American influence involved in their Pacific voyages. The physical manifestations of this behavior for Chinese sailors appear in the many cultural features of the vessels, and occasionally in the descriptions of the voyages and activities themselves. What a little bit of floating wood can tell us . . .

chapter 5

Finding Pacific Junks in History

The larger history surrounding these vessels and their individual trips across the Pacific influence what we know of them in countless ways. This context can be divided into three separate sections: first, the setting in China; second, the state of transoceanic travel; and third, the social environment on the West Coast of America. In general, these Chinese junks were procured under difficult circumstances, transported across the Pacific in dangerous conditions, and dispersed on the West Coast in a casual and informal manner. Though few documents capture the details about these junks, the historical context during the first half of the twentieth century shaped their voyages as well as our perceptions of them. They serve as a kind of bridge connecting the historical settings between China, the Pacific, and America. The junks also allow us to examine ethnographically how material culture was and is displayed in America.

Maritime Change in China

The origins of most of these Chinese vessels are surrounded by historical periods of turmoil and disruption. The periods in which the junks were procured for their voyages encompass the Republican Revolution in China, subsequent warlord rule of the divided countryside, and the outbreak of the Pacific conflict and World War II. These were not the most opportune times to journey on the Chinese coast seeking examples of traditional sailing vessels. There is very little about the early twentieth century that could be referred to as normal in the case of conditions in China. Steamships and other European vessels were transforming the trade routes in China and Southeast Asia, and home ports for these junks had become major treaty ports, undergoing social and economic change due to foreign influence. The outcome of the Opium Wars, the opening of the Suez Canal in 1869, and the transition to steam propulsion all served to increase the flow of European traffic to the China coast.

In most cases the individual stories of junks setting out across the Pacific are lost in the face of larger events. The *Sea Dragon, Free China*, and *Ning Po* stand out as the only exceptions to this rule. The *Ning Po* herself was said to have been purchased from Chinese revolutionaries, and to have played an important role in a number of political uprisings, but it remains difficult to confirm any of the junk's colorful past. The remaining junks emerge almost unnoticed from the western Pacific. The *Whang Ho* was purchased in 1905 or 1906. The *Amoy* was built in 1921. The *Fou Po II* was built in 1935. The *Hummel Hummel* was purchased in 1938, as was the *Mon Lei*. The *Cheng Ho* left the slipways the following year, 1939. Brief notice is made of the illegality of foreigners owning Chinese junks in the era before the 1911 Revolution. In the nineteenth-century selling a junk to foreigners illegally was a capital offence. The *Whang Ho* sale was delayed due to difficulties surrounding the issue of ownership and registration. The foreign ownership of Chinese junks constituted an issue that had long bothered officials in China. Customs revenue and ease of access to the many ports on the Chinese coast were determined by such things as the origins and identity of the individual vessel, and emperors had in the past expressed their concerns at so many Chinese junks being illegally sold in Southeast Asia.[1]

The *Keying*, a large junk that sailed the Indian and Atlantic oceans in 1846, also faced the same difficulties. A group of Englishmen purchased the *Keying* "by the adoption of Chinese dress as a disguise, a pretence of yachting locally, and finally some amount of fighting before Hong Kong was fetched."[2] In short, the *Keying* was stolen. "Clandestinely bought" is another phrase used by Europeans to describe the transaction.[3] It is only following the end of the Qing dynasty that sources begin to refer to the legal transfer of ownership of junks to foreign masters.

This early precaution really dates back to traditional imperial regulations on the control of coastal and overseas shipping. At various times in the Chinese past, official decrees have specifically limited both the size and design of coastal junks in an effort to curtail and control overseas activity, often reflective of periods of particular xenophobia. The most striking example of this is a mandate from the early Ming dynasty, a decree defining the reestablishment of strict Confucian morals and imperial control following the overthrow in 1368 A.D. of almost one hundred years of foreign rule by Mongol invaders (Yuan dynasty) from north of the Great Wall. All those who were found guilty of building large ships with more than two masts, or those who were found carrying contraband goods to the seacoast to trade, or those who went themselves to trade in foreign countries without official business, would be put to death—and their entire families banished to the distant interior frontier to serve with the military guards.[4] Such were the suspicions against pirates and all sea people who plundered lawful subjects of the emperor; such was the distance between the imperial bureaucracy and the coastal masses in the south.

The early Ming emperors attempted to limit or control communication between southern China and Southeast Asia, all except for official trade and diplomatic relations, which included Admiral Zheng He's armadas in the fifteenth century. Many scholars have described the noted continental perspective of China's rulers, in contrast to the active maritime trade conducted by the empire's distant (and difficult to control) southern coastal provinces. Many scholars have noted this imperial distrust of the sea. The ocean was "a vast expanse stretching to heaven, and nothing can measure its length. What is more, the boats of wicked scoundrels are like froth floating on the sea, and impossible to apprehend."[5] Unapproved contact with foreigners was forbidden. Illegal trade overseas included, of course, the vessel itself as a trade item. During the nineteenth century, extensive deforestation and the shift in local Chinese junk construction to Chinese communities in Southeast Asia spurred similar concerns regarding the sale of junks to foreigners.

Critical historical events posed many obstacles to the procurement of these junks at the time of their Pacific voyages. Given our hindsight on events of the Pacific war, the several projects involving junks either purchased or built in the late 1930s seem particularly precarious. For Americans overseas during this period, the coasts and rivers of China represented a rough frontier with elements harkening back to the days of the Wild West. Some called the coasts and interior rivers of China the most dangerous natural waterways ever sailed, featuring as they did "piracy, gun battles with warlords and armies of various factions, banditry, kidnapping, opium smuggling, gunrunning, corruption and extortion . . . far more exciting than the storied world of pulp fiction."[6]

Richard Halliburton makes many comments on the state of unrest in China and the constant stream of wartime refugees amid his plans to sail from the China coast. He also offers a rare glimpse into the problem of sailing a junk past the Japanese navy:

I've just learned one reason why the Japanese wage such a merci-
less campaign against the apparently harmless fisher-junks. In the
early days of the war the Chinese civilians were allowed to sail their
junks rather much where they chose. Then one day a Japanese airplane
carrier—an object of special hatred in China—appeared off the coast
and began to discharge its death-laden planes. The crew was so occupied that it scarcely noticed a group of small junks, busily fishing,
which drifted slowly out from shore toward the gray steel monster.
Then, when the junks and battleships were only 200 yards apart, a
Chinese mosquito boat, hitherto concealed, suddenly dashed from the
midst of the junk fleet—full speed at the carrier. Point blank it loosed a
torpedo, and struck the Japanese vessel squarely amidships. The great
carrier was so badly damaged that it had to go into dry-dock for three
months.

At once the Japanese swore vengeance on all junks—honest and otherwise. They shelled every junk they could find, set fire to the wreckage, and disposed of the crews (which in China means whole families)
by pushing them into the sea without boats or lifebelts. Even at anchor
in the harbors of the coastal cities the helpless native craft were systematically bombed—as they still are today. Knowing all this, I plan to
go first to Tokyo and formally ask the Japanese Navy to grant a safe-
conduct for the *Sea Dragon*'s journey through the war zone.[7]

Other researchers have also noted the destructive effect of the war on
the sailing junks. The general feeling of Halliburton's contemporaries ran
along the lines that "the Japs will blow that ruddy junk galley west the moment she sticks her prow into the Formosa Straits," as the British naval officers put it.[8]

Were junks difficult to find because they were vanishing? An estimate
on the number of sailing junks destroyed over several years of systematic
effort by the Japanese would prove difficult. Estimates of the numbers of
junks in China for the period preceding the conflict only produce vague information. Geographer Herold Wiens attempted to do this by averaging the
number of clearings and entries from customs records for the 1930s. Variations in the definitions of junks, vessels larger than seven tons in one region
as opposed to vessels larger than four tons in another, as well as multiple
sailings on short routes by many vessels, greatly complicated the process.
Wiens, in the end, produced an estimate of 57,536 active craft (junks and
sampans) in China for the 1930s alone. He immediately states, as well, that
the true number of junks (not sampans) could lie anywhere between 20,000

and 50,000. Annual junk carrying capacity, from this estimate, fell probably between 520,000 and 1.3 million tons.[9] Thus, any assumptions that by the late nineteenth century steam vessels had eliminated the sailing junk trade in China must be reexamined. In many locations, the shift to steam propulsion was a transition, not an immediate revolution.

The war in the Pacific had other ramifications for the junks than the beginning of their elimination. In 1940, many sailing vessels began to be fitted with engines in order to run the Japanese blockade on the China coast. Later in the war the Japanese themselves, suffering considerable losses to their merchant fleet, installed engines in their own wooden junks in order to maintain their lines of communication.[10] As noted previously, engines necessitated major departures from established junk designs.

The Japanese navy was not the only concern for Halliburton and the crew of the *Sea Dragon*. A large number of pirates had been driven south by the invading forces, and their seafaring predation had grown to an unprecedented level in the absence of any significant local coastal patrols. They were said to have watched the construction of Halliburton's junk "as a panther would regard a suckling pig."[11]

Junk Operations on the China Coast

Documents that describe in detail the nature of junk traffic in China are rare, but Andrew Watson has translated a series of articles by Japanese scholars concerning Chinese junk ownership operations. Watson describes this period, 1900–1940, as "a key transitional phase . . . when it [shipping] was absorbing the influences of various forms of modernization and on the eve of its major organizational transformation under the direction of the Communist Party."[12] True, the articles focus on a wartime situation, where activity was artificially depressed and trade restricted, not optimal conditions. But some of the information directly reveals the nature of the sailing trade occupations, the specific background of the transpacific junks.

In general, trade junks in China were owned by partnerships of related individuals in the north and live-on-board families in the south. As much as 99 percent of the junks in northern China were in partnerships with joint capital, usually made up of between ten and thirty people who were related or were old friends.[13] The boats were almost always operated under the direction of shipping brokers, or *chuanhang*, those individuals who bought and sold local products, acted as agents for distribution, provided warehouses and lodging services, hired junks, etc. Brokers belonged to a certain class of licensed merchants, *yahang*, who received special permits to act as middlemen between shippers of goods and junk operators.[14] Brokers also acted as intermediaries in the sale of junks, and may have been the contact points for Europeans seeking to procure vessels for the Pacific voyage.

In almost all aspects of business, junk ownership and operation was based on strong family or local relationships. Partners in ownership were often related, and employees of brokerage companies were usually close relations or acquaintances of the general manager, secured through recommendation. This extended to the crew, or *chuanfu*, on board the junk itself. Crew members were hired via family or locality connections.[15]

East Asian history specialists recognize the late nineteenth century as a period of open warfare between lineage groups on China's southern coast, involving all levels of economic competition, not only locally but overseas as well. Coastal Chinese, during this period, not only had ties to their family and village, but all could be strongly loyal to larger corporate identities associated with historic lineage or locality or both.[16] This suggests that it would have been very unlikely to find sailors from different regions, perhaps even different villages, coexisting on the same ship. Traveling missionary Karl Gutzlaff, among others, noticed these regional tensions on his own China voyages, witnessing serious outbreaks of violence between sailors from different areas. These battles involved small arms, and sometimes multiple junks, aligned as small, informal flotillas against enemy units.[17] The fighting could be very fierce.

As junk construction proved regionally specific, so did the crews themselves seem regionally derived. The close character of crews is further emphasized by the kinship connections that served to unite members on the ship. Selection often depended on association with the captain's clan, or on residence in the village or region where the ship was registered.[18] This degree of paternalism or affinity between captain and crew stands in sharp contrast to European vessels, where the greater social distance between the higher and lower ranks was an intentional feature, often central to maintaining strict discipline. As historian Jennifer Cushman states: "There is no evidence that the social hierarchy among the crew of a Chinese junk was governed by a codified set of regulations."[19] She describes the crew of one of Gutzlaff's vessels: the captain was a Chaozhou man, as were the sailors, his brother-in-law was the ship's clerk, and his uncle succeeded him when he left the vessel at Namoa.[20] This observation on social relations has important implications for the understanding of the structure of command on Chinese ships. Relationships on board were not formed along new lines of strict discipline, but based on kinship ranking of the home area. This implies that, unlike European ships, the captain of the junk trade vessel did not have complete authority over all the crew. Gutzlaff felt that the sailors actually exercised "full control over the vessel, and oppose every measure which they think may prove injurious to their own interest"—so much so that the captains and pilots frequently had to beg them for assistance, requesting they show better temper.[21]

Though relations might not have been strictly delineated, there were specific roles to fill in order to make the vessel work. Care must be taken, however, when comparing the roles of those officers and crew on Chinese vessels and those on European ships, for there is not always a close correspondence between the two. For instance, the captain of the Chinese vessel not only lacked absolute authority, but had very little to do with navigation during the voyage, this being the chief role of the pilot. Instead, the captain acted more as ship's merchant, or *boshang*. Gutzlaff presents a description of traditional positions on Chinese ships:

> Chinese vessels have generally a captain, who might more properly be styled a supercargo. Whether the owner or not, he has charge of the whole of the cargo, buys and sells as circumstances require; but has no command whatever over the sailing of the ship. This is the business of the Ho-chang or pilot. During the whole voyage, to observe the shores and promontories are the principal objects which occupy his attention, day and night. He sits steadily on the side of the ship, and sleeps when standing, just as it suits his convenience. Though he has, nominally, the command over the sailors, yet they obey him only when they find it agreeable to their own wishes; and they scold and brave him, just as if he belonged to their own company. Next to the pilot (or mate) is the To-kung (helmsman), who manages the sailing of the ship; there are a few men under his immediate command. There are, besides, two clerks; one to keep the accounts, and the other to superintend the cargo that is put on board. Also, a comprador, to purchase provisions; and a Heang-kung (or priest), who attends the idols, and burns, every morning, a certain quantity of incense, and of gold and silver paper. The sailors are divided into two classes; a few, called Towmuh (or head-men), have charge of the anchor, sails, &c.; and the rest, called Ho-ke (or comrades), perform the menial work, such as pulling ropes and heaving the anchor. A cook and some barbers make up the remainder of the crew.[22]

If the origins of sailors for Chinese junks could be unambiguously known, and design features also rooted in regional variation, the functional roles of commercial junks were much less defined. In all the translations of Japa-

Table 6. Average Junk Transportation Costs, 1900–1940

Mode	Japanese cents/km
Junk	1.2
Railway	2.0
Donkey or Horse	2.4
Wheelbarrow	19.0
Motor Vehicle	30.0
Porters	34.0

nese essays included in Watson's *Transport in Transition,* vessels under the control of the shipping brokers could fulfill a number of different economic functions, as their roles were not specialized.[23] Fishing junks, by and large excluded from the Japanese studies, formed a distinct functional class, and larger junks were obviously more suited for certain longer routes than smaller vessels. Teshima Masaki and Arai Yoshio find that the larger the junk, the closer the connection to "more modern structures such as transport companies, the less its connection with agriculture, and the less seasonal its form of operation."[24] Thus, it seems that by the twentieth century strict observances of monsoon patterns and established cyclical sailing routes had begun to break down in China, at least for the larger 200- to 500-ton vessels. Beyond these general observations, though, junks seem to have been flexible utilitarian tools, capable of carrying different types of cargo on multiple routes.

Finally, junks had long possessed a natural efficiency over land transportation, which has sometimes been said to apply to all water vessels, particularly for shipping bulk goods. Such efficiencies should be taken into account when describing junk operations and changes in maritime transportation. Watson concludes that junk transportation was not just cheaper than other forms, but much cheaper. Table 6 highlights comparative costs per kilometer.

The very nature of junk ownership and operation in China, then, lent this mode of transportation certain advantages in the face of accelerating change on the coast. Hayashi Tokumura describes the close, personal nature of junk traffic and extended operations even in the face of competition. One of the reasons junks continued to sail side by side with steam navigation was the solid network of personal relationships throughout the trade, particularly the "confidence inspired by same-locality origins or long-standing business contacts."[25] This seems to be an application of the same kind of phenomenon that Anthony Reid describes for Chinese junks in "The Unthreatening Alternative." The operation of sailing junks in China remained firmly entrenched in established economic and social circles, and often benefited the immediate family. It was a familiar business and much less threatening than foreign businesses. Yet this did not stop Chinese merchants and others from realizing the advantages of steam vessels.

Competition with Steam in China and the Pacific

After the mid-nineteenth century, steam navigation began to make a noticeable impact on communication across the Pacific. Steamship lines started to capitalize on the transportation of goods and passengers, capturing routes previously dominated by sail. This first appeared in coastal and river settings chiefly because of the great distances involved in oceanic travel. Until steamships achieved relative efficiency in coal consumption, represented by the technological breakthrough of triple-expansion engines and high-pressure steel Scotch boilers, they could not always compete with sail effectively on long sea routes. The English led the world in this maritime transition from sail to steam, and they had long had a commercial presence in East Asia. Steamships operated early along the coasts and up the major rivers among the sailing junks, and only later captured the bulk of transpacific trade. American and British entrepreneurs were quick to exploit the advantages of river steam navigation over the slower and established river junks, which often relied on seasonal winds and the employment of shore-side trackers to move upstream.[26]

Important coastal routes and sailing commerce along the deeper branches of major rivers were the first to feel the effects of coming modernization. Sailing junks were sometimes limited to local fisheries, or pushed out of important routes and into smaller areas of secondary economic importance. By 1873, steamships entered the trade of carrying rice from the south to Tianjin, for transhipment to the imperial capital. Eventually, steamers would monopolize this traffic.[27] Steamships would also make inroads in the lumber trade, supplanting pole junks in carrying timbers up and down the China coast. The junks, however, continued to hold their own in some areas.

Just as the business of commercial sail continued to exist for decades after the introduction of coastal and transoceanic steam, Chinese river and coastal junks persisted during this period. Edward Cunningham, managing partner of the American firm Russell and Company, noticed their most obvious advantages in 1868. Steam navigation did not rely on the wind, nor current or tide, but it was expensive. Even the lowest rates of freight on steamers had difficulty competing with the Chinese on their own small junks, "the Chinese being able to perform water carriage at a cost, lower than would be believed by the most economical of Western people."[28] According to Cunningham, the business of river steamers in China during the mid-nineteenth century had been overrated.

The 1920s and 1930s saw not just the increase in steam technology in China, but the intrusion of internal combustion gasoline and diesel engines and motorized vessels. These waited for neither the appropriate wind nor the advantageous tide, and made much better time upriver. Scheduled runs became more reliable. The older pattern of trade consisted of ships that waited on their cargo and sailed at the master's or shipping broker's convenience, and which could only give approximate dates for arrival. This slowly changed to one where vessels could be much more obedient to the schedule, departing and arriving at fixed times, more to the merchants' and passengers' approval. In the context of seasonal sailings and the periods of alternating monsoon winds, the technological advancement of the marine power plant found immediate opportunities for profit. Yet these early inroads were only supported by greater expense and reliance on higher freight rates in comparison to the junk trade, and naturally met with resistance by the numerically superior traffic on less crucial routes.

The geographic effect of steam technology on the junk traffic in China was not equal in all locations, but progressed in an inconsistent manner. The commerce of some ports benefited, while others declined. Hong Kong, with its background of foreign investment dating back to 1842, quickly saw many steamship companies and modern dockyards prosper, and the sailing trade began to fall off in the face of this change. Even such events as the Russian-Japanese War of 1904 failed to diminish trade at Hong Kong, as British steamers arrived to replace the commerce temporarily lost by the Japanese lines.[29] Arnold Wright's *Twentieth Century Impressions of Hong Kong, Shanghai, and Other Treaty Ports of China,* compiled in 1908, provides examples of this steam transition, a partial list of emerging businesses.

British, Chinese, American, French, Japanese, German, Bombay, and other commercial transportation companies required not only large steamships, but the associated dry docks and repair facilities, engineering shops, cargo boats, coaling stations, railway heads, fresh water systems, depots, wharfs, breakwaters, boiler shops, deepened channels, and other infrastructure. The first improvements to the physical shape of Hong Kong harbor itself, the Praya reclamation schemes, began in 1851; the first lighthouses there were established in 1875.[30] The days of servicing all foreign vessels at the mud docks at Whampoa, run by the Chinese without European supervision, had come to an end. Newer ships necessitated major upgrades in facilities.

A certain amount of friction accompanied such shifts in maritime operations at treaty ports. Local Chinese sailors finding employment as cargo boat

Table 7. Steam Companies and Dockyards in Hong Kong

Company name	Date in operation in Hong Kong
Peninsular and Oriental Company	1837
Apcar Line	?
Hong Kong, Canton, and Macao Steamboat Company	1865
Hong Kong and Whampoa Dock Company	1866
China Express Company	?
Eastern and Australian Steamship Company	?
American Asiatic Steamship Company	?
North German Lloyd Steamship Company	1866
Taikoo Dockyard and Engineering Company	1867
Pacific Mail Steamship Line	1867
China Navigation Company	1867
Canadian Pacific Railway Company Line	1881
China and Manila Steamship Company	?
Indo-China Steam Navigation Company	?
China and Manila Steamship Company	?
Douglas Lapraik Steamship Company	1883
Osaka Shosen Kabushika Kaisha	1884
Nippon Yusen Kaisha Line	1885
Hong Kong and Kowloon Wharf and Godown Company	1885
Norddeutscher Lloyd Line	1885
Toyo Kisen Kaisha Line	1892
Hamburg-Amerika Line	1901
Messageries Cantonaises	1907
Java-China-Japan Line	?
Kwong River Steamers	?

operators often protested against increasing regulations and taxes. Labor strikes in 1862 and 1884 and even blockades of the harbor marked the tension during the transition from the sailing trade to steamship operations. Hong Kong exemplified the greatest amount of such change.

But it was not the advantages offered by Kowloon for the establishment of a depot of this class which . . . gave promise of success to the Wharf Company, but rather the intolerable exactions of the Chinese coolie hongs and the boat people, and the delays occasioned to European traders by their antiquated methods of handling cargo. Often seven or eight days were wasted through these methods, and the advent of a European-managed concern was welcomed by the community as a means of escape from such vexations. Faced with competition, the Chinese changed their tactics, and an endless struggle ensued between the rival interests. The coolies, tallymen, and boat people would not work so well for the Company as they worked for their own countrymen; and when, as their business extended, the Company needed additional lighters, the Chinese, without reason or justification, gradually raised their charges from $4 a load to $15, and the Company were obliged to build their own fleet of lighters.[31]

The ports of Xiamen and Fuzhou, compared to Hong Kong, saw a slower transition to the steamship lines. The well-situated deep water port of Xiamen, known locally as Amoy, suffered from economic competition with Taiwan and the decline of the tea trade. And "as tea went, so did sugar . . . the local sugar was killed by the superior article prepared and grown under modern scientific methods in Java . . . the Amoy of today is thus a shadow of its former self."[32] Likewise, the tea trade declined in Fuzhou. The imposition of maritime technology spurred infrastructure in some places and at the same time played a role in the decline of others. Amid this change, sailing junks eventually found fewer niches in which to compete, yet they continued to be a factor of major significance through World War II.

Even with the increasing modernization of maritime transportation, certain roles for junks continued to remain strong. In fact, not only did oldfashioned junks hold their own, but during certain periods in the early twentieth century junk transportation actually increased within the four provinces of Anhwei, Kiangsu, Chekiang, and Kiangsi. "Economies must, to a greater or lesser extent, go through a phase in which various levels of technology and various methods of operation are found side by side, sometimes in harmony and sometimes in conflict."[33] Competition between junks and modern ships took place in a great variety of settings on an uneven playing field, and junks were not always the immediate losers, for the variety of reasons given above.

Chinese sailors had their own personal experience with steam vessels as well. They not only sailed junks on the Pacific, Chinese crews were also boarding steamships and working their way across the ocean. Eventually, the majority of the crews on the Pacific Mail Steamship Line and the Canadian Oceanic Line were Chinese sailors contracted in Canton and Shanghai at half the price of their American or Canadian counterparts. What the Chinese crewmen, the deckhands, engine crews, firemen (stokers), cooks, and stewards, thought about the random encounters at sea between Chinese junks and steamships remains unknown. The large number of Chinese crewmen on Pacific steamships represented a threat to western organized labor, and employment opportunity suffered from the anti-Chinese agitation on the coast. Eventually labor unions were successful in curtailing shipowners from contracting Chinese crews, adding significant restrictions through such things as the La Folette Seaman's Act of 1915.[34]

As a sign of these chance encounters, most of the junks headed east were reported days, if not weeks, in advance of their arrival. News came from the number of busy steamships making their way between ports. Passengers and officers of the steam liners, often incredulous, had the time to stop and offer food and assistance to the small sailing vessels. Not all the encounters between the future and the past were so amiable. Though there are very few studies that include statistical analysis of collisions at sea, many slow-moving sailing vessels, especially fishing vessels immobilized by deployed nets, were run down by steamers not only in the Pacific but worldwide. Merely the wake created by large steamships in port could and did capsize many low-built river junks.

Sailors Previously on the Pacific?

These steamships with their Chinese crews, and this selection of ten voyaging junks, had been preceded into certain parts of the Pacific Ocean by yet other Chinese mariners. Guam and the Mariana Islands possess what may be the earliest traces of Chinese sailing navigation into the Pacific. When Father Sanvitores's Spanish mission landed at Guam in 1668, they encountered the stories of two survivors of the wreck of the *Senora de la Concepcion,* a galleon that had run onto the reefs of Saipan in 1638. One was the Spanish survivor on Guam called Pedro; the other was a Chinese blacksmith who had taken up residency on Saipan, the first Chinese known to have lived in the Northern Marianas, the earliest recorded Chinese beachcomber in the Pacific. The blacksmith, however, was not the only Chinese in the area. One of the Jesuit priests wrote about a Chinese trader known as Choco, who had been voyaging between Manila and Ternate in his junk and was blown off course in about 1648 to Saipan.[35] Years later, after establishing a family, Choco relocated to Guam, where he eventually became the nemesis of Father Sanvitores. Attempts to successfully convert Choco, a.k.a. Ignacio, ultimately failed. Perhaps memories of discrimination and massacres by the Spanish against the Chinese in the Philippines had been transplanted to Guam.[36]

The story of this contact remains firmly implanted in the local lore of Guam, and there is some speculation as to what type of junk, known in the records as a sampan, actually made the landing. Suggestions center around something like the Hangzhou Bay trader, a northern-style junk from the nineteenth century that apparently was similar in decoration and design to the vessel that brought Choco to the Marianas.[37] A model was donated for display to the University of Guam in 1988. The implications of such contact are intriguing. If Chinese ships in local waters were cast into the Mariana Islands by typhoons in the seventeenth century, why not in the sixteenth? The fifteenth? Such speculation, though, is always most useful in formulating more questions rather than providing answers.

Other clues suggest the possibility of even earlier Asian maritime activity in the Pacific. Chinese sailors, perhaps from shipwrecked vessels blown off course, are said to have possibly improved irrigation methods of taro cultivation in Tonga and Samoa.[38] An endemic method in bark cloth manufacture on the island of Futuna has been attributed by some to Chinese mariners. One article, based on circumstantial evidence, argues that traces of an endemic Chinese system of divination using the Daoist trigrams and a complex mathematical selection process can be found in Micronesia, specifically on the Caroline Islands of Chuuk, Yap, Ulithi, and Puluwat.[39] Another, by E. S. Craighill Handy, draws cultural similarities between the *Tangaloa* cult of Samoa and Tonga and those of the Chinese seafarers. Handy outlines linguistic similarities between the name *Tangalo* and the southern Chinese coastal population *Tan-kah-lo* (*tanjia* or *danjia*, the *shuishangren*). He concludes that "the discovery of this correspondence in names and in cultural traits led to the conclusion that a group of seafaring Chinese, whose religion combined the strictly Chinese worship and philosophy with Buddhism, came into Polynesia."[40] Can one group instigate permanent cultural traits? Investigations from the 1920s explaining Pacific cultures in terms of diffusion from Old World civilizations are seen in a more critical light these days, for the assumption of cultural features being adopted from outside influences have frequently harbored a not-so-subtle colonial or imperial agenda. The possibilities of Chinese contact in the Pacific, nonetheless, remain interesting.

By the time the vessels in this study had begun crossing to North America, at least one Chinese shipwright was already plying his trade elsewhere in the Pacific. The Chinese merchant Lee Tam Tuck, known locally as Uncle Ah Tam, had previously established himself as an independent shipwright and merchant on Matupit Island of New Britain. He worked alongside the German colonial government, serving as a conduit for migrant southern Chinese in search of labor overseas. Many Chinese worked at Ah Tam's shipyard before moving on and finding work with the German companies or branching out and becoming independent traders.[41] By 1910, Ah Tam's empire included a wholesale and retail store, a hotel, several plantations, a gambling den, a brothel, an opium house, and two shipyards.[42]

Chinese shipwrights also built and operated junks on the beaches near Darwin, Australia. These were used in the lumber trade in the late nineteenth and early twentieth centuries.[43] The annual government reports of the Northern Territory include some brief information on their registration and tonnages, but it is still unclear whether these junks, or those from Ah Tam's shipyards, reflected specific regional designs from China. In all likelihood they did, as such craft built overseas often resembled the designs familiar to the home villages of the immigrants, as did the fishing junks built in California in the nineteenth century.

Chinese Ships and Sailors in the New World

Are nineteenth-century Pacific crossings the first to have brought Chinese vessels to America? Some in the past have suggested otherwise. There has been an infrequently recurring theme spanning nineteenth- and twentieth-century research that postulates very early transpacific contact from China. Some have, in fact, attempted experimental voyages on craft of reportedly ancient design in order to demonstrate their theories. The Chinese legend of Fusang is a common touchstone in these arguments. According to dynastic records, in 499 A.D. a Buddhist priest journeyed to a location far to the east of China, returning to tell the emperor tales of a strange and wonderful land. A second expedition to what was called Fusang, complete with colonists, never returned. Scholars conjecture today that, if indeed the voyages did occur, landfall possibilities include Alaska, Southern California, Mexico, somewhere on the Chinese coastline, and Korea. The more established opinion suggests the preferred location as Japan.

There is precedent for the study of early Chinese transpacific voyages, though it often relies on very shaky evidence. The topic was once a feature of diffusion-style studies. Stan Steiner, in *Fusang, the Chinese Who Built America,* presents one of the most accessible overviews of the nineteenth-century obsession with transpacific diffusion. Ben J. Wallace and William M. Hurley also summarize a large portion of this direction in "Transpacific Contacts: A Selected Annotated Bibliography." Such early contact has been the focus of several public collections, such as the *Across the Pacific* exhibition at New York's American Museum of Natural History in 1949, which, as anthropologist Robert Heine-Geldern expressed it, made the assumption of very early cultural contact between East Asia and America a much more acceptable subject for research.[44] Betty J. Meggers, in "TransPacific Origin of Mesoamerican Civilization," highlights a number of possible similarities between the 1200 B.C.–period Shang dynasty culture in Asia and the Olmec tradition in Central America. The use of jade, ceremonial batons, square earth platforms oriented north-south, and a number of other similarities raise questions that Meggers feels have gone unanswered not for—in her view—a lack of evidence, but for modern scholars' limited ability to form hypotheses outside the boundaries of conventional investigation. She states that, in general, terrestrial scholars habitually regard the sea as a barrier, rather than a line of communication. While there may be nothing wrong in emphasizing the ocean as highway, most Mesoamerican archaeologists do not see firm evidence of any Chinese-Pacific connection.

Joseph Needham himself, along with Lu Gwei-Djen, also investigated the difficult question of very early transpacific communication. Comparisons involving the use of jade, city architecture, artistic motifs, games such as *pachisi*, the *quipo* mnemonic tool, ziggurat-pyramid-mound-temple complexes, etc., are set forth as a collection of circumstantial evidence suggesting not colonization from Asia, but relatively minor contact and the possible diffusion of some technological and cultural traits. Both Needham and Lu express their distaste for theories that would seem to denigrate indigenous achievements, a central point for those doing diffusion studies in a postcolonial setting. They also find that the available nautical technology at the time, from the third century B.C. to the fifth century A.D., would have been quite sufficient to accomplish open ocean voyages. In this case, lugsail rigs and bamboo rafts were the tools, the design descendants of which still ply the waters both in Southeast Asia and Peru.[45]

Cultural similarities in separate localities do not prove diffusion. Trait list comparisons, while they may appear to build a case for contact, remain categorically separate from firm evidence. Sailing a replica vessel (or one assumed to be a replica) across the Pacific also does not necessarily prove any ancient crossing. In fact, those who have attempted such voyages sometimes seem to have demonstrated the opposite. There have been two attempts and two failures in experimental archaeology along these lines. Kuno Knöbl and an enterprising group of German, Danish, English, and Austrian voyagers constructed in 1972 what was, according to them, a replica of an ancient Chinese Pacific Ocean voyaging junk. The *Tai Ki*, as it was known, was roughly based on a clay model of a junk discovered in a Han dynasty tomb near Canton in 1952. Judging from its appearance, the Han dynasty second century A.D. model, with no mast or mast step, was probably a river vessel, not meant for operation on the high seas. This lack of understanding of Chinese junk designs may have been a factor in the project's failure. About halfway across the Pacific at latitude 40 degrees north, the vessel, rudder already broken and threatening to capsize, began to disintegrate and take on water. The crew was rescued by a passing freighter. Nothing really was proven one way or another.

Maritime ethnographer Tim Severin based his 1992 experimental attempt on a sailing raft rather than a plank-built junk. The *Hsu-Fu* was constructed out of giant bamboo in Vietnam, where fishermen still make the type of sailing rafts once used in ancient times around Taiwan and Southeast Asia. Following the Kuroshio Current from Hong Kong to Taiwan and then Tokyo, the raft turned to the east around latitude 40 degrees north. This voyage also ended mid-ocean, approximately one thousand miles west of Mendocino County, California, when the organic lashings holding the many poles together came apart faster than the intrepid crew could repair them.[46] Fortunately the experiment included radio and satellite navigation, and the container ship *California Galaxy* was able to rescue the team.

Divers have also sought to support this line of speculation. The case in point involves the mysterious "anchor stones" off of the Palos Verde peninsula in Los Angeles County, California, first encountered in 1973 during dredging operations. Wayne Baldwin and Bob Meistrell over the next few years came upon numerous carved stones, some with holes drilled in them "for anchor cables," scattered on the seabed in thirty to sixty feet of water.[47] It did not take long for the subject of Fusang and ancient Chinese voyages across the Pacific to make a repeat appearance, for characteristics of these stones did resemble the simple and expedient anchors used by numerous cultures, including East and South Asia seafarers. Initially this connection was given credence by reports in 1980 in *China Reconstructs,* which found that the anchor stones highlighted the *friendly intercourse* between ancient China and other regions (this source is not without its political agenda). Some American archaeologists initially held that these stones could confirm ancient contact from China.[48] Upon examination of the stones by the University of California at Santa Barbara's geology department, though, it was found that they most closely resembled Monterey shale, a local variety of rock. Furthermore, the site at Palos Verde, known in the more recent past as Portuguese Bend, featured at one time a shore whaling station, and such anchors may have been used to moor the whale boats or the whales themselves. Scholars remain rightfully skeptical and the subject has vanished from the academic scene. Kenneth L. Feder covers the phenomenon in his *Frauds, Myths, and Mysteries,* though his quick explanation that the stones were used by Chinese fishermen in the nineteenth century ignores the fact that many of these fishermen purchased iron anchors for their local California-built junks. Today, the rocks that had once almost achieved a certain amount of fame rest unmarked in a box in the parking lot of a local dive shop. The stones do bear a resemblance to some anchors, notably those used in the ancient past in South Asia and the Red Sea, but they have no resemblance to the many Chinese stone anchor stocks recovered from a number of archaeological sites.

Other records confuse the matter further. For over two and a half centuries, beginning in the 1560s, the Manila galleon trade plied the waters between the Philippines and Acapulco, ferrying the cash wealth of the Americas to the east, and luxury goods back across the Isthmus to the Spanish Main. Though migration is often overlooked in these Pacific histories, this trade brought Asian voyagers to the New World long before the English Puritans landed at Plymouth Rock in 1620. The Chinese were among the founding fathers of the city of Los Angeles. In fact, "so many Chinese had crossed the ocean by 1635 that the Spanish barbers of Mexico City had petitioned the Municipal Council to protest the competition of Chinese barbers in the capital."[49] And, though it is recorded that the Spanish built and operated galleons in the early Manila–Acapulco trade, there is little documentation that accurately describes the vessels used. Many of these ships were, after all, built in the dockyards of Cavite, and in Siam and Japan as well, by Asian craftsmen and referred to as *Naos de China,* or China Ships. The galleons were distinguishable by their very large capacities, loftiness, extremely high-ended half-moon sheer, and unusual width.[50] Author Stan Steiner classifies the galleons along the lines of Chinese junks.

> Ships from Europe were pitifully small on the vast expanses of the Pacific. They had neither the cargo space nor the weight for a journey across an ocean that was twice the width of the Atlantic, a voyage that could last as long as six months. Nor were they designed to survive the peculiar furies of monsoons and typhoons upon those treacherous and unfamiliar seas. And so the Spanish had decided to have native artisans build ships native to those seas. The shipbuilders came from China, mostly from Canton. In using their centuries-old experience in ship construction and their deep-sea knowledge, the Chinese redesigned the Spanish galleons and adapted them to the styles of the majestic seagoing junks of the Ming dynasty.
>
> In the large shipyards of Cavite on Manila Bay in the Philippines, these great galleons were entirely built by Malayan and Chinese shipbuilders. . . . Some of the galleons weighed in excess of two thousand tons, an unheard of tonnage at that time, ten times the weight of Columbus' flagship. The designing of the ships was done almost wholly by Chinese ships' engineers and architects. The hulls were built by Chi-

nese carpenters. And the metalwork and casting of cannon were done by Chinese smiths. Even the elaborate designs on Spanish baroque themes were done by Chinese artists.

No wonder the graceful crescent-shaped hulls and the huge cargo holds of the Manila galleons resembled the seagoing junks of the Ming dynasty as much as they did the many-oared galleasses of the Mediterranean for which they were named. They were more Chinese than European.[51]

Whether Manila galleons were distinguishable hybrids remains speculation. There is not much firm evidence with which to confirm Steiner's descriptions, and it is hard to imagine that overseas galleons resembled Chinese junks. It is most likely that Pacific galleons were essentially European-designed vessels with minor Asian influences, and Steiner's comparisons are of a general nature only. After all, the basic foundations of galleon and junk construction differ in major ways.

Images from later centuries are popularly, and erroneously, used to depict the undocumented vessels in the very early Manila–Acapulco trade. Archaeological investigations of wreck sites in the Pacific yield more information on the cargo, and certainly gain more notoriety by intentionally featuring the bullion and ceramic treasures, than they do the often more perishable wooden ship structure itself. The question of Asian connections to the Manila galleons tests the limits of nationalist-type histories, in this case Spanish, set within the transnational Pacific Ocean. Again the question is raised of what exactly is a European ship and what is a Chinese ship. The topic of Manila galleons also tests the limits of archaeological work in the Pacific.[52]

Closer in time to the confirmed twentieth-century voyages, there are interesting but infrequent indications that Chinese junks made landfall on the California coast as early as 1849. Artist Albert Lyman's journal records witnessing the arrival of a large Chinese junk in San Francisco on August 27, 1849. "A Chinese junk came to port yesterday and anchored a little ahead of us. Her sails are made of matting, and altogether she is a singular and queer-looking craft. Her China men on board seem to be quite active sailors."[53] Unfortunately, no further references to this rare incident have been discovered. The Spanish in the New World, though, did find it necessary to intentionally adopt a policy discouraging anyone else, including the Chinese, from conducting transpacific trade and threatening the Spanish monopoly. The leading citizens of Manila drew up such a memorial in 1586.[54]

Researcher and author Sandy Lydon is currently working on the case of the mid-nineteenth-century arrival of junks from the Pearl River Delta area.[55] Descendants of these Chinese migrants, who today live in Mendocino County, California, recall the oral tradition of several families setting out on five junks. Lydon has gathered similar oral accounts regarding Chinese Pacific vessels from multiple sources. The junk voyage originated in Hong Kong, from there moving to Manila, where (as one of the immigrant's descendants reported) they learned how to sail. The planned landfall was San Francisco, but the small flotilla was swept south along the West Coast. Two of the five junks had been lost, along with their crews, during the open ocean crossing. The remaining three refit in Mexico and then worked arduously to the north, beating into the weather and current. Two more junks wrecked somewhere along the rough Big Sur coastline, and the final boat was lost on the beach at Carmel River near Monterey. The sailors were rescued by the local Native Americans, nursed back to health, and made their way to Point Lobos, where they started a small fishing colony.[56]

Oral histories in the records of the Chinese Historical Society of America allude to similar events in the past. There is a story recorded by Mr. H. K. Wong in 1966, in which a junk or sampan arrived at Caspar Beach, four miles north of Mendocino, California, in 1852. The small boat was reportedly one of eight vessels that sailed together for America that year. Six were lost at sea, and one beached at Monterey. According to the tale, the wood from the vessel was used in the construction of the Chinese temple on Albion Street. This story was confirmed by a local post office employee, who informed the historical society that a sailor on the Caspar Beach junk was indeed his grandfather.[57]

And then, of course, there is the previously mentioned legend of the Chinese war junk fleet landing at Monterey in 1870 (see Halliburton and his *Sea Dragon*). Is this description merely a different version of the previous story of five sampans crossing the Pacific? Perhaps, but it also does not serve to make matters more clear that numerous other wrecks on the rugged Pacific northwest coastline are all referred to as China ships, including European vessels bound for East Asia or returning laden with silks and porcelains.

Surreptitious landings in remote locations, strandings, and wrecks often escaped the notice of harbor record keepers along the West Coast. None of the junk arrivals mentioned above appear in customs house documents for any official ports of entry. But there are further intriguing clues to this story. Archaeologists continue to find Chinese coins, predominantly from the Kangxi and Qianlong reign periods of the Qing dynasty, at Native American habitation sites in the Pacific Northwest.[58] Judging from the context of the artifacts from two locations and their mint dates, these coins were in use well before 1830. Some, perhaps all of these coins may be attributable to the active European fur trade between China and the northwest coast. European vessels, after all, had engaged Chinese shipwrights and sailors as early as 1788 for labor in places like Nootka Sound, Vancouver Island.[59] But some of these coins allegedly came from a mysterious shipwreck off the Oregon coastline, usually assumed to be Spanish.[60]

The Example of the Japanese Drift Junks

These are the outlines of possible early contacts with the West Coast, often featuring a generous portion of speculation. But do we know that such voyages were even feasible? The logistical possibility of such voyages, the chance that small wooden sailing vessels could cross the Pacific in a relatively short amount of time, is supported not just by the junks in this study. Whether survivors were on board or not, whether under steerage or adrift, other vessels arrived in one piece. For a number of reasons, such as control of trade and tribute and restriction of Christian influence, Japan during the majority of the Tokugawa Shogunate was a closed country. Neither foreigners nor Japanese were allowed to go in or out during the *Sakoku* (literally "country in chains") period from 1641 to 1853 A.D. The only exceptions were the minor presence of Dutch and Chinese traders at the artificially constructed Deshima Island at Nagasaki and official Japanese trade missions to China, Korea, and the Ryukyu Islands (Okinawa). An imperial edict in 1636 prohibited any Japanese vessel going abroad, and seagoing Japanese junks of sufficient size and open ocean design were destroyed.[61] The regulation specified details of ship construction suitable only to coastal transport, wide and open transoms and large, unwieldy rudders. This directly increased the number of Japanese ships disabled at sea, many of them caught by the Kuroshio Current and pulled away from their home islands into the Pacific.

In 1875 Charles Walcott Brooks, a member of the California Academy of Sciences and former consul of Japan as well as attaché of the Japanese embassy, presented an historical report on these drift junks originally entitled *Japanese Wrecks Stranded and Picked Up Adrift in the North Pacific Ocean, Ethnologically Considered as Furnishing Evidence of a Constant Infusion of Japanese Blood among the Coast Tribes of Northwestern Indians.* This was actually a follow-up report on Horace Davis's *Record of Japanese Vessels driven upon the Northwest Coast of America and its Outlying Islands,* which had come out three years earlier. Despite Brooks's nineteenth-century diffusionist overtones, he provides us with an accurate picture of more than sixty documented cases of Asian vessels lost throughout the Pacific between the years 1613 and 1875. In many cases survivors were discovered on remote coasts or on board the drifting wrecks themselves, the most famous of these being Manjiro, or John Mung. Manjiro was rescued by a whaler in 1841, received an education in America, and later served as an interpreter for Admiral Matthew Calbraith Perry in 1853 when Japan was forcibly opened by the American navy. In Brooks's findings, at least one dozen Japanese sailing junks were cast by accident onto the North American and Central American coastlines.[62] These junks were specifically designed to be unsuited for the open ocean, nonetheless many made the crossing. Interestingly, every junk reported on the coast of North America or found in the Hawaiian archipelago was identified as Japanese, not a single Chinese vessel has ever been reported as adrift. Whether this is due to misidentification or differences in vessel design or other factors remains to be discovered.

A few of the castaways in the Pacific like Manjiro played an important role in the emerging relations between America and Japan, for they brought knowledge of the West to their homeland. Most of their stories, though, are lost to us in time. There is no firm estimate of how many junks, nor how many hundreds of Japanese sailors, were castaway over the 225-year edict period, but certainly Brooks's estimate is only a very small subset of the total number. Detailed records of the unlucky seafarers following their difficult return to Japan were not kept, for they were commoners, not of noble birth. We are left with just the stories, a few artifacts, and the fact that many Asian junks of poor design crossed the Pacific and landed along the West Coast from Alaska and the Aleutian Islands to Hawai'i, Washington, Oregon, California, and Mexico. And the construction of these Japanese junks, as acknowledged by a number of maritime scholars, was heavily influenced by Chinese designs.[63] The *Yamato-gata* Japanese junk, which persisted relatively unchanged during the Tokugawa Shogunate period, featured the multi-sectional angled keel with horizontal scarfs, multiple bulkheads, and open sterns with adjustable rudders.[64]

The Welcome to the West

What sort of reception awaited the Asian Pacific traveler on the West Coast? Earlier Japanese drifters had been captured by Spanish authorities, and even taken into slavery by Native American tribes in the Pacific Northwest. The Chinese faced a different type of threat. The late nineteenth and early twentieth centuries on the West Coast of North America were a period of increasing migration to America, driven by significant social and political upheaval in Asia and the lure of gold in the California foothills. Ironically, in the years following the completion of the Statue of Liberty in New York harbor, Chinese migrants faced America's first race-based exclusion laws, banning them from entry to the western hemisphere.[65] This period of anti-Chinese agitation coincides for the most part with the arrival of the Chinese sailing junks. Perhaps as a function of this timing, in each case the attentions attendant upon these foreign vessels goes to the American owners of the Chinese vessels and not the crews, some of which did include Chinese sailors. The junk *Amoy* supposedly masked the fact that the crew members on board were Chinese; likewise the junk *Ning Po* on arrival in California.

The manner in which anti-Chinese hysteria shaped the arrival for the Chinese sailors and the Chinese junks obviously involves a number of perspectives. Unfortunately, the reactions of Chinese crew members, having just crossed the largest ocean in the world, remain unrecorded. They do not just vanish from the record; they never made the record in the first place. And understandably so, for violent anti-Chinese riots broke out across the American West during this period. For the early junks of this sample, it must be the non-Chinese sailors who act as spokesmen. Yet, while the majority of Asians were unwelcome on the coast, Chinese culture in the form of the junks themselves did make an appearance as artifacts within the grander exhibition of cultural and technological progress. American attitudes toward China and the Chinese, often expressed as part of the reactions to the junks, are the subjects of the following chapter.

The Age of the Expositions: Junks on Display

This period from the mid-nineteenth to mid-twentieth century coincides with what has been called the classic age of the international expositions. The progenitor of these massive public displays took place in London in 1851. The affair was known as the "Great Exhibition of the Works of Industry of All Nations," but more commonly called the Crystal Palace Exhibition. For a century afterward, some eighty fairs and exhibitions took place in various locations, even China. These have received scholarly attention as fertile ground for the study of nation-building, social and political histories, and ethnographic studies. During this period of anthropological imperialism, not just curious objects, but native peoples were displayed as living museum pieces. Planners with the organization known as the International Anthropological Exhibit Company did just this for the purpose of exhibiting Filipinos around the country. "It would be my idea to arrange for their stay in this country for about two years, exhibiting them at the Portland exhibition, at Coney Island, or other amusement centers, and at the larger State Fairs."[66]

Five of these large-scale exhibitions played some sort of role with the Chinese junks: the Panama Pacific International Exhibition in San Francisco in 1915; the Panama-California Exposition in San Diego in 1915–1916; the Century of Progress Exposition in Chicago in 1933–1934; the Golden Gate International Exhibition in San Francisco in 1939–1940; and the New York World's Fair in 1939. Some of these fairs featured only models or depictions of the junks, rather than complete vessels. In one case, Chicago's Century of Progress, the only connection with a Chinese vessel, in this case the *Ning Po*, was a display of carvings and statues made from timbers stolen from the aging wreck by the Boy Scouts of America. Other fairs had a more concrete presence. Chinese junks either attended these events or were struggling to make their way to them, both with varying levels of success. Actually, junks had already been placed on display before the American public, in the form of Chinese models. The collection now housed at the National Maritime Museum at Antwerp was on display at the St. Louis World's Fair in 1904.

Though the travel plans for the junk *Whang Ho* included the Lewis and Clark Exposition of 1905, due to delays the junk failed to make it to Portland in time for the event, arriving on the West Coast in 1906. Entrepreneur and entertainer W. M. Milne had attempted to make the event, hailed as the "Lewis and Clark Centennial and American Exposition and Oriental Fair," for the visitor profits. The official nature of the war junk led to delays involving the Chinese government. Somewhat ironically, the 1905 fair emphasized Portland's Asian trade connections and the potential for shortening the routes to the commercial markets of Japan and China. The *Whang Ho* arrived a year late.

In a similar manner, the Panama Pacific Exposition in San Francisco was the target destination for the junk *Ning Po*, which had aged and deteriorated to such a condition as to be unable to sustain the rough voyage under tow from San Pedro to San Francisco Bay. The *Ning Po*, already in Southern California, made the detour back to San Diego and had to settle for the smaller Panama-California Exposition, a difference of some 15 million attendees. Events such as these contributed to city coffers and gave enormous boosts to local industry. In San Diego's case, as the first major port of call for vessels passing westward through the Panama Canal, the international connections of the Pacific Rim harbor were a featured theme.

Richard Halliburton directed the entire effort behind the construction and voyage of the *Sea Dragon* toward attending the Golden Gate International Exposition, an event held on Treasure Island in celebration of the Golden Gate and San Francisco–Oakland Bay bridges in 1939. Like the earlier expositions in 1905 and 1915, the Golden Gate event featured themes incorporating both oriental and occidental motifs and ideas. Exposition promoters had contacted Halliburton as early as July 1936 with the suggestion for the junk project. In other words, the planners in this case convinced the adventurer himself to procure a junk for commercial purposes, rather than the other way around. Overseas Chinese businessmen stood as sponsors behind the fair's agents, and all three parties met repeatedly to make preparations for the junk's participation in the event. Halliburton, of course, was convinced that the junk would be the most exciting attraction at the fair.[67] What the managers did with Halliburton's unused berth at Treasure Island after he failed to show up remains unknown.

Though W. M. Milne publicly expressed his intentions to eventually take both the *Whang Ho* and the *Ning Po* through the Panama Canal and up the eastern seaboard, the only two junks of this sample to actually make this trip were the *Mon Lei* and the *Amoy*. The *Amoy* made New York harbor at the time of the World's Fair there, and the *Mon Lei*, owned by Robert Ripley, reached the eastern seaboard in 1938.

KEYING THE PROGENITOR

Whether or not the junks actually made it to these grand events on time, the expositions did act as an enticement for the vessel owners, a proven method of earning profits. Chinese junks as attractions at these kinds of events were definitely not without precedent. The large junk *Keying*, which appeared at the first Great Exposition in London in 1851 and received much publicity, represents one of the earliest and certainly most celebrated Chinese ships to appear on European shores, and it was an object of fascination for both English and American spectators alike.

The origins of the *Keying* are uncertain, though the director of the Hong Kong Maritime Museum believes she was built in Hong Kong.[68] The *Illustrated London News* for April 1, 1848, carried the graphic description:

This Junk is of the burthen of between 700 and 800 tons; her dimensions are—length 160 feet; extreme breadth, 33 feet; depth of hold, 16 feet. She is built of the best description of teak wood; and, contrary to the European plan, her planks are pinned together prior to the introduction of the ribs. She has three masts made of iron-wood: the mainmast is formed of one immense pole 90 feet long, and of a girth of about ten feet at its junction to the deck. One peculiar characteristic is the total absence of square yards or rigging. Her sails consist of stout mating, ribbed at intervals of three feet by strong bamboos, and are hoisted to the mast by a single rope of immense size, formed of plaited rattan. The mainsail is of gigantic dimensions, weighing nearly nine tons, and engaging the entire crew two hours to hoist it. The *Keying* carries three enormous anchors, made wholly of iron-wood, the cables attached to which are formed of rattans. The rudder is of most singular construction, being supported by two large ropes; two others pass from its lower end, completely under the bottom of the vessel, and secured at either bow. This rudder weighs upward of seven tons: it may be hoisted at pleasure by means of two windlasses situated on the poop.[69]

The components described reflect very traditional Chinese junk construction: adjustable rudder, horizontal windlass, no standing rigging. The newspaper's image reveals the large, forward-looking oculi of a merchant vessel, transom bow and stern, diamond-shaped fenestrations in the large rudder, the "deer's saddle" board at the bow for bringing over the underwater rudder cables, or *dule,* and just the traces of standard Fujian stern decoration. Teak wood construction suggests southern China, perhaps imported from Siam or built abroad at another location in Southeast Asia. Fujian vessels would not have been unknown in Guangdong Province and Hong Kong. Merchants from Fujian were drawn to the Guangzhou (Canton) area due to the great activity in foreign trade.

The large vessel with its thirty Chinese and twelve English crew members set out from Hong Kong for Great Britain on December 6, 1846. She was under the command of master mariner Charles Alfred Auckland Kellet of Liverpool, a navigator experienced in Australian and Chinese waters. Kellet, along with Douglas Lapraik, cofounder of the Hong Kong Bank, had "purchased" the *Keying* in Canton in August of that same year.[70] After having weathered a hurricane off the Cape of Good Hope in March 1847, the *Keying* arrived at St. Helena, where she was visited by both the governor and the naval commander of the station, and in fact by almost every person on the island. From St. Helena, instead of making London, adverse currents and winds carried the junk to New York in July, where between seven thousand and eight thousand people per day toured the first Chinese ship known to

THE CHINESE JUNK "KEYING."

Figure 54. The most celebrated junk in Europe during the nineteenth century, the *Keying* on display at Blackwall, London, in 1848. (From *Illustrated London News*, April 1, 1848, courtesy of the Guildhall Library, City of London)

have visited the United States, paying 25 cents each to go on board ($2,000 daily). She remained in New York for several months. In November she moored in Boston by the Charles River Bridge, attracting similar crowds. Finally, on February 17, 1848, the *Keying* sailed for London, recrossing the North Atlantic in a quick twenty-one days (fast even compared to American sailing packets) and eventually opening for business in London in March, where the crew soon performed their pike and shield military exercise for the Duke of Wellington.[71]

For a shilling apiece, crowds thronged on board the exotic *Keying*, visitors received by a "mandarin of rank" (Hesing, a self-appointed personage?) and a Chinese "artist of celebrity" (Sam Sing). The junk's grand saloon was furnished in the most lavish style of the Celestial Empire. The experience was said to be one of the greatest novelties in Europe at the time, and attracted no less than Her Majesty the Queen, the entire Royal Family, and "an immense number of persons, including nearly all the nobility and foreigners of distinction in London."[72] Both the Greenwich National Maritime

Museum and the Vancouver Maritime Museum today have samples of the commemorative medals that were manufactured by T. Halliday, struck following *Keying*'s arrival in London, commemorating what was seen as the first Chinese ship to reach Europe, or even round the Cape of Good Hope. Truly, there may not have been a better show around.

All was not so pleasant for the junk's crew, though. The Chinese sailors, claiming in essence that they had been "shanghaied," or kidnapped, from their intended passage to Batavia and Singapore, sued for wages, and the owners of the *Keying* were ordered by the court to sell the vessel and recompense the crew.[73] How the results of this suit apparently led to the same Chinese crew arriving again in London the following year and displaying the junk at the Great Exposition is unexplained. Tony Edwards, researching the *Keying*'s history through family ties to the Charles Kellet lineage, reports that twenty-six of the junk's Chinese crew left the vessel in New York, having signed on initially for only an eight-month voyage.[74] Were the performers in London Chinese immigrants from New York? Would that have mattered to the paying customers? (The American showman P. T. Barnum had toured England and Europe only a few years earlier.) Though the vessel's voyage focused on the Atlantic, the commercial potential of its voyage could not have gone unnoticed by American entrepreneurs in the Pacific, as witnessed by their subsequent commercial ventures.

The vessel, stolen from Chinese waters, played an interesting and somewhat informal role in the 1851 Great Exposition. Though the Chinese government had been officially invited to the exhibition, the Qing ruler had seen fit to decline, and the unused space at the fair was partially taken over by the *Keying* concession. The junk and the crew, inadvertently or otherwise, became at that moment China's impromptu and unauthorized ambassadors. China would not make an official appearance at any world exposition until the St. Louis World's Fair in 1904.[75] For the Missouri event, the nephew of the last ruling Manchu emperor and his entourage were ushered courteously across the country, while at the same time other Chinese travelers attempting to enter the United States were being detained in cages in San Francisco. The social context for junks at exhibitions and museums has a great deal to do with the way such things were and are perceived by the public.

For all the momentary excitement, the *Keying* did not endure. In 1853 the junk was towed from her mooring off Rock Ferry on the Cheshire shore and dismantled "for research" by the Redhead Harland and Brown Company. Her decks furnished the teak for two local tug boats.[76]

Contemporary Perspective on Chinese Seafaring

Sailors on Chinese junks were not the only kind of Chinese seafarers seeking foreign shores. In other words, Chinese seafaring experience has a more modern context as well. Up until about 1820, Chinese ships carried more tonnage than any other vessels in Southeast Asia.[77] With the advent of large steamships in the late nineteenth century, Chinese crews were quick to take advantage of employment opportunities in the Pacific, and soon replaced Canadian and American crews on board these vessels. Today ships are still the primary units of exchange for all nations, carrying from 90 to 95 percent of the world's trade goods. Today's modern commercial fleets, including the containerships regularly traveling back and forth across the Pacific Ocean, are manned chiefly by Asian sailors, up to 67 percent by 1987.[78] Typical complements on modern ships include a European master, Chinese officers, and a mixed Asian crew.[79] And many of today's largest, most profitable shipping lines, such as OOC and Evergreen, are owned and controlled by Taiwanese, Korean, Japanese, and Chinese companies. Six of the top ten shipping lines are based in East Asia, and China Ocean Shipping is currently the fourth largest shipper of American container cargo.[80] Some of the shipping owners are descendants of well-to-do overseas Chinese merchants, themselves descended from families of merchants once dependent on junk sails and the wind, on the arrival of vessels from the China coast. In other words, Chinese and Asian mariners have played, and continue to play, a large and important role in maritime transportation, and these transpacific sailing junks represent a part of that history.

Andre Gunder Frank, in *Reorient: Global Economy in the Asian Age*, inverts Eurocentrism with an avowedly Sinocentric flair, highlighting the Asian control of the bulk of global trade over the majority of history. Frank is not really stating something completely new in this maritime context, for other authors have made the same point. Marco Polo's well-known assertion in the thirteenth century that China possessed more ships than the rest of the world combined is a common example, but not the only one. A Dominican friar in the seventeenth century, Domingo de Navarrete, found the same to be true. "There are those who affirm that there are more Vessels in China than in all the rest of the known World. . . . I, who have not seen the eighth part of the Vessels in China, and have travel'd a great part of the World, do look upon it as most certain."[81] Gaining control of the bulk of trade with East Asia only in the mid-nineteenth century, western shipping companies continue to be hard pressed to compete successfully in trade and transportation across the Pacific.

Chinese mariners have played a more consistent role in regional maritime trade in the Pacific than is usually recognized. Certain historical elements, such as turmoil in East Asia, social upheaval and race riots on the West Coast of North America, the long distances and dangers associated with sailing vessel technology, the anthropological imperialism often inherent in various international expositions, and other influences have detracted from a clear view of this consistent role. The historical conditions surrounding these ten vessels and their trips across the Pacific influence not just what we know of these ten junks, but how we have perceived junks in general.

chapter 6

Misreading Our Guests

Public Perceptions

Judging from the public's reactions to the junks that crossed the Pacific, few people in America had an accurate appreciation of the foreign vessels or of nautical technology in East Asia. The common denominator that stands out among all the range of public reactions to the arrival of Chinese ships on the West Coast is the general lack of understanding. Americans were faced with objects that, though the functions were familiar, appeared foreign and strange. Observers expressed the general opinion that such unwieldy and ancient vessels were surely the work of a people unschooled in the nautical sciences. The sole exception to this general reaction came from the small group of nautical specialists who had written about or had direct experience with Chinese junks. Though the technical and scholarly impressions were favorable, the public perception from the mid-nineteenth to the mid-twentieth century did not vary significantly. This has only recently begun to change.

The arrival of transpacific voyaging ships of any nationality was, in the nineteenth century, much more of a noted occasion than the nearly anonymous visit of the container carriers today. This is particularly true of the arrival of the relatively exotic Chinese craft. The fact that many Americans on the West Coast had already experienced the sight of local Chinese-built vessels does not seem to have tempered the fascination with the transpacific voyagers. (Chinese migrants in California had, at least since the 1860s, been constructing Chinese fishing junks from local material for commercial operation in San Francisco Bay, Monterey, Santa Barbara, and San Diego.[1])

People were very interested in these craft and in the stories of the voyages, even though entrepreneurs sometimes overestimated the vessels' profitability. But the reasons for the public's interest did not seem to stimulate any real technological curiosity about what they were seeing.

There are established theories as to why we initially have difficulty understanding anything new and strange; our misunderstanding of foreign objects has been noted by more than a few scholars. As historian Anthony Pagden notes, that which is unfamiliar must be cast in familiar terms. In encounters the world over, attributes of European society were attached, somewhat artificially, to unfamiliar cultures. Familiar labels were used to initially describe the unknown, allowing for some measure at least of classification, serving to make "the incommensurable seem commensurable, if only for as long as it took the observer's vision to adjust."[2] While Pagden's context for the phenomenon of attachment consists of European voyagers placed in unfamiliar foreign contexts, the Chinese junks brought a bit of an unfamiliar world, if not to the Americans in Asia, to the general public on the West Coast of America. The junks represented an indirect encounter with China, with the Other, the abstraction of foreignness so often held as diametrically opposed to European society. Can the theory of attachment still apply? Was it possible in the case of the Chinese junks to use the familiar to describe the unfamiliar? Were they sufficiently similar to European and American sailing vessels, enough so to allow fairly accurate assessment? Apparently not. It was difficult for the public to do this for something so unlike familiar western vessels.

For the most part, western observers simply did not have the language or indeed the will to investigate the individual junks that made it across the ocean. Notes about the transpacific junks were often expressed in terms of negation, a listing of western features that the junks did not have. Anthropologist Richard Gould finds this to be as true of Marco Polo as it is of our more recent relations. Even Western mariners, who were generally impressed by the junk's seaworthiness, can only describe them in western nautical terms by what they seem to lack, such as keels, stem posts, stern posts, etc.[3] This is useful in deciding what a junk is not, but gives little real information on the actual object. In the case of the Chinese junks, familiar European or American measures of nautical technology, how tall the masts or how fast or how comfortable the vessel, were applied to the foreign ships, and often the junks were found wanting.

Few ever ventured beyond this type of description. An informal visit on board and confirmation of some stereotypical conclusions about the "Oriental mind" were enough for many of the public. Several basic themes, as expressed in numerous articles published at the time, will be examined here to better understand the difficulties Americans had with these unfamiliar objects cast up on their shores.

Junks as Alien Sea Monsters

That all vessels, and particularly sailing vessels, are complex artifacts that reveal not just technical but social, economic, and even political information about their culture of origin remains a basic premise of this study. This is not the same as stating that all these various parameters will be equally celebrated and appreciated. European shipowners relied on steerage passengers as their bread and butter in the transatlantic trade in the early decades of the twentieth century, and the conditions in those dark holds say something about the rigid class structure of Victorian society. But the large steam liners were celebrated for their massive engines, for the speed with which they vied for the coveted Blue Riband, and not for their anthropological significance. Vessels during the transition from sail to steam were judged by western society primarily on their technological assets and limitations, as visible evidence of industrial progress.

Chinese junks were evidence of late stages of sailing technology, but they were also the result of other influences, sometimes directly affected by social and economic politics. The works of Jennifer Cushman and others demonstrate that specific design features, such as the beam (width) and the style of rigging were determined by the need to conform to tax codes in the coastal provinces. Domestic Chinese shipping enjoyed greater mobility and freedom from foreign surcharges, thus the importance of building in the Chinese style. In short, Chinese junk designs were the result of complex forces, the process of which could be understood as logical within the context of East Asian history.

The same was often true of western ship designs, which have been influenced by social and economic vectors throughout history. But for the nineteenth-century public it was clear where European vessels derived their *logical* origins. Ever since the infusion of scientific method into the art of naval architecture, as evidenced by the drawings of Matthew Baker in the sixteenth century and the application of mathematical formulae to ship design, nautical architecture has benefited from the scientific study of buoyancy and stability and the production of the efficient European sailing and fighting machine.

Rationality and science were highlighted as the cornerstones of this type of progress, held as features perhaps that set Europeans apart from other civilizations still locked in tradition and superstition. Thus, a civilization judged as less than rational in European terms could not help but produce less than rational ship designs. American and European opinions on Chinese junks emphasize the general view of the organic and random evolution of Chinese junks. Junk creation was frequently explained by crediting natural forces without human intervention. One source refers to junks as products of the elements themselves, "Things Produced by the Work of Nature."[4] These were articles in modern engineering journals that specifically promoted this view. "The Chinaman does not experiment; it does not pay. He discovers things by accident or evolution and adopts them."[5] If a foreign culture had not been granted the comprehension of the scientific method by outside observers, then all its innovations had to be mere accidents.

Chinese junks, in this light, are not so much designed as discovered, not so much built as grown. Sources repeatedly refer to them in terms that go far beyond the mundane state of inanimate units of transportation. Junks seemed to be anything but plain old vessels. They were variously labeled as unique, fantastic, strange, picturesque, teakwood tubs, crazily built little ships, relics of the past centuries, peaceful, and queer old hulks. Likewise, the junks were all at once fabled, famous, infamous, celebrated, venerable, quaint, reprobates, and floating heaps of lumber. They were beautiful barnacled objects of Oriental art, notorious, improbable, utterly absurd, and slightly delightful, an awesome thing. This is not a phenomenon limited to China. Regarding Moken boats, also perceived as exotic objects by nineteenth-century western observers, Jacques Ivanoff sums up reaction as "torn between technical fascination and cultural revulsion."[6]

Making them more animate yet, "sea monsters" seems to be one common assessment of Chinese junks. The *Ning Po* was commonly believed to be, at the time of her initial visit to the West Coast, modeled after the Chinese idea of a sea monster. This idea continues to the current day, in articles from the late 1980s. Authors continue to paint the vessel as some kind of dragon. "Her open bow (with her sides joined at the waterline, but widely spread apart at the deck) was built to look like a mouth, the two disks on both bows formed the eyes, masts and sails resembled fins, and her exaggerated high stern formed the tail of the beast."[7] The attributes of the *Ning Po* were transferred to all Chinese vessels. Learned minds back in the 1920s held that "to a Chinaman every junk is a fish."[8] To be fair, westerners had, as early as the sixteenth century, conceptualized their vessels' hulls as the hybrid offspring of a cod and a mackerel, based on the drawings of Baker, an English shipwright. Both are simply representations of the vessel as metaphor. Surely the serpent-headed Viking longships of legend and the sculpted northern European boat coffins that bore leaders to the afterlife entered a similar metaphorical realm, and were not really considered designed from sea monsters.

This particular equation of junks as dragons or sea monsters has decidedly negative overtones for westerners. The object is imbued with its connotation; the serpent-headed craft were predators. Analysis of seafaring myth points to examples of this stereotype. Folk tales of dragon junks place them in the class of devil ships, "because to the student of folk tales there can be no more significant symbol or embodiment of evil than the dragon or serpent. The Junk . . . is the very spirit of evil moving upon the face of the waters, a terror so real that it conquers even cupidity and curiosity."[9] That piracy was (and is) so frequent in Southeast Asia has not helped the popular reputation of junks in the West. Even tourists visiting the graceful junk *Amoy* at the waterfront in Victoria in 1922 would have agreed. "As far as folks here were concerned such a craft was associated with Chinese pirates and all previous knowledge had been gained from prints in books."[10]

Strangely enough, the fact that Chinese junks were higher at the stern than the bow was considered a noteworthy and backward feature. "True to the Oriental way of doing things, in direct opposition to the Occidental, this craft [*Ning Po*] was navigated from the stern; and the captain stood on the sea-monster's elevated tail to direct the vessel's movements."[11] Such an emphasis seems odd, given the fact that for hundreds of years European sailing ships featured elevated stern decks, and all such vessels, commercial or military, were navigated or conned from the quarterdeck.

The general western impression of East Asian sailing vessels is not one very informed by the historical circumstances of their development. A lack of understanding of East Asian history, both in Japan and China, led observers of the many drifting and broken Japanese junks in the Pacific, and of the shallow coastal designs of the Chinese junks, to arrive at incorrect conclusions as to the abilities of Asian shipwrights. For many westerners, the simple fact was that the Japanese and Chinese did not appear to know how to build oceangoing vessels. Yet, the same design influences often dictated the shape of western vessels. In an attempt to control smuggling in the eighteenth century, "any boat built to row with more than four oars found upon land or water within the counties of Middlesex, Surrey, Kent or Sussex, or Ipswich, or any boat rowing with six oars found upon land or water, in any other port, or within two leagues of the coast of Britain, was subject to forfeit."[12]

Such measures are not surprising, for this was one of a few ways that land-bound governments can attempt to control a seagoing population. There is very little that any entity can do to control the actions of captains or crews, once a ship is five or fifty or five hundred miles from the shore. Limiting the construction or design of the vessel, the single necessary tool available to seafarers, in an attempt to curb certain activities is one of the few options. The most extreme case comes from China. In the seventeenth century the Qing government, in order to combat the southern Chinese rebel pirate organization of Zheng Chenggong (Ming dynasty loyalists), forcibly removed its own coastal population from numerous provinces and erected barriers across the inland rivers so that "not an inch of board may set out to the ocean!"[13] No seafaring and no vessels at all! The intention was to deny Zheng's fleets material for repair, to deny them their vessels. This was the ultimate in retribution by a land-bound government against a seafaring population. No one knows the true dimensions of suffering caused by the Qing coastal zone prohibition, and the policy did not have complete success due to Zheng Chenggong's strong overseas connections. Nevertheless, it highlights the fact that seafarers, to a level unknown in any other human activity, are completely dependent upon the technological artifact of the ship. Hydrographic science and economics are not the only influences upon ship design.

That places like Japan and China had a long history of discrete maritime codes, formed by the interaction of complex political and economic forces that dictated specifics of ship construction, was a measure of their intense seafaring activities, not a sign of their lack of skills. For westerners, though, junks simply looked like fish. Indeed, some did resemble such creatures, but this short-term reaction had the effect of obscuring a clearer understanding of their physical evolution.[14]

Junks as Ancient History

The popular assertion that Chinese junks are ageless vessels, little changed through thousands of years, and all of "ancient" lineage, denotes a similar lack of appreciation of a dynamic history in East Asia. No one in America seemed at all sure what era such vessels represented. The *Amoy* voyage in 1922 was immediately compared to seafaring in northern Europe, circa 800 A.D. "Surely an exploit comparable only to the intrepid voyages of old! Let the shades of the Vikings guard jealously their laurels, with such as Captain Waard and his Chinese mate about the Seven Seas!"[15] The *Whang Ho,* the "most curious object in the nature of a vessel that has ever entered the harbor," was a "typical Chinese war craft of many many generations ago."[16] (Occasionally, observers were actually pretty close to correct as to the approximate age, but by guess.) The *Free China,* arriving in San Francisco in

1955, sailed "out of the storied past."[17] The crew members, though, were apparently on a mission only some four or five hundred years old, as they were "bound eastward around the world, reversing Magellan."[18] The *Hummel Hummel* was obviously "emulating venturesome Chinese pirates who sailed their junk to these shores from ancient Cathay long before Columbus crossed the Atlantic."[19] The *Ning Po* was old enough to "claim existence before the famous Flying Dutchman came into being."[20] The Flying Dutchman, of course, refers to the tale of Captain van der Decken, who, frustrated in his attempts to round the Cape, fired his pistol at the constellation of the Southern Cross, and was condemned to sail those seas for eternity. Indeed, in all that time the *Ning Po* had seen so many evil deeds that the "ancient ghosts of those who died in horror aboard her must swirl around that spot on Ballast Point like a spectral cyclone, yet unseen by the crews of the sleek new yachts that now anchor year round in Catalina Harbor."[21] And regarding the transpacific junks' distant cousin *Keying* in London in 1848:

> Talk of the wisdom of our ancestors! Here is a sample of the ship-building wisdom and skill of the ancestors of the Chinese which may have dated from the earliest ages of the world. Certainly never before did so unwieldy and misshapen a vessel traverse the Indian and Atlantic oceans. . . . The junk *Keying* is of precisely the same build as the vessels which carried the "Celestials" three thousand years ago. . . .[22]
>
> Thousands of years have passed away, since the first Chinese junk was constructed on this model; and the last Chinese junk that was ever launched, was none the better for the waste and desert of time. In all that interval, through all the immense extent of the strange kingdom of China—in the midst of its patient and ingenious, but never advancing art, and its diligent agricultural cultivation—not one new twist or curve has been given to a ball of ivory; not one blade of experience has been grown.[23]

The problem here is twofold. The first and underlying misconception is that China represents a civilization void of history, an unchanging tradition stretching back into the formless past. This general bias is a distinct development of the process of history and historiography from the nineteenth century. It has been set forth by some of the major influential thinkers of the past, and is a fallacy that, except for the maritime realm, has been more or less laid to rest.

The second part of this misperception of history is more complex, for in terms of the past several centuries, *though not the past millennia*, the perception of junks as changeless ancient vessel designs does not seem to be too wide of the mark. One the one hand, a clear bias has labeled the Chinese past as changeless, and on the other hand, though there is obviously evolution over time, there has not been much significant change in sailing junk design in the past several hundred years, particularly when compared to design changes in the West. These two facts combine to confuse the picture of the historical development of sailing junks in China. In short, people have been too loose with the word *ancient*. Worcester himself falls somewhat into this camp, though he is careful to apply the description ancient to only certain features. "The junk, therefore, like so many customs and contrivances in China, has survived down the ages as a sort of perpetual and useful anachronism and is in many essentials very little altered from its ancient prototypes."[24]

"We are faced with the oldest state in existence, and yet with one which has no past, but exists at the present time in exactly the same way as we hear of it from antiquity. . . . To this extent, China has no real history."[25] With this, the German philosopher Georg Wilhelm Friedrich Hegel identified China as being at the beginning of the evolution of civilizations, yet stalled somehow and unable to move forward. Status for Oriental people was defined against advanced societies, the great civilizations he termed the Graeco-Roman and the modern, or Germanic. Hegel also applied geography to the classification and ranking of societies, not as bands of northern, temperate, or southern climate, but as eastern and western divisions. For Hegel, the true divisions between men were based on internal, moral principles. "The course of the sun is a symbol of the course of the human spirit; and as the light of the physical sun travels from the east to the west, so does the light of the sun of the self-consciousness. Asia is the determinate east or absolute beginning, and Europe the determinate west or end of history."[26]

As strange as these statements appear today, they were not seen as so odd at the time they were made. Historiography and the scientific investigation of history came to the fore in the nineteenth century. Civilizations, interpreted as coherent units, were seen to rise and fall, an understanding influenced by concepts of Social Darwinism. "The British rule the whole world with their trade; they have opened East India and China to Europe, and all these empires are almost submitting to the European spirit."[27] Foreign nations, thus, without the technological advancements of steam and steel and modern transportation, occupied the back seat on the train of modern history. Leopold von Ranke himself, considered by some as the father of the practice of modern history, regarded China, for instance, as a "nation of eternal stagnation."[28] These very same sentiments seemed confirmed at the world expositions, where evidence of the backwardness of Chinese technology, sometimes in the form of the occasional sailing junk, was available for tour. An anonymous observer at London's Great Exhibition stated, "We need envy nothing that they have. . . . Their porcelain has been known from time immemorial, and in everything else the Chinese are so stationary, that they may be considered as the most ancient workmen on the earth."[29]

It might also be said that where there is no Chinese history, there is no reason to study the Chinese past. General ignorance of junks has led to rather large errors being published about them. For example, "The square-sailed junk of China has not altered for thousands of years" includes a sail type never featured on Chinese vessels.[30] There is, simply, a lot of bad history when it comes to the nautical world. "The Chinese sailor has held to his square sail junk from the earliest times down to the present day. It may have been his refusal to adopt fore-and-aft sails that prevented the wide spreading of a Chinese civilization by long voyages and overseas colonization."[31]

Chinese junks, in this analysis then, were no more than antiquarian curiosities, evidence of the backwardness of Chinese mariners, useful only in comparison to modern-day progress. Today, old ideas about the stagnation of East Asian civilizations have been vanquished, but we still like to imagine traces of an ancient past, even if we have to include simple but efficient working craft from the nineteenth century in that category. From G.R.G. Worchester himself, "here is a chance to let an old China hand take you to one of the great rivers of the world for a last look at a timeless land just before time there ceased to stand still."[32] Where has time ever really stood still?

Such a modern and sympathetic intention to capture a frozen moment of the past, making that "historical snapshot" represent a sort of timeless reality, is reflected by the term *the ethnographic present*. A type of illusion is noted by anthropologist Renato Rosaldo: the ethnographic present is a perspective that voids all questions of change over time and renders foreign cultures artificially frozen in the present tense. This phenomenon provides a single, unchanging picture of an assumed static and unchanging society, accepting this as accurate contemporary description. It denies change. It is an illusion that accomplishes the same thing nineteenth-century historiographers attempted, making the very real dynamic nature of history vanish for China.

Quite often some of the pitfalls of the ethnographic present prove difficult to avoid. Given the lack of a plethora of sources for this study, sources used for analytical purposes, such as Worcester's *Classification of the Principal Chinese Sea-Going Junks,* are exactly the kind of instant snapshots that attempt to freeze the image of a changing process, the evolution of junk design. Searching for individual construction features or patterns within the overall evolution of vessel designs helps, for features can continue to change while the "Chinese-ness" of the junk pattern is not invalidated. The ethnographic present is a fallacy, albeit a useful one generally inherent in classification schemes, and when in use should be acknowledged.

There is uncertainty in the time line of Chinese nautical evolution, to say the least. Several scholars do indicate evidence of meaningful changes in junk design both throughout the long span of Chinese history and within the scope of the late imperial era.[33] Gang Deng and Worcester and Needham and others have developed portions of this time line. J. Richard Steffy of Texas A&M indicates that important areas are still unclear, that "we still know nothing about transitions in construction or the methods by which they built those fabled great ships of the Orient."[34] Not all agree on the exact dates when changes in junk design became evident, but the fact remains that Chinese vessels, like those of other cultures, changed in response to a variety of factors. These same scholars point out that junks were stable in design in recent centuries not because they were ancient, but because they were advanced.

Chinese junks had, relative to European history, met all the design requirements demanded of them by their operating environment very early on indeed. By the end of the Song dynasty, they had already achieved the major technological changes needed to remain efficient for hundreds of years. Gang Deng divides the entire span of Chinese nautical development into three major phases: first, the rudimentary period of 6000 B.C. to 1030 B.C.; second, the period of progress from 770 B.C. to 1279 A.D.; and third, a period of status quo, from 1279 A.D. to 1911 A.D.[35] This broad classification can be broken down in more detail in terms of individual ship designs. The *lochuan,* or multi-decked ship of the Han to Sui periods, gave way to the *fuchuan,* or Fujian ship, from the Tang to Song, and finally the *shachuan,* or shallow draft sand ship,[36] encompassing the late imperial era. Each of these broad transitions brought technical innovations. "Thus, it is no exaggeration to say that after the twelfth century A.D. Chinese sailors were technically capable not only of sailing to but also returning from the Pacific and Indian Oceans."[37] Gang Deng estimates that the majority of design advancements, roughly 70 percent, took place before the fourth century A.D. By the end of the Song dynasty, the remaining 30 percent of major advancements had been completed. The point that the major technological changes in junk design occurred prior to western maritime contact in East Asia reinforces the very basic design differences between Chinese and western ship designs.

The solid bulkheads, multiple decks, axial rudder, multiple fore-and-aft lug sails, and mariner's compass represented major achievements in vessel use and design, and these were all well known in China at a time when western mariners were steering single-masted, square-sailed cogs with oars and defending themselves against raiders in dragon-headed galleys. The next major step in nautical technology for Europe was the oceanic ship of discovery, capable of crossing oceans with the trade winds. Carracks and early galleons were the first European vessels to show up in East Asia. Further refinements led to the faster "race-built" galleons of the English, and the more economical *fluit* vessels of the Dutch. Following that, the European vessel design of the frame-built, multi-masted armed cargo ship did not change radically until the advent of marine steam power and iron hull construction. Sailors on sixteenth-century galleons would be pretty surprised, but perhaps not at a total loss, if transported to the decks of a Royal Navy frigate in the Napoleonic era. When European vessels arrived in China, the Chinese already had achieved their own kind of equivalent stability in design. The Industrial Revolution and the transition to iron hulls and steam power changed the playing field.

For numerous reasons that go far beyond the scope of this study, the nineteenth-century industrial take-off, capitalism, was a European phenomenon. Steam power on board wooden sailing vessels, initially outfitted with side paddle wheels, soon found its more technologically compatible expression in stiffer iron-hulled ships with screw propellers. Chinese junks remained the same. The fact that the Chinese junk design remained relatively unimproved positioned these vessels to serve as the backdrop, the comparative "Other" to the measure of European nautical evolution. Historian Kenneth Pomeranz states, "it is China, more than any other place, that has served as the 'other' for the modern West's stories about itself."[38] Though his analysis leaves out discussions of many specific maritime topics, the same forces Pomeranz defines can be seen shaping contemporary views of the maritime past. Chinese junks could represent all that was traditional and less efficient and backward in comparison to modern nautical advancements. Junks could be all that modern European vessels had left behind.

Capitalism and nation-building are powerful themes in the study of history, neither of which may be particularly conducive to Chinese junks. It might be argued that nationalist-style history, associated with figures such as Hegel and von Ranke and the birth of modern history in the nineteenth century, is by nature biased against, or at least ill-suited toward, topics that are by nature transnational, as in "maritime." The maritime voyagers of not just China but many nationalities operated (and operate) oftentimes between borders and national institutions. There have been serious efforts by the nation-state to settle maritime nomads ashore and have these populations conform to land-based societal norms, efforts that are not always initially successful. In short, a tension exists between the modern nation with its nationalist histories and the more fluid realities of the maritime realm.

Fortunately, more attention is beginning to be paid to sometimes hard-to-define regional maritime histories. James Warren's work on the Sulu region in Southeast Asia serves as an example of a study cast in distinctly maritime parameters. The outlines of Warren's zone cannot be found drawn on any map, but are more indicative of the seasonal monsoon winds and the cruising ranges of the Suluwesi vessels. His work reflects a maritime perspective, the fluid and dynamic struggle for labor resources (coastal populations), rather than the conquest of territory. Epeli Hau'ofa has painted a meaningful maritime perspective for the Pacific Islands. William Skinner redefined familiar borders and united southern China with Southeast Asia in a common regional approach to the South China Sea maritime realm. These scholars have redrawn the boundaries of our perceptual maps in ways that better recognize the sea.

It is a question of national boundaries versus the fluid nature of the ocean. In the volume of the *Geographical Review* devoted to maritime analysis, "Oceans Connect," historian Jerry Bentley reinforces the idea that focusing on national narratives distracts us from larger scale processes that have "deeply influenced both the experiences of individual societies and the development of the world as a whole."[39] Bentley goes on to note that the arena of cultural interaction, though less developed as an approach, might benefit from such ultra-national perspective. This requires breaking beyond the permeating influences of von Rankian–style histories, histories that "make limited provision for processes of commercial, biological, and cultural exchange."[40] These are the influences that limited our ability to comprehend the transpacific junks, and to understand how and when they have changed over time.

What would have influenced that change in China? Are there reasons that many of the designs of Chinese junks remained stable in recent times? Scholars have addressed the steady state of China's trade technology in the days of junks and sails, taking into account broader economic forces. The picture for the late imperial era, according to scholar J. C. van Leur, is of quantitative, not qualitative evolution. Conditions, in van Leur's analysis, simply did not conspire to demand technological change. In his view, trade in China served as an historical constant. The fixed rhythm of arrivals and departures and the changing monsoon set the stage, and "the only alterations were quantitative ones within the given framework. . . . However, one needs to remember in the first place," van Leur continues, "that ship construction develops to a much higher level in connection with and dependence on warfare than within the commercial framework."[41] In the case of western ship development, this is a commonly held presumption. Stout galleons capable of maneuvering relatively quickly and carrying a large number of heavy cannon definitely played a role in European warfare. That European maritime trade existed in a state of armed tension, and that this tension spurred development, is undeniable.

It would not be correct to maintain that sailing junks in recent centuries experienced no change at all. Junks had changed in the past, and continued to change throughout the period of European contact, continuing to adopt some new technologies. The major design elements remained constant during a time when the nautical technology of the European world changed dramatically. Junks changed some of the features or language within the consistent pattern, while European ships changed the entire pattern. From this point of view, Europeans were not completely wrong in assuming ancient or at least very old models for contemporary junks. The only problem was that observers made their assumptions not from historical information of comparative technological evolution, but from inherently flawed historiography. In short, in interpreting the age of these artifacts, westerners were somewhat right for all of the wrong reasons.

Junks as Floating Museums of Fascinating Atrocities

Interpretations of their cultural meanings, though, were much more problematic. For anyone who has visited a *Ripley's Believe It or Not!* wax museum, the attraction of various torture devices and grisly scenes is easy to recall. Something in our common nature makes us vulnerable to dark and horrible fascinations. Junks fulfilled the Ripley function in America. Both the *Whang Ho* and the *Ning Po* served as warehouses and museums for a collection of weaponry and devices reportedly well-worn with use in East Asia. Museums of the period reflected not the thematically designed educational institutions of today, but the entertainment options of the nineteenth century, haphazardly collected assortments of random and exotic items aimed at stimulating the senses. At London's first Great Exposition in 1851, the Chinese junk *Keying* was available for public examination. Colors shown from every side, huge gaudy shields hung on deck between jingals (a heavy musket, hybrid cross between cannon and arquebuses). Inside, the grand saloon was arranged as a museum, filled with all sorts of curiosities. And nearby, if one felt so inclined, a small chapel containing the idols "which those serious Orientals who lounge about the deck are in the habit of worshipping."[42]

The *Ning Po* in 1912 continued in this tradition, being advertised as "a floating museum of ancient Chinese arms, instruments of torture, and quaint historical relics."[43] The junk carried a selection of implements guaranteed to excite the casual visitor:

> Here, also are shown some of the modes of torture that were prac-ticed in China. The *Kee-long* is the wooden cage in which persons accused of piracy or crimes against the government were suspended without food or water until death came. Other torture instruments on boards included a two-handed sword, a big beheading knife, iron flairs (bone crushers), thumb screws, the *Kang* double and single-boards that were fitted about the neck, a "weazened rusty little gun" 3-feet long, estimated to be 400 years old and a capstan whose iron bands litter the decks.[44]

Items were added to the collection as time passed, and one or two sources note the inaccuracy of a beheading block on the junk, as no such item was used in the Chinese traditional execution. No tour of the pirate vessel would have been complete without venturing below decks, though, and the appro-priate accommodations were made.

> Back of the officer's quarters and mandarin's cabin is the old smug-gler's chamber of horrors. In this dungeon dark compartment there was originally only one very small entrance and the compartment itself a deep well of darkness, extending clean to the hold.
>
> Finding it impractical to show visitors such a ventless, rayless place, the exhibitors of the ship sawed a large section out of the thick wall, and put floorings across the deep chasm. Even then the way amidst the thick blackness of the gruesome chamber cannot be found without the aid of a lantern. By means of its feeble rays one may perceive on its outer wall the marks of the shelves that once had been there—shelves where the prisoners were placed until they either divulged the secret of their wealth or treasure to the outlaws who had captured them or died of starvation or lack of air in that horrible place. They were literally laid on the shelf, with the prospect of dropping to the depths below if they became restless in their narrow beds.
>
> After looking at this place, beheading knives did not appear so for-bidding to me.[45]

This theme found its counterpart ashore, for it was typical for the grand fairs to feature such dark obsessions for the regular visitor, whether junks were available for display or not. "As a result of objections raised by a member of the local Chinese business community and by the Chinese consul, the directors agreed to close one portion of the Chinese Village—the Underground Chinatown concession, operated by theatre executive Sid Grauman, which depicted a 'chamber of horrors' including opium dens."[46] It was what the public wanted to see.

Contradictory Impressions

The various attitudes toward the Chinese and the junks occasionally combined to produce what appear today as amazingly contradictory conclusions. It is a reaction similar to the familiar fallacy of "presentism," the amazement that comes with the discovery that people of other times were capable of doing some of the things we do today. We are amazed at the Egyptians' ability to lift stone, as reflected in the television programs on the building of the pyramids, and the realization that Egyptians accomplished their feat by mastering the ramp fills us with wonder. We are amazed at the sailing junk's ability to sail, to do exactly what it was designed to do. Yet, conclusions about the skills of Chinese shipwrights and seafarers have not benefited significantly from the demonstration. It seems odd to be surprised that ships floated, that sailors sailed.

Dickens, writing about the junk *Keying* in the *Examiner*, marveled "that seafarers who knew nothing of shipbuilding or navigation managed to bring the craft to London in the first place."[47] The ship, in this case, was not a ship at all.

> If there be any one thing in the world that it is not at all like, that thing is a ship of any kind. So narrow, so long, so grotesque, so low in the middle, so high at each end . . . with no rigging, with nowhere to go aloft, with mats for sails, great warped cigars for masts, gaudy dragons and sea monsters disporting themselves from stem to stern, and, on the stern, a gigantic cock of impossible aspect, defying the world . . . it would look more at home at the top of a public building, at the top of a mountain, in an avenue of trees, or down in a mine, than afloat on the water.[48]

The ship, as defined, meant of course the European-style ship. Notes on the *Keying* provide examples of the phenomenon of Pagden's attachment.

Apparently, the fact that the vessel had arrived from China under its own sail power did not go far in clearing up its identity. Likewise, even the more technical venue of the journal *Mariner's Mirror* proved to be afflicted by the same puzzling juxtaposition. The *Keying* persisted as "a vessel which, though constructed on lines and equipped in a fashion not associated with ocean passages, proved herself a very good sea boat. Much of the contemporary information fails in technical clearness, and no scientific account of the *Keying* seems to have been written."[49] Here one apparently finds that typical large Chinese junks, "not associated with ocean passages," seemed to be adapted to the environment almost by accident. If large junks the size of the *Keying*, some 160 feet long and 33 feet in beam, sailing between Southeast Asia and China, were not adapted to the ocean, what then was their function? This was not a phenomenon confined to China. European travelers in the late nineteenth century had difficulty equating the apparent backwardness of Moken culture in Southeast Asia with the design of the Moken boat, so perfectly adapted to their environment.[50]

This curious attitude may be a holdover of the earlier European opinion that the Chinese never indulged in blue-water sailing. At the time of European contact in East Asia, the general maritime resistance to private overseas business had limited shipwrights to the production of shallow draft coastal vessels, leading to the mistaken European impression that Chinese sailors were incapable of crossing large bodies of water. In this contradictory fashion, Chinese ships were not ships and Chinese sailors were not sailors.

> How the flowery region ever got, in the form of the junk *Keying*, into the latitude and longitude where it is now to be found is not the least part of the marvel. The crew of Chinamen aboard the *Keying* . . . had not enough on board to keep them from the bottom, and would most indubitably have gone there, but for such poor aid as could be rendered by the skill and coolness of a dozen English sailors, who brought this extraordinary craft in safety over the wide ocean.[51]

The general opinions regarding the skill of Chinese sailors are also to be found in abundance in the nineteenth-century literature of those who traveled in China.

All of these basic contradictions add up to a dual perspective: Chinese junks are at once fascinating and improbable. Though the *Ning Po* was best summed up as an object modeled on a sea creature by some, its own fame has made the junk somewhat immortal in the eyes of Southern Californians. The story of the junk continues to be reworked in popular magazines. The model of the *Ning Po* has now taken its place alongside models of the *Bounty*, the *Sovereign of the Seas,* Viking longships, etc. For tourists who visit the two or three institutions that happen to have the representations, the *Ning Po* has become the stand-in for all Chinese junks, the single representation of the entire species.

Perspectives on "Entangled" Junks

It is clear that ships, whether they are junks or schooners or steamships, embody more significance for various seafaring cultures than mere transportation machines. One need only read about the *Titanic.* And it is clear that oceans have acted as seaways for the transmission of not just technology but culture. Is there any fixed relationship between the mode of transportation and the message? Do objects, such as Chinese junks, laden with cultural features specific to the long history of Chinese seafaring, carry with them any inherent and unchanging cultural meaning? Can we expect that they would have been understood? Anthropologist Nicholas Thomas answers "no." In Thomas's view, cultural meaning stems from the original society, and is not easily transmitted through the trade of just the actual object. The language barrier between cultures comes immediately to mind as a natural obstacle to cultural contact; "there was a gap in the sense that there was no developed language through which their relevance . . . could be specified."[52] Without language, without relevance, artifacts become trivialized. Their meanings become tangled up in a failed cultural translation. Chinese junks were tossed into that much larger category of foreign curiosities reserved for ethnographic collections. Regarding this loss of relevance for objects in nineteenth-century collections, Thomas states:

> The artifacts of non-Western peoples were known over a long period as "curiosities." Occasionally, this term, or "curios," also embraced certain kinds of antiques and classical relics, and (in the absence of the qualifier "artificial") even natural specimens—coral, bones, and mineral samples. . . . This is to express, perhaps in extreme terms, a tension between a scientifically controlled interest in further knowledge and an unstable "curiosity" which is not authorized by any methodological or theoretical discourse, and is grounded in passion rather than reason.[53]

One single observation, from a functional standpoint, applies universally to all ten vessels that crossed the Pacific: none of the Chinese junks continued to be what they once were. All of these objects shifted function and lost their original meaning in their journey over the Pacific, despite the permanent features built into their very keels and carved into their sides. What were cargo carriers and fishing vessels and war junks became pleasure yachts and tourist attractions and floating museums. Commercial vessels became movie sets and dressed in a variety of make-believe disguises. Even the junks that were built under the overall direction of Europeans in Asia display this cultural hybridism. The *Cheng Ho*, built for scientific cruising, took its form from what was imagined to be an early Ming dynasty *baochuan* or treasure galleon. Why use a Ming galleon, or what someone said represented a Ming galleon, for scientific cruises? Except for the sentiment of wishing to preserve *something*, this question goes unanswered.

Chinese junks were treated much as any artifact would have been, put on display at a museum or exhibition. These junks, in a certain sense, were portable sites—in archaeological terms, loci of human activity. Sailors fill the role of inhabitants for these locations, and as any nautical archaeologist can testify, aspects of their work, food processing, leisure hours, cargo, etc., can all be revealed in the patterns and physical remains of their homes. Sites are complex entities and often demand well-thought-out research designs and slow, deliberate investigation in order to maximize the return of information.

Had our approach to these artifacts or "sites" been more systematic and rational, it would have produced a much more informative record than the handful of carnival postcards and tourist brochures of curiosities left to us. Who would appreciate, in a casual manner, the star-shaped patterns of nails, the long history of the oculi, the Chinese written *chengyu* on the junks themselves? The statue in the joss house was just another pagan idol. What other interpretation was necessary for the setting at a public fairground?

Armchair Sailors and the Tourist "Gaze"

John Urry, in *The Tourist Gaze*, remarks: "Tourism is a leisure activity. Post modernism involves a dissolving of boundaries, not only between high and low cultures, but between different cultural forms. The post tourist does not have to leave their home in order to see the typical objects of the tourist gaze."[54] A bit of China itself had come before the tourist, not to be analyzed, but simply to be experienced in juxtaposition to the modern technological wares of the western nations. This is what promoters like W. M. Milne and Robert Ripley were selling. Images of the junks were captured in tourist postcards, that ubiquitous and easily reproducible tourist souvenir essential to the casual act.

The fairs and expositions on the West and East Coasts of North America played a role in the journey of the Chinese junks. These fairs have become a subject for study in their own right. The anthropological assessment of foreign peoples, a charting of the physical and social evolution of the various races, was often a major theme at these expositions. Fairs were no longer, as they had once been, intended for the mere trade and sale of goods, but as anthropologist Burton Benedict states, "They were selling ideas: ideas about the relations between nations, the spread of education, the advancement of science."[55] Thus, primitive products and tribes were juxtaposed with gleaming examples of modern industry for obvious purposes. Exhibitions during this period, then, were not specifically held to investigate historical or technological facets of artifacts. They were, in the words of Umberto Eco:

> . . . an enormous gathering of evidence from Stone to Space Age, an accumulation of objects useless and precious, an immense catalogue of things produced by man in all countries over the past ten thousand years, displayed so that humanity will not forget them. . . . The merchandise is "enthroned . . . with an aura of amusement surrounding it." A boat, a car, a TV set are not for sailing, riding, or watching, but are meant to be looked at for their own sake. They are not even meant to be bought, but just to be absorbed by the nerves, by the taut, excited senses, as one absorbs the vortex of projected colors in a discotheque.[56]

And often in an attempt at a comprehensive arrangement of the objects of the world, the logic behind the specific selection of goods could be lost. Though the discipline of anthropology may have been present, the end result at the fairs could be confusion.

Two other exhibits dealt with human social life in an evolutionary mode. One was a history of human habitations shown in full scale models ranging from Stone Age caves to Persian palaces and from wigwams to Chinese pagodas. The other was an international retrospective Exposition of Labor and of the Anthropological Sciences, which began with the skeletal remains of early hominids, ranged through the Paleolithic and Neolithic, touched upon all major civilizations of recorded history, and then surveyed the liberal arts, sciences, trade, transportation, and military arts.[57]

This is a tall order to present in any meaningful context, especially given the often random nature of the exotic collections. With the possible exception of the *Fou Po II*, chosen intentionally by maritime ethnographer De

Bisschop, very little work apparently went into the selection of each particular junk type. As is clear from the individual stories of the voyages, usually whatever was quickly available and cheap, happened to look seaworthy, and satisfied the whim of the particular owner came across the Pacific. Richard Halliburton, for instance, working directly for the promoters of the San Francisco Exposition, arrived in China with no preconceived criteria on what to obtain. Nicholas Thomas points out:

> A lack of specified interest is also apparent from the actual practices of collecting, in that the explorers did not make systematic effort to acquire either representative samples of a totality or artifacts of particular kinds. . . . These points suggest that what was important about collecting, was not so much what could be said about or done with the specimens collected but the way that collected material attested to the fact of having visited remote places and observed novel phenomena.[58]

This applies to the selection of junks on the Chinese coast. Junks were obtained as trinkets and displayed as objects from a monolithic and homogeneous land, not as specific artifacts from distinct regions. This is not surprising, for most of these vessels were not part of any research agenda. The immediate reason for most of these voyages would appear to be financial profit. The entrepreneurs who brought the early Chinese junks across the Pacific must have been well aware of the profit-making potential that such events represented. Gaining access to a dock anywhere within the vicinity of one of these fairs could be a guarantee of better returns, a get-rich-quick scheme. Sometimes the intentions of their voyages had little to do with the results.

In the Eyes of the Beholder

Nicholas Thomas's observations on the processes of perception seem to hold true for the general case of Chinese junks. Regarding the colonial exposition of 1886:

> This is to remind us, once again, of the crucial role of material culture and of the optical illusion that it constantly offers us: we take the "concrete and palpable" presence of a thing to attest to the reality of that which we have made it signify; our fantasies find confirmation in the materiality of things that are composed more of objectified fantasy than physical stuff.[59]

This is quite a statement. Given the prevailing anti-Chinese views of the late nineteenth century, junks were anything from floating prisons to sea monsters to direct threats to American seaborne trade. The physical reality of the visiting junks did little to change American attitudes, perceptions that involved much more than the handful of vessels. Reactions to junks mimicked reactions to Chinese immigration. In the popular media of the time, Chinese sailing junks, a symbol of Chinese sailors who competed for jobs with American crewmen, can be seen implicated in the destruction of American commerce. A striking image in Philip P. Choy, Lorraine Dong, and Marlon K. Hom's *The Coming Man* captures this spirit. Set on the rocky coast, the familiar female persona of Lady Liberty impales herself on her own sword as ancient Chinese junks sail past the sinking ships of modern American merchant vessels. The caption reveals that the American ship of state, American commerce, is gliding noiselessly toward her doom. In the state of tension between two cultures involved in economic competition these junks symbolized the encroachment of the hordes of uncivilized Chinese immigrants.

Junks arriving from across the Pacific were simply curiosities used to confirm what most visitors already knew to be true about "Orientals" or "Mongolians" before ever stepping on board. Even though the physical form of the junk was filled with specific cultural features, the interpretation of the artifact was a kind of blank slate, to be filled in by the entrepreneur or shipowner. Nine out of the ten junks selected in this study were not built for public exhibition, but only ended up fulfilling that role through a combination of forces generally termed the agency of display. Junks briefly became ethnographic objects through certain processes, which scholars have labelled detachment and contextualization. Once purchased in China and detached from their original functions, they were displayed on the West Coast in the context of the museum artifact, juxtaposed with modern shipping. The exposition of ethnographic objects, from this point of view, is fundamentally theatrical, neither objective nor scientific.[60] Almost any exotic artifact could be placed on board the vessel and sold to the public.

What is significant about a relatively small wooden craft that brings visitors from afar across the largest ocean on the planet? Significance is in the eyes of the beholder. In America these odd Asian vessels were remarked briefly upon and then scrapped, abandoned, or sold into private hands. The effort to understand these foreign vessels in America never failed, because the effort was never made. These were, in the national sense after all, someone else's history. Chinese junks in America, no matter the long individual histories of Asian immigrants, were not part of the selective American story, nor were they a part of the narrow and selective tale of the evolution of ships.

Junks were available to become anything that the American imagination desired them to be, and this was never what they had once been. Regarding American culture, sometimes it seems that the most immediate use for odd objects detached from their original meanings seems to be for profit and sales. The most recent incarnation for the adaptable junk is a floating dockside boat and bed by the name of *Mei Wenti*, available for $220 per night.

> Boats and the water are the stuff my dreams are made of . . . so imagine my delight upon hearing that I could spend a night on an authentic Chinese junk in Long Beach Harbor. . . . Inside, the junk is comfy and compact. The galley is surprisingly spacious and fully equipped, including refrigerator, microwave, coffee maker, electric rice cooker and a table carefully laid with lacquer rice bowls and chopsticks, wineglasses and fresh flowers.[61]

The real junkmen never had it so good. The authentic junk comes complete with diesel engines and gleaming controls set in polished wood. It is a fantasy out of time and place, and the tourist is drawn to it not to learn about the vessel, but to be able to say she spent a night on board a junk. What really distinguishes this vessel from a replica at Disneyland? The *Mei Wenti* costs more.

Perhaps some of the above statements regarding the whims of American perceptions and the nature of the tourist act involve more jaded and cynical supposition than is healthy, but there remains one reality: almost all the junks have slipped away. These Chinese vessels have not been, and might not be any time soon, protected by any preservation efforts or institute. The *Keying* was broken up for scrap, the *Ning Po* burned and looted, the *Free China* abandoned and then carved up, and the Beihai junk has barely escaped the blackberry bushes of Portland, Oregon. Most efforts to find a permanent home for these artifacts have been unsuccessful.

This chapter began by raising Anthony Pagden's question of whether it is possible to ever really understand elements of foreign culture, and by extension, Chinese junks. Pagden's thesis has been noted by some as being fatalistic, setting forth an insurmountable barrier, a basic "incommensurability" between different human societies. He states "literally nothing that does not come within the range of our own cultural experience, and hence within the range of our own language, can have any meaningful existence for us."[62] This is perhaps a bit strong, but do these junks confirm this barrier? It does indeed seem to be the case, judging from the popular misconceptions surrounding Chinese junks in America, that we have struggled with the difficulty of incommensurability. Nothing meaningful is learned from a series of hollow metaphors about sea monsters. It remains a fact that the only institution in America to take a serious interest in these junks is *Ripley's Believe It or Not!* But we did learn something about these vessels. We learned at least enough to know that we have been confused, and perhaps more.

The only ones who were able to gain any real appreciation for the qualities of the Chinese vessels were those with a penchant for nautical topics, including the crew members themselves—the true junk mariners, and historians, preservationists, and archaeologists. In this sense, maritime specialists moved outside the usual boundaries of their own cultures, and were able to take part in a maritime exchange of culture, a shared heritage across the Pacific. Cultures may not be as monolithic as Pagden sometimes suggests. Mariners, whose experiences, geographical scope, and very language set them apart, are capable of crossing some cultural bridges otherwise inaccessible.

chapter 7

Views from the Vanishing Deck

Conclusions

This study takes the stories and the primary artifacts of transpacific Chinese vessels and attempts a broad description, weaving together a number of different but closely related disciplines. Ships can be directly interpreted as physical records of the past, and these junks allow us to glimpse several things: some of the seafaring history in East Asia, the technological analysis of ship design, the complex nature of the ship as a cultural artifact, the historical setting that shaped each voyage across the Pacific, and an ethnographic analysis of the ways these junks were perceived in the West. They are (or were) the record of the Chinese seafarer's responses to the environment, including the physical, social, cultural, economic, and political environment. These junks and our interpretation of them raise a number of different themes within both Chinese and American history, large-scale patterns in technological change, maritime folklore, modes of armed and unarmed trade, and the politics of perception. The history and culture that these junks have been associated with represent the true cargo they brought across the Pacific.

First of all, it is usually no easy feat to sail anything across the Pacific. The voyages captured here for the most part share the adventure of the crossing, the personalities and the challenges, as well as the investigation into the long-range capabilities of East Asian craft. The historical circumstances surrounding these junks shaped their Pacific voyages. Yet, the cumulative effect of historical influences stacks up against the clear transmission of Chinese junk culture, whether technical or cultural, across the ocean. At the time these junks were procured, sailing operations in China had not vanished, but were undergoing large-scale changes, stimulated by foreign influence, war, and the adaptation to modern technology. The junks were not, then, representative of contemporary transportation, but slowly becoming "foreign" artifacts themselves in their own home. Steamships were dominating the transpacific routes, and commercial sail, while not having been immediately replaced, was in decline. And the social environment in America, with its anti-Chinese agitation and exclusion laws, certainly did not lead to the open reception of these vessels or to any serious interest in their significance.

The junk cultural "exchange" would seem to have been truncated fairly early on. The junks, interpreted as documents, went unread by the majority of the public. The exchange went only as far as the small group of maritime experts who found it worthwhile to write about the junks, but no further. We can speculate about why this happened, or did not happen as the case may be. The timing was wrong; the period of anti-Chinese exclusion met the period of steamship innovation, and neither boded well for the traditional wooden sailing vessels; the practice of history in the past featured easily definable nationalistic topics. Transpacific junks fall into the cracks between nations and between national histories.

The junk experience in America went beyond the specific setting of expositions and entrepreneurs, and involved more basic and deep-rooted aspects of perception and display. From the very beginning of their western encounter, entertainment rather than serious understanding proved to be the common explicit goal. This took the vessels out of the technical world of nautical evolution, away from the context of Chinese maritime history, and placed them into a museum-like setting, isolated from history and open to free-wheeling interpretation. Entrepreneurs spun tales designed to please the tourists. According to modern scholars, something deeply imbedded in our human psyche gives us a tendency to gawk unknowingly at foreign objects, especially when these have been, for one reason or another, predefined for us as exotic curiosities and not legitimate subjects for our attention. Observers were more than able to fill in the gaps in understanding—with multiple theories on junks as sea monsters, as ageless artifacts, as almost anything except what they actually were. For the public, perhaps their apparent backwardness highlighted our own advances? In material culture terms, Mumford's "democratic, man-centered, relatively weak" objects did not fare well compared to vessels designed for a "more authoritarian, system-centered, immensely powerful" setting.[1]

The physical analysis of Chinese junk construction goes beyond these single voyages and accomplishes two things: first, an understanding of the construction patterns of the vessels in a larger context of nautical evolution, both within their own culture, exploring certain changes through time, and in comparison to western vessels; and second, an interpretation of those patterns, reading their "language," opening the door to understanding the significance of these vessels at a variety of levels (for example, regional, northern versus southern junk; functional, merchant versus fishing junk; and global, armed trade patterns versus unarmed trade patterns).

These transpacific junks were representative, each to a greater or lesser degree, of broader established maritime traditions from East Asia. From patrol vessels of the Green Banner army, to Fujian long-distance traders, to a variety of regional fishing vessels, including those of the *shuishangren* boat people, these vessels were the physical record of the skills of the Chinese seafaring population. Chinese junks that fit into the established pattern language of the Chinese shipwright functioned well. The odd few fanciful eastern/western motorized creations, such as Halliburton's *Sea Dragon*, often proved unsatisfactory to the shipwrights of both cultures. These appear to challenge the definitions of traditionally Chinese junks. The basic construction patterns that trace their origins through hundreds of years of evolution suggest a conservative, slow-to-change nautical tradition among shipwrights. Such a tendency might provide a kind of buffer against extreme design changes. This nautical evolution, nonetheless, is capable of being influenced by external events, such as the Ming maritime ban and the subsequent dominance of coastal sailing vessels, or such as the need for power vessels during wartime. These junks show some of these established patterns, and the consequences of radical change. No other "documents" capture this particular aspect of the past in quite the same way.

These junks also record elements of the folklore and popular religion of the coastal population. And though the functional features of junks were so different from European ships, many of the cultural features, though appearing so odd, reveal strikingly similar practices between different maritime cultures. Along these lines of comparative maritime ethnography perhaps lies a kind of common denominator for seafaring cultures, practices closely tied to human responses to the shared hazards of the ocean environment.

The responses by individual seafarers to their environment may be similar, but the responses by empires and nations may be a world apart. Armed maritime trade has become a measure used, almost unconsciously by some, to define nautical development and maritime history on the stage of the world's oceans. These junks represent an older, unarmed tradition, such as was common among the junk trade between China and Southeast Asia, which was in place before the European maritime influence and the rise of the modern ship design. Confusion still exists between the practice of armed expansion and the physical vessels themselves. Some equate the two, concluding that China, not being a practitioner of naval expansion, must have abandoned ocean vessels hundreds of years ago; others note the difference but, having separated the cannon from the ship, conclude nonetheless that all vessels were equal. Both positions seem to suffer from a lack of detailed awareness of the relationships between nautical technology and maritime activity, between the tools and the modes of operation. Activity on the seas is determined, to a certain extent, by the characteristics of the vessels used. Chinese junks do not represent designs borne from conflict, but private vessels dedicated to cargo space.

This type of interpretation raises its own issue pertinent to junks and Chinese maritime history. Rank and the social privileges of command on board European vessels do not seem to find an equivalent system on Chinese junks. European captains of the smallest seagoing vessels represented both symbolic and real expressions of ultimate authority, responsible for all on board their ships. Can this strict command be associated with the burgeoning powers of the state? Is such a structure symptomatic of emerging nation-states, nautical officers symbolic representatives of the king? If so, the social structure of European vessels would be well-suited to state-sponsored armed expansion, while familial relations on Chinese junks reflect private, informal social systems. Long periods of overseas trade in China, thanks to coastal prohibitions and imperial regulations (and lack of state recognition or support for overseas Chinese communities in Southeast Asia), were dominated by private trade, with the exceptions of official tributary missions. Sometimes years of this private trade verged on outright smuggling. Perhaps it is not surprising that the social structure of nautical command in China reflects the influences of village and lineage rather than the state. Maritime-oriented nations that relied on armed trade for existence, such as England and America, produced the aggressive doctrines that provided for domination of the seas. For western nations, these were epitomized by the codified theories of Alfred Thayer Mahan, author of the pivotal *The Influence of Sea Power upon History* in the late nineteenth century. Those which merely tolerated commercial activity yet ultimately restricted aggressive maritime expansion, such as China, faced nautical defeat at the hands of the British and French and westernizing Japanese navies.

The material culture or pattern language approach that emphasizes "reading history into the object" can help to elicit a broader understanding of Chinese junks. The pattern language, as applied by Steven Lubar, originally highlighted technology and the ties between machines and the formation of industrial culture. Here it has been modified to fit a pre–industrial complex cultural artifact. The junk is a cultural and technological text, as meaningful to the social scientist as to the nautical architect. Emphasizing the pattern language approach serves to highlight the intentional design process of the craftsmen involved, the patterns and language of a pre-industrial population. Ships do not just "happen," styles of vessels do not simply blossom accidentally from the environment—they are the result of human choices made for specific reasons over an extended period of time. Admittedly, applying an untried modification of a particular approach to a topic with difficult and scarce sources to begin with leads to some innovation along the way— a diverse and "democratic" list of references at the very least! But hopefully the result is a deeper understanding of junks and the possibilities for historic craft in general.

Unfortunately, as far as heritage preservation goes, this type of understanding was not a factor at the time the strange Chinese craft arrived at their destinations in America. Junks did not manage to find any permanent destination overseas, any serious presence; the transpacific junks were a vanishing feature of someone else's maritime past. There was a momentary type of cultural exchange across the Pacific Ocean, but one that faced numerous obstacles, one in which meanings shifted and transmission was unclear. Melvin Kranzberg, founder of The Society for the History of Technology, points to our own changing perceptions of technology as one of the major causes for this confusion. Kranzberg states that for most of our past there has been little separation between art and technology. Archaeological artifacts bear this out, providing both artists and technologists material for study. Early crafts were an expression of both artistic and technical ability. The term *technology* as separate from artistic expression only became widespread in the nineteenth century.[2] Chinese junks were bearers of a pre-industrial pattern language. They not only faced the complications of perception and display mentioned above, but they were cultural and even artistic transport machines from an early age, entering an industrial society that was moving toward no longer supporting the perspectives of culture and technology within a single object. We value technology and progress, sometimes at the expense of understanding our own historical origins.

Clearly, junks are being used blatantly in this study as launching points, as stepping stones, opening the door to a variety of historical topics, such as trade and technology, maritime traditions and social structure, religion and politics, etc. The junk is a microcosm, and by looking into the details, one can find the linkages to the larger setting. Taking an analogy in time, it is possible to go forward from the junk's construction and investigate the manner in which they were used and perceived. Moving backward from their construction, one can find the precedents of their shape, the design traditions and social and economic influences, and something of the plans in the thoughts of the shipwrights. The history contained within the study of material culture should not be a subject apart from, but one merged with, the components of the rest of the maritime story, our common maritime heritage. In this case, inclusion is an absolute necessity, for the few vessels left are our last tangible links to a very broad maritime past.

Regarding these junks, we, the foreign observers, have a history of allowing our cultural perceptions of the Asian "Other," along with the justified celebration of our own technological progress, to cloud our vision, thus causing us to overlook the details and significance of this rare material record. Those specialists who based their findings on pragmatic observations and archaeological projects often ended up with quite a different view than the general public. Thanks to the recent work by the historians, anthropologists, sociologists, and archaeologists, this situation is now beginning to change.

Still, as post-industrial folk, we have a tendency to see the junk, and boats in general, purely as technology, purely as a machine, and we usually focus only on that aspect, leaving much of the less tangible culture and history in the ship's wake. It is the potential to combine both of these views, the technical object and historical craft, in a single artifact that highlights the special nature of traditional sailing vessels, in this case the Chinese sailing junk. It is a potential revealed through the very few remaining junks themselves, through reflections of others in historical photographs and documents, and, if you care to get wet, in the potential for underwater discoveries of historical wreckage on the ocean floor.

Notes

Chapter 1. Junks, Not Just Floating Wood

1. Kirshenblatt-Gimblett, *Destination Culture*, 23.
2. Paul Chow, interview by the author, August 7, 2000.
3. Wright, *Hart and the Chinese Customs*, 400.
4. Worcester, *Junks and Sampans*, back leaf.
5. Needham, *A History of Science and Civilization in China,* vol. IV, part 3, 380.
6. Worcester, *Sail and Sweep*, xiv.

Chapter 2. The Journeys Across the Pacific

1. See Lewis and Wigen, "A Maritime Response to the Crisis in Area Studies," 167, for an overview of the Pacific basin in contemporary area studies.
2. See Tate, *Transpacific Steam*, 25. Even after the advent of steam power, 35 degrees north provided the smoothest Pacific passage in both directions. Junks and other sailing vessels usually called at Yokohama prior to setting out for the West Coast rather than leaving directly from Chinese ports.
3. Joseph Needham states that the current was then called *Wei Lu.* See Knöbl, *Tai Ki,* 46.
4. See Kirch, *On the Road of the Winds,* for a recent summation of this migration.
5. Gang, *Chinese Maritime Activities,* 144. Such contrast serves to make Admiral Zheng He's early Ming dynasty voyages even more exceptional.
6. Biel, *Down with the Old Canoe,* 7.
7. "Heavy Tax for the *Whang Ho,*" *San Francisco Chronicle,* December 8, 1906, 15.
8. "Curious Vessel Bought of Viceroy of Nankin Comes into this Port," *San Francisco Chronicle,* December 9, 1906, 51. Chatterton, in *Sailing Ships and Their Story,*

313, adds, "This craft, which was over a hundred years old . . . was previously a pirate ship."

9. *China: Catalogue of the Collection of Chinese Exhibits at the Louisiana Purchase Exposition, St. Louis 1904*, 300. Mexican and Spanish dollars have a long history of common currency in the Pacific.

10. "Junk's Long Trip," *Victoria Daily Times*, January 4, 1908, 8. This puts the junk sailing north along California's coast in the wintertime, into the waves, wind, and current along a treacherous foggy coast—a sure testament to the soundness of the vessel and the skill of the crew.

11. "The *Whang Ho*'s Captain Wanted," *San Francisco Chronicle*, June 7, 1908, 52; and Borden, *Sea Quest*, 225.

12. "The *Whang Ho*'s Captain Wanted," *San Francisco Chronicle*, June 7, 1908, 52.

13. Borden, *Sea Quest*, 226.

14. Hager and Hager, "The *Ning Po*," 193. Numerous other articles have expanded on the shaky foundation of facts.

15. Phillips, "A Peaceful Pirate," 327–31. Wooden vessels of any design more than one hundred years old are extremely rare, and much of the comment on the *Ning Po* has focused on the nature of the large junk's construction, and the hardwoods employed by the Chinese shipwrights.

16. Raymenton, "The Venerable *Ning Po*," 52.

17. Hampton, "Saga of the *Ning Po*," 23.

18. Phillips, "A Peaceful Pirate," 327–28. Biographies of Chinese Gordon fail to record this minor incident.

19. Hoyle, "*Ning Po* in Avalon Bay," 1. Mr. Hoyle spent years as guide and caretaker on board the *Ning Po*. The British warship is often cited erroneously as the H.M.S. *Calliope*.

20. Hager and Hager, "The *Ning Po*," 195.

21. "Ancient War Junk Spoken by Liner," *San Francisco Chronicle*, February 12, 1913, 10.

22. Kennedy, "The Infamous *Ning Po*," 266. Several sources record that the junk traveled north as far as Washington and Oregon, but this is not corroborated by any documents at those ports.

23. Hager and Hager, "The *Ning Po*," 198.

24. Brown, "*Ningpo*," 22. The Meteor Company ran the fleet of glass-bottom boats at Catalina.

25. Hager and Hager, "The *Ning Po*," 202.

26. Brown, "*Ningpo*," 22.

27. Ibid., 274. Movies filmed at Catalina in the 1920s and 1930s include *King of Kings, Old Ironsides, Treasure Island, Hurricane, Sadie Thompson,* and *Mutiny on the Bounty.*

28. Lawson, "Catalina's Pirate Ship," 27. Such pilfering would today be considered a violation of cultural resource preservation laws.

29. Borden, *Sea Quest,* 226. Though only a few years since the *Ning Po* and the *Whang Ho* had made it to the West Coast, the *Amoy* was mistakenly reported as the first Chinese vessel to cross the Pacific, as she was also mistakenly reported later to be the first Chinese vessel on the East Coast.

30. "Rivals Viking Voyages of Old," *Daily Colonist,* September 20, 1922, 12. It is not clear exactly what Captain Waard did in show business.

31. Ibid.

32. "Romantic Craft Ends Thrilling Trip from China," *Victoria Daily Times,* September 19, 1922, 15.

33. Ibid.

34. "Rivals Viking Voyages of Old," *Daily Colonist,* September 20, 1922, 12.

35. Ibid.

36. Susan Buss, Vancouver Maritime Museum Librarian, personal communication to the author, October 23, 2005.

37. "Crowds Throng to See Chinese Junk," *Daily Colonist,* September 21, 1922, 12.

38. "Rivals Viking Voyages of Old," *Daily Colonist,* September 20, 1922, 12.

39. "Chinese Junk Sails for Nanaimo; Final Destination New York," *Daily Colonist,* September 29, 1922, 12.

40. Borden, *Sea Quest,* 226; "Chinese Junk *Amoy* Now at Los Angeles," *Daily Colonist,* May 5, 1923, 19. Nilson self-published the book *The Story of the Amoy* in 1924.

41. "Buys Chinese Junk *Amoy* for Pleasure Yacht," *Daily Colonist,* August 31, 1924, 1.

42. "Junk *Amoy* Will Tour the Globe," *Daily Colonist,* May 23, 1926, 17.

43. "Junk *Amoy* Held 'On Suspicion,'" *Daily Colonist,* August 11, 1926, 15.

44. Personal communication with the author, November 16, 2004. Nilson's cousin reportedly has located the wreck of the *Amoy* in the Pamlico Sound, but no further details are currently available.

45. De Bisschop, *Tahiti Nui.*

46. Borden, *Sea Quest,* 229–30. Borden includes a large passage selected from De Bisschop's journal. Haddon and Hornell's *Canoes of Oceania* offers the most concise summary of Polynesian migration theories popular among the academic community in the early decades of the twentieth century.

47. An ill omen. The remains of this wreck were visible above the water until the 1990s, and the shipwreck site is still marked on modern charts.

48. "Adventurous Quartet Reaches Port After 85 Days Under Sail," *Daily Sun Long Beach,* October 4, 1938, 1.

49. Petersen, "We Crossed the Pacific in a 36-foot Junk!" Misc. document, J. Porter Shaw Library, San Francisco Maritime National Historic Park.

50. Japanese sailing junks had, for centuries, been carried all the way across the Pacific by this very current. See Brooks, "Report of Japanese Vessels Wrecked in the North Pacific Ocean."

51. The teredo worm, *Teredo navalis,* more commonly known as the shipworm, is a bivalve mollusk of the family Teredinidae, notorious for damaging wooden ships by boring long cylindrical holes in keels and hull planks.

52. Borden, *Sea Quest,* 238.

53. Halliburton, *Richard Halliburton,* 381.

54. Root, *Halliburton,* 19.

55. Ibid., 22. The corporation hoped for proceeds from ticket sales, souvenirs, radio spots, stamps, merchandise, marketing via letters to school children, and movies.

56. Halliburton, *Richard Halliburton,* 430.

57. Ibid., 433.

58. Root, *Halliburton,* 268.

59. Ibid., 274.

60. Borden, *Sea Quest,* 233.

61. "Down to the Sea in Junks," Reno Chen's collection.

62. "Planes and Yachts Greet Ripley Today as City's Sirens Herald Welcome," *Times Union,* August 8, 1947, 1.

63. Frank Pierce Young, personal communication with the author, October 3, 2000.

64. Philip Budlong, Mystic Seaport Museum, personal communication with the author, October 6, 2000.

65. Norman Brouwer, personal communication with the author, October 3, 2000.

66. Fairchild, *Garden Isles of the Great East,* 14–15.

67. Borden, *Sea Quest,* 238. An intentional allusion to the earlier vessel?

68. Degener, "The Last Cruise of the *Cheng Ho,*" 197.

69. Fairchild, *Garden Isles of the Great East,* 15. Old Admiral Zheng He never had it so good.

70. Ibid., 71.

71. Ibid., 226.

72. Borden, *Sea Quest,* 239.

73. Degener, "The Last Cruise of the *Cheng Ho,*" 197.

74. Ibid., 198.

75. Borden, *Sea Quest,* 239.

76. Tomasetti, "Final Report: A Survey of a Wrecked Vessel at Kona Coast State Park," 2.

77. Wendy Coble (Naval Historical Center), in communication with the author, October 12, 2000.

78. Ibid.

79. Borden, *Sea Quest,* 240.

80. Much of the following information comes from a series of interviews conducted by the author with crew members in California in August 2000.

81. Calvin Mehlert, former U.S. vice-consul of Taiwan and crewman of junk *Free China*, communication to the author, Palo Alto, Calif., August 14, 2000.

82. Worcester, citing the American-sponsored *Shanghai Evening Post*, in *Sail and Sweep*, 85.

83. Paul Chow, Taiwanese fisherman and navigator of the junk *Free China*, communication to the author, Los Angeles, August 7, 2000.

84. One condition of the support was that the junk be named after "Keelung," or *Free China*, for the propaganda value. Paul Chow readily agreed to this, scrapping his plan of naming her *Dragon Seed*, a reference to the novel *The Good Earth*; Chow, *The Junk Story*, unpublished manuscript, Los Angeles, 2000, 132.

85. Ibid., 66. Vessel names like this in China sometimes reflect characters carved onto the vessel for luck, rather than individual labels or names. Some hold that before western-style registration, Chinese junks did not have names; see Hommel, *China at Work*, 337.

86. Chow, *The Junk Story*, 54.

87. One source records the approximate cost of Fuzhou coastal trading junks, those 90 feet long, as 1,000 Mexican dollars in 1904; *China: Catalogue of the Collection of Chinese Exhibits*, 255–56.

88. Ibid., 101. One wonders whether they were aware of the junks that had already successfully crossed.

89. Ibid., 125. Benny Hsu's great-grandfather had owned over three hundred fishing junks in Swamei near Swatow. That seems to be the closest sailing connection any of the crew could produce.

90. Ibid., 162.

91. Ibid., 193. Tillers were broken due to strain caused by failure to lower the mainsail, rather than any design flaw; Chow interview, August 7, 2000.

92. There may be some question as to just how seriously Paul Chow, Reno Chen, and the rest of the crew really were in attending the race, compared to how seriously they were interested in getting visas to America.

93. Ch'ung and Bell, "The Four Seas Are One Family," 32.

94. Bond, "Dragon Eyes for Freedom," 24.

95. Kevin Wallace, "Chinese Junk Finally Docks in San Francisco," *San Francisco Chronicle*, August 9, 1955, 1. T. K. Chang alludes to a much bigger commercial junk arriving in the Bay Area in the 1850s (Lyman's citation in 1849?), but no known records explain this.

96. "Taipei Hails *Free China* Daring Crossing; Nation Cheers," *China News*, August 10, 1955.

97. Chow interview, August 7, 2000.

98. Correspondence between legal counsel Mark S. Hamilton of the San Francisco Maritime Museum Association and Mr. Paul Chow, navigator of junk *Free China*, October 26, 1960. The junk became the Six Companies' "white elephant."

99. "China Crew's 2-Mast Junk Given to S.F.," *San Francisco Examiner*, July 22, 1956, 14.

100. Ibid.

101. "Chinese Junk at Oyster Point," *The Post,* vol. 20, no. 23, 1966.

102. Al Dring, Harry Dring's son, personal interview with the author, April 10, 1996. Harry Dring's plan, never realized, was to sail the *Free China* to Tasmania.

103. Mehlert interview, August 14, 2000.

104. Guy Lasalle Jr., interview with Beihai junk donor by the author, August 25, 2000, Portland, Ore. Mr. Lasalle now manages a Nike factory in Guangzhou. Lasalle Jr.'s interest in junks predates the museum commission, though. Guy Lasalle Sr. served in the merchant marine in China.

105. Ibid.

106. Bridgeford, "Acquiring a Junk."

107. Worcester, *Classification,* 170.

Chapter 3. Reading the Junks Themselves

1. Kemp, *The Oxford Companion to Ships and the Sea,* 437.

2. Ibid.

3. See Mack and Connell, *Naval Ceremonies, Customs, and Traditions*; Brown and Daniel, *Sea-Lingo: Notes on the Language of Mariners and Some Suggestions for Its Proper Use*; Ozaki, *Japanese-English Dictionary of Sea Terms*; and *Yinghan hanghai cidian* (English-Chinese Maritime Dictionary).

4. Ronan, *The Shorter Science and Civilization in China,* 75.

5. Ibid., 76.

6. Zhou Shide, "Shipbuilding," 481.

7. Lubar, "Machine Politics," 209.

8. Alexander et al., *A Pattern Language,* introduction.

9. Ibid.

10. McGrail, *Boats of the World,* 374.

11. Greenhill and Morrison, *The Archaeology of Boats and Ships,* 78; Hornell, *Water Transport,* 90; Ronan, *The Shorter Science and Civilization in China,* 69.

12. Possible exceptions to the raft origins of the junk are noted in Johnstone, *The Sea-Craft of Prehistory,* 186–87.

13. Hornell, *Water Transport,* 88.

14. Ronan, *The Shorter Science and Civilization in China,* 65.

15. McGrail, *Boats of the World,* 374.

16. Ronan, *The Shorter Science and Civilization in China,* 85–86.

17. Green, "The Ship from Quanzhou, Fujian Province, People's Republic of China," 296.

18. Gang, *Chinese Maritime Activities,* 24.

19. McGrail, *Boats of the World,* 367.

20. Ibid., 364, 369, 371.

21. Gould and Foster, *Junks,* 10.

22. McGrail, *Boats of the World,* 364.

23. Gould and Foster, *Junks,* 18.

24. Ibid., 8.

25. Delgado, "Relics of the Kamikaze," 37.

26. Randall Sasaki, Ph.D. candidate, Texas A&M, personal communication to the author, October 23, 2005. Further details of the project can be found at http://nautarch.tamu.edu/shiplab/randall/Randall%20Index%20002.htm.

27. McGrail, *Boats of the World*, 377. McGrail interprets Marco Polo's record as indicating, at most, Chinese vessels of 130 feet in length. The archaeological evidence supports vessels at least this length.

28. Ibid., 378.

29. Barker, "The Size of the 'Treasure Ships' and Other Chinese Vessels," 273–75. Barker estimates vessel length at over two hundred feet. There are, however, other nontechnical reasons to question the Ming dynastic records on the subject of *baochuan* length. Do we know the real unit of measurement for Song period China? Did the scribes record the length in the historic annals correctly? About 230 feet might be the current maximum accepted length for Chinese junks.

30. Green, "The Ship from Quanzhou," 282.

31. Li, "Archaeological Evidence for the Use of 'chu-nam' on the 13th Century Quanzhou Ship, Fujian Province, China," 277–83; Ronan, *The Shorter Science and Civilization in China*, 115.

32. Du Halde, *The General History of China*, 284–85.

33. Gould and Foster, *Junks*, 19.

34. Needham, *Science and Civilization*, 664.

35. Muir, *One Old Junk Is Everyone's Treasure*, 104.

36. Ronan, *The Shorter Science and Civilization in China*, 66.

37. Green, "Eastern Shipbuilding Traditions," 1–6; Green, "The Song Dynasty Shipwreck at Quanzhou, Fujian Province, People's Republic of China," 253–61; Green, "The Shinan Excavation, Korea," 293–301.

38. Zhang, *Zhongguo Gudai de Zaochuan he Hanghai*, 77.

39. Chen, *Zhongguo Fanchuan yu Haiwai Maoyi*, 148.

40. McGrail, *Boats of the World*, 375.

41. Ibid., 371.

42. Kemp, *The Oxford Companion to Ships and the Sea*, 443.

43. Gang, *Chinese Maritime Activities*, 27–28.

44. Ibid., 28–29; also Zhou, "Shipbuilding," 480–82.

45. Worcester, *Sail and Sweep*, 16.

46. Gould and Foster, *Junks*, 22–23.

47. Gang, *Chinese Maritime Activities*, 27–28.

48. Flecker, "The Bakau Wreck," 229.

49. Gang, *Maritime Sector*, 12.

50. Ibid.

51. Woodman, *The History of the Ship*, 51; Needham, *Science and Civilization*, 594. See also London, *Tales of the Fish Patrol*.

52. McGrail, *Boats of the World*, 375.

53. Zhang, *Zhongguo Gudai de Zaochuan he Hanghai,* 52.

54. Worcester, *Sail and Sweep,* 24.

55. Hornell, *Water Transport,* 88.

56. Needham, *Science and Civilization,* 632–33.

57. Johnstone, *Sea-Craft of Prehistory,* 190–91.

58. Worcester, *Sail and Sweep,* 22.

59. McGrail, *Boats of the World,* 374.

60. Mott, *The Development of the Rudder.* Mott examines exclusively the Mediterranean World between the Roman period and the Age of Discovery.

61. Johnstone, *Sea-Craft of Prehistory,* 191. See also Christides, "The Transmission of Chinese Maritime Technology by the Arabs to Europe."

62. Mumford, "Authoritarian and Democratic Technics," 2.

63. Reid, "The Unthreatening Alternative," 14.

64. Pomeranz, *The Great Divergence,* 112.

65. Ibid., 287.

66. Cipolla, *Guns, Sails, and Empires,* 140.

67. Reid, "The Unthreatening Alternative," 13. The EIC, or British East India Company, capacity before 1833 was less than thirty thousand tons.

68. Diamond, *Guns, Germs, and Steel,* 258.

69. Worcester, *Junks and Sampans,* 342.

70. Worcester, *Sail and Sweep,* 27.

71. Worcester, "The Chinese War Junk," 22–24.

72. Rawlinson, *China's Struggle for Naval Development,* 3.

73. *China: Catalogue of the Collection of Chinese Exhibits at the Louisiana Purchase Exposition, St. Louis 1904,* 300.

74. Worcester, *Junks and Sampans,* 342.

75. Rawlinson, *China's Struggle for Naval Development,* 6.

76. Ibid., 344.

77. Worcester, "The Chinese War Junk," 24.

78. Ibid.

79. Gardiner, ed., *The Line of Battle,* 151.

80. Teng and Fairbank, *China's Response to the West,* 109. The rear-opening rifles here refer to breach-loading cannon.

81. Cardwell, "Pirate Fighters of the South China Sea."

82. Paul Chow, personal communication with the author, November 13, 2000. This is in contrast to the western tradition of placing the "head" for the crew at the bow of the sailing vessel (hence the term *head* for marine toilet). Western ships also had heads at the stern, but typically for officers only.

83. Worcester, *Junks and Sampans,* 187.

84. Johnson, *Shaky Ships,* 82.

85. Gang, *Maritime Sector,* 44.

86. Maze, *The Maze Collection.*

87. Gould and Foster, *Junks,* 34.

88. Donnelly, "Foochow Pole Junks," 226.

89. Pomeranz, *The Great Divergence*, 171.

90. Worcester, *Junks and Sampans*, 191.

91. Crawfurd, *Journal of an Embassy*.

92. Pomeranz, *The Great Divergence*, 226.

93. Worcester, *Junks and Sampans*, 190.

94. Donnelly, "Foochow Pole Junks," 227. The same Chinese-style windlass can be seen on the *guangchuan*-style war junk, typified by the *Whang Ho*.

95. Worcester, *Sail and Sweep*, 43.

96. Donnelly, "Foochow Pole Junks," 227.

97. Johnson, *Shaky Ships*, 28.

98. Gang, *Maritime Sector*, 7; Zhou, "Shipbuilding," 479.

99. Worcester, "The Amoy Fishing Boat," 304.

100. Worcester, *Classification*, 95.

101. McGrail, *Boats of the World*, 364.

102. Du Halde, *The General History of China*, 283.

103. Maze, *The Maze Collection*, 1938.

104. McGrail, *Boats of the World*, 375.

105. The terminology here comes from a mid-nineteenth-century shipbuilding document (chapter 5).

106. Worcester, "The Amoy Fishing Boat," 306.

107. Jarrett, "The Chinese Junk," 28.

108. Captain Waard of the junk *Amoy*, upon his arrival in British Columbia, in "Rivals Viking Voyages of Old," *Daily Colonist*, September 20, 1922, 12.

109. Du Halde, *General History of China*, 279. This praise is of dubious origin. No doubt many a Chinese vessel, like all others, eventually leaked like a sieve.

110. Borden, *Sea Quest*, 229.

111. Petersen, "We Crossed the Pacific in a 36-foot Junk!" Misc. document, J. Porter Shaw Library, San Francisco Maritime National Historic Park.

112. Ibid.

113. Worcester, *Sail and Sweep*, 17.

114. Worcester, *Classification*, 50.

115. Ibid., 59.

116. Worcester, *Sail and Sweep*, 17.

117. Ibid., 18.

118. Gould and Foster, *Junks*, 63–64.

119. Borden, *Sea Quest*, 233.

120. Worcester, *Classification*, 109.

121. Ibid.

122. Borden, *Sea Quest*, 238.

123. Worcester, *Junks and Sampans*, 312.

124. Worcester, *Classification*, 69.

125. Chow, *The Junk Story*, 66.

126. Chow interview, August 7, 2000.

127. Ibid.; Dring interview, April 10, 1996.

128. Worcester, *Junks and Sampans,* 162.

129. Waters, "Chinese Junks: The Hangchow Bay Trader and Fisher," 29.

130. Worcester, *Junks and Sampans,* 164.

131. Worcester, *Classification,* 170.

132. Needham, *Science and Civilization,* 620. Ancient Formosan sailing rafts featured daggerboards.

133. Soan Thao Hon-Hop Boi, *Hai Thuyen Thanh Thu . . . Junk Blue Book.*

134. See White, *The Sea Gypsies of Malaya,* 261.

135. Anderson, *The Selungs of the Mergui Archipelago,* 2.

136. Ivanoff, *The Moken Boat,* 95, 132.

137. Gang, *Maritime Sector,* 52.

138. See Ho Ke-en, "The Tanka or Boat People of South China," in *Symposium of Historical Archaeological and Linguistic Studies on Southern China, South-East Asia and the Hong Kong Region,* 120–24.

139. Antony, *Like Froth Floating on the Sea,* 9–10.

140. Tsai, *Hong Kong in Chinese History,* 45.

141. Sather, *The Bajau Laut,* 327.

142. Danton, *Culture Contacts of the United States and China,* 41.

143. Lasalle Jr. interview, August 25, 2000.

144. Ta Chen, *Chinese Migrations, with Special Reference to Labor Conditions,* 13; Crawfurd, *Journal of an Embassy,* 49.

145. van Leur, *Indonesian Trade and Society,* 126.

146. Crawfurd, *Journal of an Embassy,* 415.

147. Wiens, "Riverine and Coastal Junks in China's Commerce," 257.

148. Yoneo Ishii, ed., *The Junk Trade from Southeast Asia,* 2–3.

149. Needham, *Science and Civilization,* 405. Needham refers to this single image as one of the best pictures of a Chinese ship in the Chinese style to be found.

150. Frank, *Reorient,* 96.

151. Reid, "The Unthreatening Alternative," 13; and Gang, "What Did Seas and Oceans Mean to the Chinese in the Past Millennia?"

152. Cushman, *Fields from the Sea,* 78.

153. McPherson, "China's Trade with the Indian Ocean to the 19th Century," 57.

154. Gang, *Maritime Sector,* 9–10. Zhou Shide states that Zheng He's vessels, at over 450 feet in length, were the largest of the *shachuan.* He goes on to say, however, that most of the vessels in the Ming naval fleet were *fuchuan.* The exact distinctions between the two remain blurred; Zhou, "Shipbuilding," 480–81.

155. Gang, *Chinese Maritime Activities,* 28.

156. McGrail, *Boats of the World,* 374.

157. Flecker, "The Bakau Wreck," 224.

158. Schlegel, "On the Invention and Use of Firearms and Gunpowder in China, Prior to the Arrival of the Europeans," 9.

159. Fu, ed., *A Documentary Chronicle of Sino-Western Relations (1644–1820)*, 317, citing the Qianlong emperor, in a decree to Ministers of the Grand Council, May 25, 1721.

160. Blusse, *Strange Company*, 106, drawing from data in the *Xiamen Zhi II*, 178.

161. King and Hattendorf, eds., *Every Man Will Do His Duty*, 322, quoting sailor George Little.

162. Hornell, *Water Transport*, 86.

163. Murray, "The Kwangtung Water World."

164. Ronan, *The Shorter Science and Civilization in China*, 210, 272.

165. Diamond, *Guns, Germs, and Steel*, 258.

Chapter 4. The Living Culture of Chinese Vessels

1. Lubar, citing Lewis Mumford, in "Machine Politics," 205.

2. Ivanoff, *The Moken Boat*, 110, 125.

3. Cowburn, *The Warship in History*, 107.

4. Beck, *Folklore and the Sea*, xiii.

5. McGhee, "Towards a Postcolonial Nautical Archaeology," http://www.shef.ac.uk/assem/3/3mcghee.htm.

6. Gould, citing Michael Schiffer, *Archaeology and the Social History of Ships*, 9.

7. Ivanoff, *The Moken Boat*, quoting Nooteboom, 1.

8. Aubert and Arner, "On the Social Structure of the Ship," 200, 208.

9. Westerdahl, "The Maritime Cultural Landscape," 5.

10. Ebrey and Gregory, eds., *Religion and Society in T'ang and Sung China*, 12.

11. Beck citing Cooper, in *Folklore and the Sea*, 279.

12. Worcester, *Junks and Sampans*, 124.

13. Gray, *China*, 260–61.

14. For more information on the cult of Mazu, see Watson, "Standardizing the Gods."

15. Ibid., 297.

16. Duyvendak, "The True Dates of the Chinese Maritime Expeditions," 345. This was an interesting official statement for Zheng He, considering the fact that he was a Muslim (though many eunuchs were Buddhists).

17. Interview of Chinese merchant in Sausalito, California, by the author, April 22, 1995.

18. Eberhard, *A Dictionary of Chinese Symbols*, 183.

19. *China: Catalogue of the Collection of Chinese Exhibits at the Louisiana Purchase Exposition, St. Louis 1904*, 281.

20. Werner, *A Dictionary of Chinese Mythology*, 226.

21. Eberhard, *A Dictionary of Chinese Symbols*, 135.

22. Bottignolo, *Celebrations with the Sun: An Overview of Religious Phenomena among the Badjaos*, 69.

23. Waters, "Chinese Junks: The Antung Trader," 52.

24. Chow interview, March 27, 2001.

25. Beck, *Folklore and the Sea,* 5.

26. Gutzlaff, *Journal of Three Voyages,* 97.

27. Saso, correspondence between Beijing Center and Ching Lim of Catalina Island Museum, July 4, 1997.

28. Worcester, *Junks and Sampans,* 118.

29. Beck, *Folklore of the Sea,* 14.

30. Gray, *China,* 257.

31. Hommel, *China at Work,* 337.

32. Blusse, citing the *Xiamen Zhi V,* in *Strange Company,* 106.

33. Worcester, *Sail and Sweep,* 25.

34. Kani, *A General Survey,* 74–75.

35. Beck, *Folklore of the Sea,* 259.

36. Hornell, *Water Transport,* 285.

37. Beck, *Folklore of the Sea,* 15.

38. Ibid., 288.

39. Donnelly, "The Oculus in Chinese Craft," 339.

40. "The Song Dynasty Shipwreck Excavated at Quanzhou Harbor," *Wen Wu.*

41. Green, "The Song Dynasty Shipwreck," 254.

42. Eberhard, *A Dictionary of Chinese Symbols,* 72, 188.

43. Moll and Laughton, "The Navy of the Province of Fukien," 376.

44. Baker, *Folklore of the Sea,* 36.

45. Eberhard, *A Dictionary of Chinese Symbols,* 315.

46. Worcester, *Junks and Sampans,* 191.

47. Eberhard, *A Dictionary of Chinese Symbols,* 280.

48. Jackie Wesolosky, Honolulu Academy of Arts, personal communication with the author, April 3, 2001.

49. Eberhard, *A Dictionary of Chinese Symbols,* 277.

50. Biedermann, *Dictionary of Symbolism,* 186; Morgan, *Chinese Symbols and Superstitions,* 77.

51. Eberhard, *A Dictionary of Chinese Symbols,* 152.

52. Biedermann, *Dictionary of Symbolism,* 185–86.

53. Chen, *Zhongguo Fanchuan yu Haiwai Maoyi,* 144

54. Patrick Smith, marine science student at the University of California, Berkeley, in communication with the author, 1997.

55. Muir, "One Old Junk Is Everyone's Treasure," 112.

56. Ivanoff, *The Moken Boat,* 19.

57. Anderson, "The Happy Heavenly Bureaucracy," 15.

58. Baker, *Folklore of the Sea,* 74.

59. Werner, *A Dictionary of Chinese Mythology,* 192.

60. Beck, *Folklore of the Sea,* 287.

61. Kani, *A General Survey,* 77.

62. Eberhard, *A Dictionary of Chinese Symbols,* 42.

63. Fortune, *A Residence Among the Chinese,* 405–6.

64. Scarth, *Twelve Years in China*, 118.

65. Ivanoff, *The Moken Boat*, 17.

66. Kani, *A General Survey*, 73.

67. Beck, *Folklore of the Sea*, 101.

68. Ibid., 58.

69. Moll and Laughton, "The Navy of the Province of Fukien," provides a translation of this document.

70. Chen, *Zhongguo Fanchuan yu Haiwai Maoyi*, 415.

Chapter 5. Finding Pacific Junks in History

1. Clark, "The Politics of Trade and the Establishment of the Quanzhou Trade Superintendency"; Chan, "The Smuggling Trade Between China and Southeast Asia during the Ming Dynasty."

2. Brindley, "The '*Keying*,'" 311.

3. Altick, *The Shows of London*, 294.

4. Woodside, "Early Ming Expansionism," 49.

5. Antony, citing He Changling in 1827, in *Like Froth Floating on the Sea*, 139.

6. Grover, *American Merchant Ships on the Yangtze*, xv.

7. Halliburton, *Richard Halliburton*, 402–3.

8. Root, *Halliburton*, 20.

9. Wiens, "Riverine and Coastal Junks in China's Commerce," 262–63.

10. Worcester, *Classification*, xiii. This, in Worcester's view, was the beginning of the end. "Due to their independence of tides and favourable winds, this type of vessel may be expected in future to be seen in increasing numbers on the coasts and rivers of China."

11. Ibid.

12. Watson, trans., *Transport in Transition*, iii.

13. Koizumi, "The Operation of Chinese Junks," 7; Nakamura, "Shipping Brokers in North China," 26.

14. Hayashi, "The Shipping Brokers and Transport Companies of Soochow," 35.

15. Kosaka and Nakamura, "Junk Ownership and Operation in North China," 55.

16. Also see Leung, "Regional Rivalry in Mid-Nineteenth-Century Shanghai."

17. Gutzlaff, *Journal of Three Voyages*, 138.

18. Cushman, *Fields from the Sea*, 99–100.

19. Ibid., 101.

20. Ibid., 100.

21. Gutzlaff, *Journal of Three Voyages*, 96.

22. Ibid., 95.

23. Koizumi, "The Operation of Chinese Junks," 13.

24. Teshima and Arai, "Junk Crews in Soochow," 68.

25. Hayashi, "The Shipping Brokers and Transport Companies of Soochow," 35.

26. Liu citing Cunningham, in *Anglo-American Steamship Rivalry in China*, 67.

27. Wiens, "Riverine and Coastal Junks in China's Commerce," 249.

28. Liu citing Cunningham, in *Anglo-American Steamship Rivalry,* 68.

29. Wright, ed., *Twentieth Century Impressions of Hong Kong, Shanghai, and Other Treaty Ports of China,* 192.

30. Ibid., 194.

31. Ibid., 200.

32. Ibid., 280.

33. Koizumi, "The Operation of Chinese Junks," iv.

34. Schwendinger, "Chinese Sailors, America's Invisible Merchant Marine"; Schwendinger, *Ocean of Bitter Dreams.*

35. Ballendorf, "The Chinese as Pacific Explorers," 78.

36. Rogers, *Destiny's Landfall,* 49.

37. Ballendorf, "The Chinese as Pacific Explorers," 79.

38. Langdon, "Castaways," 71.

39. Lessa, "Chinese Trigrams in Micronesia," 356.

40. Handy, "Polynesian Religion," 325.

41. Wu, *The Chinese in Papua New Guinea,* 21. A Chinese shipbuilding company in the 1930s would carry on in Ah Tam's wake, providing vessels for the New Guinea coastal trades.

42. Ibid., 52.

43. Nick Burningham, Duyfken 1606 Replica Foundation, personal communication with the author, July 14, 1998.

44. Knöbl, *Tai Ki,* 31.

45. Edwards, "Sailing Rafts of Sechura," 368; Severin, *The China Voyage.*

46. Severin, *The China Voyage,* 313.

47. Frost, "The Palos Verdes Chinese Anchor Mystery," 27.

48. Pierson and Moriarty, "New Evidence of Asiatic Shipwrecks Off the California Coast."

49. Steiner, *Fusang, the Chinese Who Built America,* 81.

50. Schurz, *The Manila Galleon,* 195.

51. Steiner, *Fusang, the Chinese Who Built America,* 81–82. It is not clear how Steiner knows what Ming dynasty vessels looked like.

52. Jinky Smalley of East Carolina University's Maritime Studies Program has worked on a thesis investigating Asian shipbuilding influences in Manila galleons.

53. Camp, citing Lyman, in *San Francisco,* 259.

54. Schurz, *The Manila Galleon,* 301.

55. Lydon, *Chinese Gold.*

56. Sandy Lydon, personal communication with the author, July 29, 2000.

57. *Bulletin of the Chinese Historical Society of America,* 3; Linda Bentz, Los Angeles County researcher, personal communication with the author, January 21, 2001.

58. Beals, "Chinese Coins in Six Northwestern Aboriginal Sites," 58.

59. Bancroft, *History of the Northwest Coast.*

60. Gibbs, *Shipwrecks of the Pacific Coast.*

61. Maekawa and Sakai, eds., *Kaigai Ibun*, 11. The edict repealing the prohibition was not issued until 1861.

62. Brooks, "Report of Japanese Vessels," 50.

63. Purvis, "Ship Construction in Japan," 7.

64. Greenhill and Morrison, *The Archaeology of Boats and Ships*, 108. Oddly, though, Greenhill and Morrison downplay the importance of keels on Chinese vessels, placing Chinese junks under the raft family, and Japanese junks in the log boat tradition. In their analysis, "Japanese boatbuilding seems to have owed nothing to China."

65. Chen, *The Chinese of America*.

66. Rydell, *All the World's a Fair*, 194.

67. Halliburton, *Richard Halliburton*, 399.

68. Tony Edwards, *Keying* researcher, personal communication to the author, August 17, 2005.

69. *Illustrated London News*, April 1, 1848.

70. Charles Kellet, not to be confused with Henry Kellet, the British naval officer; Tony Edwards, personal communication with the author, August 17, 2005.

71. Altick, *The Shows of London*, 255.

72. *Illustrated London News*, July 29, 1848.

73. Altick, *The Shows of London*, 294.

74. Tony Edwards, personal communication to the author, August 17, 2005.

75. Cortinovis, "China at the St. Louis World's Fair," 59.

76. Tony Edwards, personal communication to the author, August 17, 2005.

77. Reid, "The Unthreatening Alternative," 13.

78. Clifford B. Donn, in introduction to Chapman, *Trouble on Board*, xxvi.

79. Cuyvers, *Sea Power*, 64–66.

80. Paine, "Aspects of a Global Maritime History," 137.

81. Ronan, citing Dominican friar Domingo de Navarrete, 1669, *The Shorter Science and Civilization in China*, 89.

Chapter 6. Misreading Our Guests

1. Nash, "American-Built Chinese Junks," 111–12; Nash, in "The Chinese Shrimp Fishery of California."

2. Pagden, *European Encounters with the New World*, 36.

3. Gould, *Archaeology and the Social History of Ships*, 192.

4. Ting, trans., "Things Produced by the Work of Nature."

5. Winterburn, "The Chinese Junk," 425.

6. Ivanoff, *The Moken Boat*, 4.

7. Lawson, "Catalina's Pirate Ship," 26.

8. Donnelly, "Chinese Junks," 319.

9. Bassett, *Wander-Ships*, 92.

10. "Romantic Craft Ends Thrilling Trip from China," *Victoria Daily Times*, September 19, 1922, 1.

11. Phillips, "A Peaceful Pirate," 329.

12. Walker, *The Modern Smuggler*, 23.

13. Cheng, "Cheng Ch'eng-Kung's Maritime Expansion and Early Ch'ing Coastal Prohibition," 242.

14. Worcester, *Junks and Sampans*, 191.

15. "Rivals Viking Voyages of Old," *Daily Colonist*, September 20, 1922, 12.

16. "Curious Vessel Bought of Viceroy of Nankin Comes into this Port," *San Francisco Chronicle*, December 9, 1906, 51.

17. "Junk Comes Sailing out of Storied Past" *San Francisco Chronicle*, August 10, 1955, 18.

18. Ibid.

19. "Adventurous Quartet Reaches Port After 85 Days Under Sail," *Daily Sun Long Beach*, October 4, 1938, 1.

20. "Ancient War Junk Spoken by Liner," *San Francisco Chronicle*, February 12, 1913, 10.

21. Hampton, "Saga of the *Ning Po*," 25.

22. London *Examiner*, May 20, 1848, cited in Altick, *The Shows of London*, 333.

23. London *Examiner*, June 24, 1848, cited in Altick, *The Shows of London*, 403.

24. Worcester, *Sail and Sweep*, 5.

25. Franke, citing Hegel, in *China and the West*, 142.

26. Barnes, citing Hegel, in *A History of Historical Writing*, 196.

27. Franke, citing von Ranke, *China and the West*, 142.

28. Ibid.

29. Sparling, *The Great Exhibition*, 27.

30. Winchester, ed., *Shipping Wonders of the World*, 668.

31. Ibid.

32. Worcester, *Junks and Sampans*, front leaf.

33. See Elvin, "Skills and Resources in Late Traditional China," 98.

34. Steffy, *Wooden Ship Building and the Interpretation of Shipwrecks*, 126.

35. Gang, *Chinese Maritime Activities*, 22.

36. Gang, *Maritime Sector*, 7.

37. Gang, *Chinese Maritime Activities*, 58.

38. Pomeranz, *The Great Divergence*, 25.

39. Bentley, "Sea and Ocean Basins as Frameworks of Historical Analysis," 213.

40. Ibid., 221.

41. van Leur, *Indonesian Trade and Society*, 85, 87.

42. Altick, *The Shows of London*, 296.

43. From the brochure printed for visitors, in Catalina Maritime Museum collection.

44. Hager and Hager, citing Phillips, in "The *Ning Po*," 195. The "weazened" gun, in Phillips's article, is said to be 3,600 years in age, a little early for the development of firearms.

45. Ibid., 329.

46. Rydell, *All the World's a Fair,* 228.

47. Altick, *The Shows of London,* 297.

48. London *Examiner,* June 24, 1848, cited in Altick, *The Shows of London,* 403.

49. Brindley, "The '*Keying,*'" 305.

50. Ivanoff, *The Moken Boat,* 4.

51. London *Examiner,* June 24, 1848, cited in Altick, *The Shows of London,* 403.

52. Altick, *The Shows of London,* 131.

53. Ibid., 126–27.

54. Urry, *The Tourist Gaze,* 82. The concept of the "gaze" is borrowed from Michel Foucault's concept of the "medical gaze."

55. Benedict, *The Anthropology of World's Fairs,* 2.

56. Eco, *Travels in Hyper-Reality,* 292, 294.

57. Benedict, *The Anthropology of World's Fairs,* 32.

58. Thomas, *Entangled Objects,* 138, 141.

59. Ibid., 176.

60. Kirshenblatt-Gimblett, *Destination Culture,* 3.

61. Ellen Clark, "Junket of a Junk," *Los Angeles Times,* August 6, 2000, 5.

62. Pagden, *European Encounters with the New World,* 174.

Chapter 7. Views from the Vanishing Deck

1. Lubar, "Machine Politics," 206.

2. Kranzberg, "Confrontation or Complementarity?" 333–34.

Glossary

Comparative English and Chinese Nautical Terminology

The accessible published Chinese nautical dictionaries, mentioned in the text, generally feature modern terminology of steam- and diesel-powered vessels, but not the rich vocabulary from the days of the wooden sailing junks. There is partial information, though, available from a variety of separate sources. The problems in sorting out this terminology are legion. In almost every instance where comparisons can be made between similar translations, exact Chinese terminology differs. This, in addition to the noted regional variations in nautical language, ensures that any attempt to create a nautical glossary for junks is bound to remain at this stage somewhat general in nature. Needham himself drew attention to the fact that shipwrights, practical men, never committed anything to writing. The scholars, who knew nothing about shipbuilding, could only invent and repeat commentary on technical terms that they perhaps only half understood.

This glossary represents only some of the basic technical terms included in this study, juxtaposing English and Chinese versions where possible. Information has been gleaned from a variety of miscellaneous sources. Some of the colorful descriptions in the following table come from various standard Chinese dictionaries, some from manuscript #5 in the Hirth collection in the Royal Library of Berlin, a document written around 1850 by a Chinese naval official. Other sources include Mathews' *Chinese-English Dictionary*, the *Liu Qiu Guo Zhi Lue* in Needham's *Science and Civilization in China*, Chen's *Zhongguo Fanchuan yu Haiwai Maoyi*, Worcester's *Junks and Sampans of the Yangtze*, the *English-Chinese Maritime Dictionary* (ECMD), and the *Oxford-Duden Pictorial English-Chinese Dictionary*.

Comparative English and Chinese Nautical Terminology

English	Chinese	Description	Characters	Citation
anchor	ding, or mao	ding is for a wood/stone anchor, and mao is for one of metal	椗, 碇, 錨	Ronan 78
batten	ban tiao	"wood strip," longitudinal stiffening element attached to sails	板條	Oxford 490
beam	zheng heng	breadth of vessel at widest point	正橫	ECMD 61
berth	ding bo	"anchor mooring," space for vessel next to dock or quay	椗泊	*Zongguo Gudai de* ... 52
boat	chuan	boat, in West any vessel usually shorter than 60 feet, as opposed to a ship	船	Mathews' 204
bollards	jiang jun zhu	"two generals," symmetrical posts for securing lines (ropes)	將軍柱	Needham 413
bow	chuan tou	"boat head," forward or front end of vessel	船頭	DeFrancis 86
bulkheads	cang bi	"cabin wall," the vessel's vertical interior partitions	艙壁	ECMD 88
bulkhead (forward)	long kou liang	"dragon mouth bulkhead," first watertight bulkhead at forward end of vessel	龍口梁	Needham 411
bulkhead (at main mast)	shi feng liang	"wind-using bulkhead," adjacent to mainmast and mast partners	使風梁	Zhou 486; Needham 411
bulkhead (stern)	duan shui liang	"cut water bulkhead," watertight partition just forward of transom	斷水梁	Zhou 486; Needham 411
bulwark gate	shui xian men	"water spirit door," door in side of vessel	水仙門	Ronan 79; Needham 407
chapel	shen tang	"spirit hall," shrine	神堂	Ronan 78
chunam	you shi hui	"oil stone ash," caulking material for Chinese junks	油石灰	Worcester 35
compass cabin	zhen fang	"needle place," referring to the magnetized needle of the compass	針方	Ronan 78
daggerboard	chui ban long gu, or zhong cha ban	"lower(able) board dragon bone," or "center insert board," adjustable stabilizer housed in slot, resists leeward drift when sailing	垂板龍骨 中插板	Oxford 284

English	Chinese	Description	Characters	Citation
deck	jia ban, chan	"shell board" or "deck," or "planks"	甲板, 橇	Needham 412
deck beams	heng liang	"horizontal cross beam," solid interior structural timbers	橫梁	Needham 411
fenestrations		diamond-shaped holes cut into rudder and keel of Chinese junks		
fore-and-aft sails		sails carried on masts or spars oriented to the major axis of the vessel		
foremast	qian wei	"front mast," closest to the bow	前桅	
foremast sail (mat)	tou peng	head awning or sail	頭蓬	Ronan 78
frames	chuan lei gu	"boat rib bones," transverse curved structural timbers, or ribs, of the hull	船肋骨	Oxford 285
freeboard	qiang	vertical measure of hull side above the waterline	檣	Needham 412
gallows frames	peng jia	"sail support boards," frame(s) above deck to support batten sails when lowered	蓬架	Hirth; Chen 415
gudgeon		female part of European rudder attachment		
gunwale	zheng fang	"straight timber," uppermost longitudinal members along sides of hull	正枋	Needham 412
halyards	xian	lines or ropes used to raise and lower sails	弦	Needham 411
hatchway	huo cang kou	"goods hold opening," referring to cargo hatches	貨艙口	ECMD 100
hold	shui mi ge cang	"watertight partitioned room," lower cargo compartment	水密隔艙	Chen Xiyu 63
hull	chuan shen, shui di ban	"boat body," or "bottom water boards," boards being the hull planks	船身, 水底板	Chen 415
keel	long gu	"dragon's bone," the main longitudinal timber at the very bottom of the ship	龍骨	Hirth
keel (fore)	tou long gu	"head dragon bone," keel section near bow	頭龍骨	Chen 415

continued

English	Chinese	Description	Characters	Citation
keel (mid)	zhong long gu	"middle dragon bone," midship keel section	中龍骨	Chen 415
keel (stern)	wei long gu	"tail dragon bone," aft keel section toward the stern	桅龍骨	Chen 415
keelson	nei long gu	"inner dragon bone," main longitudinal element running above keel and interior of hull	內龍骨	ECMD 31
leeboards	pi shui ban	"overside water boards," adjustable keel-boards mounted on the side of vessels	披水板	
lines	liao	ropes on board sailing ships	繚	
lines for sails	liao si, peng liao	"wind silk," running rigging, the ropes used to manipulate the sails	繚絲, 蓬繚	Mathews' Chen 415
mainmast	da wei, or zhong wei	"big mast" or "middle mast," midship location	大桅, 中桅	Mathews'
mainsail (mat)	da peng	"large awning" or sail	大蓬	Ronan 78
mast	wei	mast	桅	Mathews'
mast partners	wei jiazi, di long	"mast tongs," vertical side-by-side supports of mast built into vessel, also called "ground dragon" (horizontal)	桅夾子, 地龍	Mathews' Needham
mizzenmast	wei wei	"tail mast," stern-most mast of ship	尾桅	Mathews'
mizzen sail (mat)	wei song	"tail sail," sail nearest stern of ship	尾送	Ronan 78
oculus	long mu	"dragon eye," painted or carved eyes on the bow quarters. Bow quarters above the eyes were known as "eyebrows"	龍目	Ronan 79; Chen 415; Needham
pine	sha mu	pine tree	杉木	Worcester
port side	zuo xian	"left ship side," sometimes called "horse door side," left side of vessel when facing forward	左舷	ECMD 42
rigging	wei gong sheng lian	mast pole rope	桅槓繩練	Mathews' 1048

English	Chinese	Description	Characters	Citation
rudder	duo	rudder	舵	Ronan 78
rudder cables	du le	"belly straps," fore-and-aft underwater cables attached to rudder	肚 勒	Ronan 78; Needham 405
rudder post	duo tou	"rudder head," upper section of the rudder post	舵 頭	Oxford 490
sail	fan	"sail"	帆	Mathews' 253
sailors	chuan fu	"boat crew"	船 夫	Mathews' 204
sampan	san ban	"three boards," generic term for small skiff or boat	三 板	Worcester 42
scantling	cai liao chi cun	material measurements (width and thickness) of main structural elements in wooden ship building	材料尺寸	ECMD 481
scarf	jie kou	"joint cut," joining connection between two timbers	接 口	
sheer	xian hu xian	"ship arc line," curving sweep of line of hull	舷弧線	ECMD 497
shipwright	zao chuan shi	"boat building expert"	造 船 師	Mathews' 204
starboard side	you xian	"sail spread side," right side of vessel when facing forward	右 舷	ECMD 423
stern	wei	aft or back end of vessel	尾	
strake	ban	"board," hull plank	板	
taffrail deck	jiang tai	"general's platform," the uppermost rail and highest deck across the stern transom, poop deck	將 台	Chen 415; Needham 405
thole pins		"tongs," fulcrum for operating oars over sides of vessel		Hirth
tiller	duo bing	"rudder handle"	舵柄	Oxford 490
transom (stern)	wei ban	"stern boards," transverse end of vessel	尾 板	Oxford 285
transom (bow)	tou ban	"head boards," prow or bow transom, also called tuo lang ban or "wave protection boards"	頭 板, 托 廊板	Oxford 285; Chen 415

continued

English	Chinese	Description	Characters	Citation
transom (bow, lower portion)	tuo lang ban	"wave lifting board," referring to hydro-dynamic influence of transom bow on junks	托浪板	Needham 406
wales (lower)	zou ma	"running horse," thickened strake, often semi-rounded (unfinished) log running length of hull	走馬	Chen 415; Hirth
wales (upper)	shui she	"water snake," wale above the "running horse"	水蛇	Chen 415; Hirth
winch	jiao che	"twisting machine," synonym for windlass	絞車	Chen Xiyu 107
windlass	liao, da xiao liao niu	"winders," deck equipment for hauling on lines, also "large and small winding ox	繚, 大小繚牛	Ronan 78

Bibliography

Abu-Lughod, Janet. *Before European Hegemony: The World System A.D. 1250–1350*. New York: Oxford University Press, 1991.

Alexander, Christopher, Sara Ishikawa, and Murray Silverstein. *A Pattern Language: Towns, Buildings, Construction*. New York: Oxford University Press, 1977.

Alexander, D. N. Correspondence with Catalina Island Museum regarding *Ning Poo* [*sic*], n.d., Catalina Maritime Museum collection.

Alexander, William. *Image of China*. London: Jupiter Books, 1980.

Altick, Richard D. *The Shows of London*. Cambridge, Mass.: Belknap Press, 1978.

Anderson, Eugene N. "The Boat People of South China." In *Asian Folklore and Social Life Monographs*, edited by Lou Tsu-k'uang, 1–10. Taiwan: Orient Cultural Service, 1972.

———. "The Happy Heavenly Bureaucracy: Supernaturals and the Hong Kong Boat People." In *Asian Folklore and Social Life Monographs*, edited by Lou Tsu-k'uang, 11–25. Taiwan: Orient Culture Service, 1972.

Anderson, John. *The Selungs of the Mergui Archipelago*. London: Trubner, 1890.

Antony, Robert J. *Like Froth Floating on the Sea: The World of Pirates and Seafarers in Late Imperial South China*. Berkeley: Institute of East Asian Studies, University of California, 2003.

"Archeological Report, Song Dynasty Galleon (Quanzhou) of Fujian Province." Song Shipwreck group, Department of History, Xiamen University, 1987.

Armentrout-Ma, L. Eve. "Big and Medium Business of Chinese Immigrants to the United States, 1850–1890: An Outline." In *Chinese Historical Society of America Bulletin* 13, no. 7 (1978): 1–9.

———. *Chinese and GGNRA, 1849–1949: Guests of Choice, Guests of Necessity*. Unpublished manuscript in J. Porter Shaw Library collection, San Francisco Maritime National Historic Park.

———. "Sampans, Junks and Chinese Fishermen in the Golden State." Pamphlet prepared for the San Francisco Maritime National Historic Park, San Francisco, 1979.

Aston, Richard James. "The Merchant Shipping Activity of South China, 1644–1860." Master's thesis, University of Hawai'i, 1967.

Aubert, Vilhelm, and Oddvar Arner. "On the Social Structure of the Ship." *Acta Sociologica* 3, no. 4 (1965): 200–219.

Audemard, L. *Les Jonques Chinoises* (The Chinese Junk), vols. 1–4. Rotterdam: Museum Voorland en Volkenkunde en het Maritiem Museum "Prins Hendrik," 1962.

Baker, Margaret. *Folklore of the Sea.* London: David and Charles, 1979.

Baldwin, J. "A Look Inside China." *Wooden Boat Magazine* 49 (1982): 108–10.

Ballendorf, Dirk Anthony. "The Chinese as Pacific Explorers." *Asian-Pacific Culture Quarterly* 17, no. 2 (1989): 78–82.

Bancroft, Hubert Howe. *History of the Northwest Coast,* vol.1. San Francisco: A. L. Bancroft and Company, 1884.

Barber, Larry. "Chinese Junk Awaits Portland Home." *Freshwater News,* Portland, Ore., 1997.

Barker, Richard. "The Size of the 'Treasure Ships' and Other Chinese Vessels." *Mariner's Mirror* 75, no. 1 (1989): 273–75.

Barnes, Harry Elmer. *A History of Historical Writing.* Norman, Okla., 1937.

Bassett, Wilbur. *Wander-Ships: Folk-Stories of the Sea.* Chicago: Open Court Publishing Company, 1917.

Beals, Herbert K. "Chinese Coins in Six Northwestern Aboriginal Sites." *Historical Archaeology* 14 (1980): 58–73.

Beck, Horace. *Folklore and the Sea.* Middletown, Conn.: Wesleyan University Press, 1973.

Benedict, Burton. *The Anthropology of World's Fairs: San Francisco's Panama Pacific International Exposition of 1915.* Berkeley: Lowie Museum of Anthropology, 1983.

Bentley, Jerry H. "Sea and Ocean Basins as Frameworks of Historical Analysis." *Geographical Review* 89, no. 2 (1999): 213–25.

Bentz, Linda. "Redwood, Bamboo and Ironwood: Chinese Junks of San Diego." *Mains'l Haul* 35, nos. 2 and 3 (1999): 14–22.

Biedermann, Hans. *Dictionary of Symbolism: Cultural Icons and the Meanings Behind Them.* New York: Meridian, 1989.

Biel, Steven. *Down with the Old Canoe: A Cultural History of the Titanic Disaster.* New York: W. W. Norton and Co., 1996.

Blusse, Leonard. *Strange Company: Chinese Settlers, Mestizo Women, and the Dutch in VOC Batavia.* Dordrecht, Holland: Foris Publications, 1986.

Bond, Cliff. "Dragon Eyes for Freedom." *California Monthly Magazine* (October 1955): 21–25.

Borden, Charles A. *Sea Quest: Global Blue-Water Adventuring in Small Craft.* Philadelphia: Macrae Smith Company, 1967.

Bottignolo, Bruno. *Celebrations with the Sun: An Overview of Religious Phenomena among the Badjaos.* Manila: Ateneo de Manila University Press, 1995.

Bowen, Richard LeBaron, Jr. "Eastern Sail Affinities." *American Neptune* 13, no. 3 (1953): 185–211.

Brewington, M. V., and Dorothy Brewington. *The Marine Paintings and Drawings in the Peabody Museum.* Salem, Mass.: Peabody, 1968.

Bridgeford, Robert G. "Acquiring a Junk." *Portland Children's Museum Newsletter.* Portland, Ore., 1991.

Brindley, H. H. "The '*Keying.*'" *Mariner's Mirror* 8, no. 10 (1922): 305–14.

Brooks, Charles Walcott. "Report of Japanese Vessels Wrecked in the North Pacific Ocean." In *Proceedings of the California Academy of Sciences,* 50–66. San Francisco: California Academy of Sciences, 1875.

Brouwer, Norman J. *International Register of Historic Ships.* Annapolis: Naval Institute Press, 1985.

Brown, Alexander Crosby. *Sea-Lingo: Notes on the Language of Mariners and Some Suggestions for its Proper Use With Gossary of animal terms by J. Nelson Daniel.* Newport News: Mariner's Museum, 1980.

Brown, William F. "*Ningpo:* Chinese Pirate Junk." *Mains'l Haul* 29, no. 4 (1993): 19–23.

Bulletin of the Chinese Historical Society of America 1, no. 2 (1966).

Buys, C. J., and S. O. Smith. "Chinese Batten-Lug Sails." *Mariner's Mirror* 66, no. 3 (1980): 233–46.

Camp, William. *San Francisco: Port of Gold.* Garden City, N.Y.: Doubleday, 1947.

Cardwell, Robert. "Pirate Fighters of the South China Sea." *National Geographic* 89, no. 6 (May 1946): 787–92.

Caulfield, Marjorie. Correspondence with Catalina Island Museum regarding *Ning Po* junk, April 15, 1991, Catalina Maritime Museum collection.

Chan Cheung. "The Smuggling Trade Between China and Southeast Asia during the Ming Dynasty." In *Symposium on Historical, Archaeological, and Linguistic Studies on Southern China, South East Asia and the Hong Kong Region,* edited by F. S. Drake, 223–27. Hong Kong, 1967.

Chapman, Paul K. *Trouble on Board: The Plight of International Seafarers.* Ithaca, N.Y.: ILR Press, 1992.

Chatterton, Edward. K. *Sailing Ships and Their Story.* Argosy-Antiquarian: Philadelphia, 1968.

Chen, Jack. *The Chinese of America: From the Beginnings to the Present.* San Francisco: Harper and Row, 1981.

Chen, Reno. Interview with crew member, purser of junk *Free China* by the author, Palo Alto, Calif., August 14, 2000.

Chen Xiyu. *Zhongguo Fanchuan yu Haiwai Maoyi* (Chinese Sailing Junks and Overseas Trade). Xiamen: Xiamen University, 1991.

Cheng K'o-Ch'eng. "Cheng Ch'eng-Kung's Maritime Expansion and Early Ch'ing Coastal Prohibition." In *Development and Decline of Fukien Province in the 17th and 18th Centuries,* edited by Eduard B. Vermeer, 217–44. Leiden: E. J. Brill, 1990.

China: Catalogue of the Collection of Chinese Exhibits at the Louisiana Purchase Exposition, St. Louis 1904. St. Louis: Shallcross Print, 1904.

Chou Houang. *Liu Qiu Guo Zhi Lue* [Account of the Liu-Qiu Islands]. 1757. In *A History of Science and Civilization in China* vol. 4, part 3, by Joseph Needham, 382. London: Cambridge University Press, 1943.

Chow, Paul. Interview with crew member, navigator of the junk *Free China* by the author, Los Angeles, September 7, 2000.

———. *The Junk Story.* Unpublished manuscript, Paul Chow collection, Los Angeles, 2000.

Choy, Philip P., Lorraine Dong, and Marlon K. Hom, eds. *The Coming Man: 19th Century American Perceptions of the Chinese.* Seattle: University of Washington Press, 1994.

Christensen, Arne Emil, ed. *The Earliest Ships: The Evolution of Boats into Ships.* Annapolis: Naval Institute Press, 1996.

Christides, Vassilios. "The Transmission of Chinese Maritime Technology by the Arabs to Europe." *American Neptune* 52, no. 1 (1992): 38–45.

Ch'ung, Marco, and Charles Bell. "The Four Seas Are One Family." *Motor Boating* 96, no. 6 (1955): 30–33.

Cipolla, Carlo M. *Guns, Sails, and Empires: Technological Innovation and the Early Phase of European Expansion, 1400–1700.* New York: Pantheon Books, 1965.

Clark, Hugh R. "The Politics of Trade and the Establishment of the Quanzhou Trade Superintendency." In *China and the Maritime Silk Route: Proceedings of the UNESCO Quanzhou International Seminar on China and the Maritime Routes of the Silk Roads*, 376–94. Fuzhou: UNESCO, 1991.

Clark, Paul, and Zhang Wei. "A Preliminary Survey of Wreck Sites in the Dinghai Area, Fujian Province, China." *International Journal of Nautical Archaeology* 19, no. 3 (1990): 239–41.

Clowes, G. S. Laird. *The Story of Sail.* London: Eyre and Spottiswoode Publishers, 1936.

Collins. "Chinese Fishing Craft." In *Bulletin of the United States Fish Commission* 9 (1892), document in J. Porter Shaw Library collection, San Francisco Maritime National Historic Park.

Cortinovis, Irene E. "China at the St. Louis World's Fair." *Missouri Historical Review* 72, no. 1 (1977): 59–67.

Couling, Samuel. *Encyclopaedia Sinica.* Shanghai: Kelly and Walsh, 1917.

Cowburn, Philip. *The Warship in History.* New York: Macmillan Company, 1965.

Cox, Bill. "The Notorious *Ning Po.*" *High Country* 5, no. 20 (1972): 24–31.

Crawfurd, John. *Journal of an Embassy from the Governor General of India to the Courts of Siam and Cochin China.* London: HenryColburn, 1828.

Cushman, Jennifer Wayne. *Fields from the Sea: Chinese Junk Trade with Siam during the Late Eighteenth and Early Nineteenth Centuries.* New York: SEAP, 1993.

Cuyvers, Luc. *Sea Power: A Global Journey.* Annapolis: Naval Institute Press, 1993.

Dalton, Govinda. Interview with current owner of junk *Free China* by the author, Berkeley, April 15, 1996.

Danton, George H. *The Culture Contacts of the United States and China.* New York: Columbia University Press, 1931.

Dars, Jacques. *La Marine Chinoise du Xe siecle au XIVe siecle.* Paris: Economica, 1992.

Day, Clarence Burton. *Chinese Peasant Cults: Being a Study of Chinese Paper Gods.* New York: Paragon Book Gallery, 1974.

De Bisschop, Eric. *Tahiti Nui.* New York: McDowell, Obolensky, 1959.

De Braganza, Ronald Louis Silveira, ed. *The Hill Collection of Pacific Voyages.* San Diego: University of California at San Diego, 1983.

De Francis, John. *ABC Chinese-English Dictionary.* Honolulu: University of Hawai'i Press, 1996.

Degener, Otto. "The Last Cruise of the *Cheng Ho.*" *Journal of the New York Botanical Garden* 44, no. 525 (1943): 197–214; no. 526 (1943): 221–33.

Delgado, James P. "Relics of the Kamikaze." *Archaeology Magazine* 56, no. 1 (2003): 36–41.

Dening, Greg. *Mr. Bligh's Bad Language: Passion, Power and Theatre on the Bounty.* Cambridge, U.K.: Cambridge University Press, 1992.

Diamond, Jared. *Guns, Germs, and Steel: The Fates of Human Societies.* New York: W. W. Norton and Company, 1997.

Dillon, Richard H. "Transpacific Voyage in a Junk." *Ships and the Sea* 7, no. 1 (1957): 54.

Donnelly, Ivon A. *Chinese Junks: A Book of Drawings in Black and White.* Shanghai: Kelly and Walsh, 1920.

———. "Chinese Junks." *Mariner's Mirror* 9, no. 10 (1923): 318–20.

———. "Foochow Pole Junks." *Mariner's Mirror* 9, no. 8 (1923): 226–32.

———. *Chinese Junks and Other Native Craft.* Singapore: Graham Brash, 1924.

———. "The Oculus in Chinese Craft." *Mariner's Mirror* 12, no. 3 (1926): 339–40.

Doran, Edwin, Jr. "The Junk." *Oceans* (May 1978): 13–20.

Dring, Albert. Interview with son of Harry Dring, past owner of the junk *Free China* by the author, San Francisco, April 10, 1996.

Du Halde, P. *The General History of China.* London: John Watts, 1753.

Duyvendak, J.J.L. "The True Dates of the Chinese Maritime Expeditions in the Early 15th Century." *T'oung Pao* 34 (1938): 341–412.

Earl, George Winston. *The Eastern Seas, or Voyages and Adventures in the Indian Archipelago in 1832–33–34.* London: Wm. H. Allen and Co., 1837; reprint, London: Oxford University Press, 1971.

Eberhard, Wolfram. *A Dictionary of Chinese Symbols: Hidden Symbols in Chinese Life and Thought.* London: Routledge, 1983.

Ebrey, Patricia Buckley, and Peter N. Gregory, eds. *Religion and Society in T'ang and Sung China.* Honolulu: University of Hawaii Press, 1993.

Eco, Umberto. *Travels in Hyper-Reality.* London: Pan Books, 1987.

Edwards, Clinton R. "Sailing Rafts of Sechura: History and Problems of Origin." *Southwestern Journal of Anthropology* 16, no. 3 (1960): 368.

English-Chinese Maritime Dictionary. New York: French and European Publications, Inc., 1994.

Epidendio, George. "The Death of China Camp." *San Francisco Magazine* (October 1962): 17–21.

Ellis, C. Hamilton. *Ships: A Pictorial History from Noah's Ark to the USS United States.* New York: Pebbles Press, n.d.

Elvin, Mark. *The Pattern of the Chinese Past.* Stanford: Stanford University Press, 1973.

———. "Skills and Resources in Late Traditional China." In *China's Modern Economy in Historical Perspective,* edited by Dwight Perkins, 85–113. Stanford: Stanford University Press, 1975.

Fairbridge, Rhodes W. *The Encyclopedia of Oceanography.* New York: Reinhold Publishing Company, 1966.

Fairchild, David. *Garden Isles of the Great East: Collecting Seeds from the Philippines and Netherlands India in the Junk Cheng Ho.* New York: Charles Scribner's Sons, 1943.

Feder, Kenneth L. *Frauds, Myths, and Mysteries: Science and Pseudoscience in Archaeology.* London: Mayfield Publishing Company, 1999.

Findling, John E., ed. *Historical Dictionary of World's Fairs and Expositions, 1851–1988.* New York: Greenwood Press, 1990.

Fitch, R. F. "Life Afloat in China." *National Geographic* 51 (1927): 665–86.

Flecker, Michael. "Excavation of an Oriental Vessel of c. 1690 off Con Dao, Vietnam." *International Journal of Nautical Archaeology* 21, no. 3 (1992): 221–44.

———. "The Bakau Wreck: An Early Example of Chinese Shipping in Southeast Asia." *International Journal of Nautical Archaeology* 30, no. 2 (2001): 221–30.

Foisie, Jack. "Junk *Free China* Due Here Today." Misc. document, junk folder, J. Porter Shaw Library collection, San Francisco Maritime National Historic Park.

Fortune, Robert. *A Residence Among the Chinese: Inland, on the Coast, and at Sea.* London: John Murray Publishers, 1857.

Frank, Andre Gunder. *Reorient: Global Economy in the Asian Age.* Berkeley: University of California Press, 1998.

Franke, Wolfgang. *China and the West.* Columbia: University of South Carolina Press, 1967.

Franks, Jeremy. "Eighteenth-Century Chinese Vessels at Canton: The Paintings at Skarva, Sweden." *Mariner's Mirror* 83, no. 1 (1997): 21–40.

Frost, Frank J. "The Palos Verdes Chinese Anchor Mystery." *Archaeology* 35, no. 1 (1982): 23–28.

Fu, Lo-shu, ed. *A Documentary Chronicle of Sino-Western Relations (1644–1820).* Tucson: University of Arizona Press, 1966.

Gang Deng. "What Did Seas and Oceans Mean to the Chinese in the Past Millennia?" Paper presented to the Second Annual Conference of the World History Organization, Victoria University of Wellington (New Zealand), June 1993.

———. *Chinese Maritime Activities and Socioeconomic Development, c. 2100 B.C.– 1900 A.D.* London: Greenwood Press, 1997.

———. *Maritime Sector, Institutions, and Sea Power of Premodern China.* Westport, Conn.: Greenwood Press, 1999.

Gardella, Robert. "The Maritime History of Late Imperial China: Observations on Current Concerns and Recent Research." *Late Imperial China* 6, no. 2 (1985): 48–67.

Gardiner, Robert, ed. *The Line of Battle: The Sailing Warship, 1650–1840.* London: Conway's Maritime Press, 1992.

Gerstenberger, Heide. "Men Apart: The Concept of 'Total Institution' and the Analysis of Seafaring." *International Journal of Maritime History* 3, no. 1 (1996), 173–82.

Gibbs, James A. *Shipwrecks of the Pacific Coast.* Portland, Ore.: Binford and Mort Publishing, 1957.

Gibson, David. Correspondence with Catalina Island Museum regarding Wang-ye cult statue and *Ning Po*, n.d., Catalina Island Maritime Museum collection.

Gleason, Duncan. *The Islands and Ports of California.* New York: Devin-Adair Company, 1958.

Godley, Michael R. "China's World's Fair of 1910: Lessons from a Forgotten Event." *Modern Asian Studies* 12, no. 3 (1978): 503–23.

Gordon, Robert B. "The Interpretation of Artifacts in the History of Technology." In *History from Things: Essays on Material Culture,* edited by Steven Lubar and W. David Kingery, 74–94. Washington and London: Smithsonian Institution Press, 1993.

Gould, Albert S., Jr., and Gerald J. Foster. *Junks—Construction and Regional Characteristics.* China Lake, Calif.: U.S. Naval Ordnance Test Station, 1965.

Gould, Richard A. *Archaeology and the Social History of Ships.* Cambridge, U.K.: Cambridge University Press, 2000.

Gray, John Henry. *China: A History of the Laws, Manners, and the Customs of the People.* London: Macmillan and Company, 1878.

Green, Jeremy. "The Song Dynasty Shipwreck at Quanzhou, Fujian Province, People's Republic of China." *International Journal of Nautical Archaeology* 12, no. 3 (1983): 253–61.

———. "The Shinan Excavation, Korea: An Interim Report on the Hull Structure." *International Journal of Nautical Archaeology* 12 (1983): 293–301.

———. "Eastern Shipbuilding Traditions: A Review of the Evidence." *Bulletin of the Australian Institute for Maritime Archaeology* 10, no. 2 (1986): 1–6.

———. "Arabia to China: The Oriental Traditions." In *The Earliest Ships: The Evolution of Boats into Ships,* edited by Arne Emil Christensen, 89–109. Annapolis: Naval Institute Press, 1996.

———. "The Ship from Quanzhou, Fujian Province, People's Republic of China." *International Journal of Nautical Archaeology* 27, no. 4 (1998): 277–301.

Greenhill, Basil, and Ann Giffard. *Travelling by Sea in the Nineteenth Century.* New York: Hastings House Publishers, 1972.

Greenhill, Basil, and John Morrison. *The Archaeology of Boats and Ships: An Introduction.* Annapolis: Naval Institute Press, 1995.

Grover, David H. *American Merchant Ships on the Yangtze, 1920–1941.* Westport, Conn: Praeger, 1992.

Gutzlaff, Karl Friedrick. *Journal of Three Voyages along the Coast of China in 1831, 1832, and 1833.* London: Frederick Wesley and A. H. Davis, 1834.

Hager, Everett, and Anna Marie Hager. "The *Ning Po*, a Fabled Chinese Junk in Southern California Waters." In *Brand Book XV: Los Angeles, the Westerners*, edited by Anthony L. Lehman, 193–203. Glendale, Calif.: Los Angeles Corral, 1978.

Halliburton, Richard. *Richard Halliburton: His Story of His Life's Adventures, as Told in Letters to His Mother and Father.* New York: Bobbs-Merrill Company, 1940.

Hamilton, Mark S. Correspondence between legal counsel of San Francisco Maritime Museum Association and Paul Chow, navigator of junk *Free China*, October 26, 1960, Paul Chow collection.

Hampton, Ralph. "Saga of the *Ning Po.*" *Sea Classics*, n.d., Catalina Island Maritime Museum collection.

Handy, E. S. Craighill. "Polynesian Religion." *Bernice P. Bishop Museum Bulletin*, no. 34. Honolulu: Bishop Museum, 1927.

Hansell, Nils. Correspondence between chairman of Operation Sail and Paul Chow, navigator of junk *Free China*, February 17, 1964, Paul Chow collection.

Hau'ofa, Epeli. "Our Sea of Islands." In *A New Oceania: Rediscovering Our Sea of Islands*, edited by Eric Waddell et al., 2–16. Suva: University of the South Pacific, 1993.

Haws, Duncan. *Ships and the Sea: A Chronological Review.* New York: Thomas Y. Crowell Company, 1975.

Hayashi Tokumura, "The Shipping Brokers and Transport Companies of Soochow." In *Transport in Transition: The Evolution of Traditional Shipping in China*, translated by Andrew J. Watson, 35–52. Ann Arbor: University of Michigan, 1972.

Heine, William C. *Historic Ships of the World.* New York: G. P. Putnam's Sons, 1977.

Herron, Richard D. "Spencer's Junks of Central China: Understanding Five Models." *Nautical Research Journal* 40, no. 3 (1995): 148–58.

"History of the Port of Quanzhou in the Song and Yuan Dynasties," *Wen Wu* (Song Shipwreck group, Department of History, Xiamen University) 10b (1975): 19–23.

Ho Ke-en, "The Tanka or Boat People of South China." In *Symposium of Historical Archaeological and Linguistic Studies on Southern China, South-East Asia and the Hong Kong Region*, edited by F. S. Drake, 120–24. Hong Kong: Hong Kong University Press, 1967.

Hommel, Rudolf P. *China at Work: An Illustrated Record of the Primitive Industries of China's Masses, Whose Life Is Toil, and Thus an Account of Chinese Civilization.* New York: John Day Company, 1937.

Hoobler, Dorothy, and Thomas Hoobler. *The Chinese American Family Album*. New York: Oxford University Press, 1994.

Hornell, J. "The Origin of the Junk and Sampan." *Mariner's Mirror* 20, no. 3 (1934): 331–37.

———. *Water Transport: Origins and Early Evolution*. Cambridge, U.K.: Cambridge University Press, 1946.

Hoyle, C. A. "*Ning Po* in Avalon Bay: The Celebrated Chinese Pirate Ship Now on Exhibition." *Catalina Islander Magazine* (July 1916): 1–2.

Hunter, J. R. "Maritime Culture: Notes From the Land." *International Journal of Nautical Archaeology* 23, no. 4 (1994): 261–64.

Iritani, Evelyn. *An Ocean Between Us*. New York: William Morrow, 1994.

Ivanoff, Jacques. *The Moken Boat: Symbolic Technology*. Bangkok: White Lotus Press, 1999.

Jack-Hinton, Colin. "Junks and the Chinese Trader." *Hemisphere* 13, no. 1 (1969): 8–14.

Jarrett, Charles. "The Chinese Junk." *For an' Aft* (vol. and year unknown): 23–33.

Johnson, Wim. *Shaky Ships: The Formal Richness of Chinese Shipbuilding*. Antwerp: National Maritime Museum of Antwerp, 1994.

Johnstone, Paul. *The Sea-Craft of Prehistory*. Cambridge, Mass.: Harvard University Press, 1980.

Kani, Hiroaki. *A General Survey of the Boat People of Hong Kong*. Hong Kong: Chinese University of Hong Kong, 1967.

Keith, D. H. "A Fourteenth-Century Cargo Makes Port at Last." *National Geographic* 156, no. 2 (1979): 230–43.

———. "A Fourteenth-Century Shipwreck at Sinan-gun." *Archaeology* 33, no. 2 (1980): 33–43.

Keith, Donald H., and Christian J. Buys. "New Light on Medieval Chinese Seagoing Ship Construction." *International Journal of Nautical Archaeology* 10, no. 2 (1981): 119–32.

Kemble, John Haskell. *San Francisco Bay: A Pictorial Maritime History*. Cambridge, Md.: Cornell Maritime Press, 1957.

Kemp, Peter, ed. *The Oxford Companion to Ships and the Sea*. London: Oxford University Press, 1978.

Kennedy, Don H. "The Infamous *Ning Po*." *American Neptune* (1969): 262–74.

King, Dean, and John B. Hattendorf, eds. *Every Man Will Do His Duty: An Anthology of Firsthand Accounts from the Age of Nelson, 1793–1815*. New York: Henry Holt and Company, 1997.

Kirch, Patrick V. *On the Road of the Winds: An Archaeological History of the Pacific Islands Before European Contact*. Berkeley: University of California Press, 2000.

Kirshenblatt-Gimblett, Barbara. *Destination Culture: Tourism, Museums, and Heritage*. Berkeley: University of California Press, 1998.

Knöbl, Kuno. *Tai Ki: To the Point of No Return*. Boston: Little, Brown and Company, 1975.

Koizumi Teizo, "The Operation of Chinese Junks." In *Transport in Transition: The Evolution of Traditional Shipping in China*, edited and translated by Andrew J. Watson, 1–14. Ann Arbor: University of Michigan, 1972.

Kosaka Torizo and Nakamura Yoshio. "Junk Ownership and Operation in North China." In *Transport in Transition: The Evolution of Traditional Shipping in China*, edited and translated by Andrew J. Watson, 53–56. Ann Arbor: University of Michigan, 1972.

Kranzberg, Melvin. "Confrontation or Complementarity?: Perspectives on Technology and the Arts." In *Bridges to the Future: A Centennial Celebration of the Brooklyn Bridge*, edited by Margaret Latimer, Brooke Hindle, and Melvin Kranzberg, 333–45. New York: New York Academy of Sciences, 1984.

Laai, Yi-faai. "The Part Played by the Pirates of Kwangtung and Kwangsi Provinces in the Taiping Insurrection." Ph.D. diss., University of California, 1950.

Laird, Cecil. "Chinese Fishermen's Rich History Revealed." *Soundings* (December 1979): 19.

Lamley, Harry J. "Lineage Feuding in Southern Fujian and Eastern Guangdong Under Qing Rule." In *Violence in China: Essays in Culture and Counterculture*, edited by Jonathan N. Lipman and Stevan Harrell, 27–64. New York, SUNY Press, 1990.

Langdon, Robert. "Castaways." In *The Cambridge History of the Pacific Islanders*, edited by Donald Denoon et al., 69–74. Cambridge, U.K.: Cambridge University Press, 1997.

Lasalle, Guy, Jr. Interview with Beihai junk donor by the author, Portland, Ore., September 25, 2000.

Lasalle, Guy, Sr. Interview with Beihai junk donor's father by the author, Portland, Ore., September 28, 2000.

Lawson, Stephen. Correspondence with Catalina Island Museum regarding *Ning Po* junk, October 12, 1987, Catalina Island Maritime Museum collection.

———. "Catalina's Pirate Ship: The *Ning Po*." *Discover Diving Magazine* (July/August 1988): 25–28.

Lee, Murray K. Interview with curator of San Diego Chinese Historical Museum by the author, San Diego, August 8, 2000.

Lessa, William A. "Chinese Trigrams in Micronesia." *Journal of American Folklore* 82, no. 326 (1969): 353–62.

Leung Yuen Sang, "Regional Rivalry in Mid-Nineteenth-Century Shanghai: Cantonese vs. Ningpo Men." *Ch'ing-shih wen-t'i* 4, no. 8 (1982): 29–51.

Lewis, Martin W., and Karen Wigen. "A Maritime Response to the Crisis in Area Studies." *Geographical Review* 89, no. 2 (1999): 161–69.

Li Guo-Qing. "Archaeological Evidence for the Use of 'chu-nam' on the 13th Century Quanzhou Ship, Fujian Province, China." *International Journal of Nautical Archaeology* 18, no. 4 (1989): 277–83.

Lilius, Aleko E. *I Sailed with Chinese Pirates*. New York: D. Appleton and Company, 1931.

Lin Ch'ing Yuan. *Fujian Chuan Zheng Ju Shi Gao*. Fuzhou, 1986.

Lin Shimin, Du Genqi (translator), and Jeremy Green. "Waterfront Excavations at Dongmenkou, Ningbo, Zhe Jiang Province, PRC." *International Journal of Nautical Archaeology* 20, no. 4 (1991): 299–311.

Liu, Kwang-Ching. *Anglo-American Steamship Rivalry in China, 1862–1874.* Cambridge, Mass.: Harvard University Press, 1962.

Liu Ben-an. "Three Recently Discovered Shipwrecks in China." In *Sunken Treasures: Underwater Archaeology in China* (conference papers), University of California, Los Angeles, Center for Pacific Rim Studies, October 14, 1995.

Liu Han-po. *Fishing Sampans in Taiwan.* Taipei: Taiwan Fisheries Bureau, 1963.

Liu Sufen. "Qing chao zhongye beiyang de haiyun" (North sea ocean shipping during the Qing dynasty middle period). In *Zhongguo haiyang fazhan shilun wenji*, vol. 4 (Collected historical works on Chinese overseas development), 101–25. Taipei: Academia Sinica, 1991.

——. "Jindai beiyang zhong wai hangyun shili de jingzheng 1858–1919" (Influence of shipping competition between China and foreign countries in the north sea 1858–1919). In *Zhongguo haiyang fazhan shilun wenji*, vol. 5 (Collected historical works on Chinese overseas development), 301–57. Taipei: Academia Sinica, 1993.

London, Jack. *Tales of the Fish Patrol.* New York: Macmillan Company, 1905.

Lovegrove, H. "Junks of the Canton River and the West River System." *Mariner's Mirror* 18, no. 3 (1932): 241–53.

Lower, J. Arthur. *Ocean of Destiny: A Concise History of the North Pacific, 1500–1978.* Vancouver: University of British Columbia Press, 1978.

Lubar, Steven. "Machine Politics: The Political Construction of Technological Artifacts." In *History from Things: Essays on Material Culture*, edited by Steven Lubar and W. David Kingery, 197–215. Washington and London: Smithsonian Institution Press, 1993.

Lydon, Sandy. *Chinese Gold: The Chinese in the Monterey Bay Region.* Santa Cruz: Capitola Book Company, 1985.

Mack, William P., and Royal W. Connell. *Naval Ceremonies, Customs, and Traditions.* Annapolis: Naval Institute Press, 1980.

MacMullen, Jerry. "Last of the Junk Fleet." *Westways Magazine* 35, no. 12 (1943).

Maekawa Bunzo and Sakai Junzo, eds. *Kaigai Ibun* (A Strange Tale from Overseas). Los Angeles: Dawson's Book Shop, 1970.

Mahan, Alfred Thayer. *The Influence of Sea Power upon History 1660–1783.* New York: Dover, 1987.

Marshall, Don B. *California Shipwrecks: Footsteps in the Sea.* Seattle: Superior Publishing, 1979.

Mathews, R. H. *Mathews' Chinese-English Dictionary.* Cambridge, Mass.: Harvard University Press, 1947.

Mayers, W. F. "Chinese Junk Building." *Notes and Queries from China and Japan* 1 (1867): 170.

Maze, Sir Frederick. *The Maze Collection of Chinese Junk Models in the Science Museum, London.* London: Science Museum, 1938.

McGhee, Fred. "Towards a Postcolonial Nautical Archaeology." University of Texas paper, delivered at Society for Historical Archaeology conference, Washington, D.C., 1997; *Assemblage* 3 online e-journal, http://www.shef.ac.uk/assem/3/3mcghee.htm, accessed October 15, 2005.

McGrail, Sean. *Boats of the World: From the Stone Age to Medieval Times.* Oxford: Oxford University Press, 2001.

McPherson, Kenneth. "China's Trade with the Indian Ocean to the 19th Century: A Study in Cyclical Relationships." In *China and the Maritime Silk Route: Proceedings of the UNESCO Quanzhou International Seminar on China and the Maritime Routes of the Silk Roads,* 55–64. Fuzhou: UNESCO, 1991.

Medhurst, W. H. *The Foreigner in Far Cathay.* London: Edward Stanford, 1872.

Meggers, B. J. "TransPacific Origin of Mesoamerican Civilization: A Preliminary Review of the Evidence and Its Theoretical Implications." *American Anthropologist* 77, no. 1 (1975): 1–27.

Mehlert, Calvin. Interview with former vice-consul of Taiwan, crew member of junk *Free China* by the author, Palo Alto, Calif., August 14, 2000.

———. 90-minute 16mm color film footage of transpacific voyage of junk *Free China.*

Miller, Stuart C. "The American Trader's Image of China, 1785–1840." *Pacific Historical Review* 36, no. 4 (1967): 375–97.

Mitman, Carl W., ed. *Catalogue of the Watercraft in the United States National Museum.* Washington: Government Printing Office, 1923.

"Models of Chinese Junks." *Yachting Monthly and Motor Boating Magazine* (December 1938).

"Models of Chinese Junks: Sir F. Maze's Gift to Science Museum." *London Times,* October 27, 1938.

Moll, F., and L. G. Carr. Laughton. "The Navy of the Province of Fukien." *Mariner's Mirror* 9, no. 10 (1923): 364–76.

Moodie, David. "Fire Bending with the Dragon's Tongue." *Wooden Boat Magazine* 44 (1982): 104–6.

Morgan, Harry T. *Chinese Symbols and Superstitions.* Detroit: Gale Research Company, 1972.

Morse, Hosea Ballou. *The Trade and Administration of the Chinese Empire.* London: Longmans, Green and Company, 1908.

Mott, Lawrence W. *The Development of the Rudder: A Technological Tale.* College Station: Texas A&M University Press, 1997.

Muir, John C. "One Old Junk Is Everyone's Treasure: The Excavation, Analysis, and Interpretation of a Chinese Shrimp Junk at China Camp State Park." Master's thesis, Sonoma State University, 1999.

Mumford, Lewis. "Authoritarian and Democratic Technics." *Technology and Culture* 5 (1964): 1–8.

Murray, Dian H. *Pirates of the South China Coast, 1790–1810*. Stanford, Calif.: Stanford University Press, 1987.

———. "The Kwangtung Water World." Conference Proceedings pamphlet excerpt, 145–70. Nankang: Academia Sinica, 1999.

Nakamura Yoshio, "Shipping Brokers in North China." In *Transport in Transition: The Evolution of Traditional Shipping in China*, translated by Andrew J. Watson, 15–34. Ann Arbor: University of Michigan, 1972.

Nash, Robert A. "American-Built Chinese Junks." *Nautical Research Journal* 4, no. 7 (1952): 111–12.

———. "A California Sampan from Marin County." *Bulletin of the Chinese Historical Society* 4 no. 1 (1969): 2–3.

———. "The Chinese Fishing Industry in Baja California." Paper read at the Baja California Symposium IX *Asociacion Cultural de las Californias*, May 1, 1971. San Diego Historical Society Library and Manuscripts Collection.

———. "The Chinese Shrimp Fishery of California." Ph.D. diss., University of California at Los Angeles, 1973.

Needham, Joseph. *A History of Science and Civilization in China* vol. 4, part 3; vol. 5, part 7. London: Cambridge University Press, 1971.

Needham, Joseph, and Lu Gwei-Djen. *Trans-Pacific Echoes and Resonances: Listening Once Again*. Singapore: World Scientific, 1985.

Ng Chin-Keong. *Trade and Society: The Amoy Network on the China Coast, 1683–1735*. Singapore: Singapore University Press, 1983.

Nimmo, H. Arlo. *The Sea People of Sulu*. San Francisco: Chandler Publishing Company, 1972.

Nooteboom, Christiaan. *Trois problemes d'ethnologie maritime*. Rotterdam: Museum voor Land—en Volkenkunde en het Maritiem Museum "Prins Hendrik," 1952.

Ogden, Adele. *Trading Vessels on the California Coast, 1786–1848*. Copy of four-volume manuscript donated to Bancroft Library, University of California at Berkeley, 1979.

O'Shaughnessy, Eleanore. Correspondence with Catalina Island Museum regarding *Ning Po*, July 21, 1993, Catalina Island Maritime Museum collection.

Oxford-Duden Pictorial English and Chinese Dictionary. Hong Kong: Oxford University Press, 1988.

Ozaki, C. *Japanese-English Dictionary of Sea Terms*. Berkeley: University of California Press, 1943.

Pagden, Anthony. *European Encounters with the New World*. New Haven, Conn.: Yale University Press, 1993.

Paine, Lincoln. "Aspects of a Global Maritime History." *Nautical Research Journal* 43, no. 3 (1998): 131–38.

Parry, Horace. *The Discovery of the Sea*. New York: Dial Press, 1974.

Petersen, E. Allen. *Hummel Hummel*. New York: Vantage Press, 1952.

———. "We Crossed the Pacific in a 36-foot Junk!" Document in J. Porter Shaw Library collection, San Francisco Maritime National Historic Park, n.d.

Phillips, Della. "A Peaceful Pirate." *Overland Monthly* 19, no. 4 (1917): 327–31.

Pierson, Larry J., and James R. Moriarty III. "New Evidence of Asiatic Shipwrecks Off the California Coast." In *Underwater Archaeology: The Challenge Before Us,* edited by Gordon P. Watts, 88–95. San Marino, Calif.: Fathom Eight Publications, 1981.

Pietri, J. B. *Voiliers D'Indochine.* Saigon: S.I.L.I., 1949.

Pin-tsun Chang. "Maritime China in Historical Perspective." *International Journal of Maritime History* 4, no. 2 (1992): 239–55.

Plummer, Katherine. *The Shogun's Reluctant Ambassadors: Japanese Sea Drifters in the North Pacific.* Portland: Oregon Historical Society Press, 1991.

Pomeranz, Kenneth. *The Great Divergence: China, Europe, and the Making of the Modern World Economy.* Princeton, N.J.: Princeton University Press, 2000.

Pritchard, L. A. "The *Ning Po* Junk." *Mariner's Mirror* 9, no. 3 (1923): 89.

Prown, Jules David. "The Truth of Material Culture: History or Fiction?" In *History from Things: Essays on Material Culture,* edited by Steven Lubar and W. David Kingery, 1–20. Washington and London: Smithsonian Institution Press, 1993.

Purvis, F. P. "Ship Construction in Japan." *Transactions of the Asiatic Society of Japan* 47 (1919): 1–34.

Rawlinson, John L. *China's Struggle for Naval Development, 1839–1895.* Cambridge, Mass.: Harvard University Press, 1967.

Raymenton, H. K. "The Venerable *Ning Po.*" *San Diego Historical Society Quarterly* 4, no. 4 (1958): 50–53.

"The Reconstruction of the Ship After Recovery." *Wen Wu* (Song Shipwreck group, Department of History, Xiamen University) 10d (1975): 28–34.

Reid, Anthony. "The Unthreatening Alternative: Chinese Shipping in Southeast Asia, 1567–1842." *Review of Indian and Malaysian Affairs* 27 (1993): 13–32.

Rogers, Robert F. *Destiny's Landfall: A History of Guam.* Honolulu: University of Hawai'i Press, 1995.

Ronan, Colin A. *The Shorter Science and Civilization in China: 3* (abridgement of Joseph Needham). Cambridge, U.K.: Cambridge University Press, 1986.

Root, Jonathon. *Halliburton: The Magnificent Myth.* New York: Coward-McCann, 1965.

Rosaldo, Renato. *Culture and Truth: The Remaking of Social Analysis.* Boston: Beacon Press, 1993.

Rydell, Robert W. *All the World's a Fair: Visions of Empire at American International Expositions, 1876–1916.* Chicago: University of Chicago Press, 1984.

Sandmeyer, Elmer Clarence. *The Anti-Chinese Movement in California.* Chicago: University of Illinois Press, 1991.

Saso, Michael. Correspondence between Beijing Center and Ching Lim of Catalina Island Museum, July 4, 1997, regarding Wang-ye cult figure. Catalina Island Maritime Museum collection.

Sather, Clifford. *The Bajau Laut: Adaptation, History, and Fate in a Maritime Fishing Society of Southeastern Sabah.* Oxford, U.K.: Oxford University Press, 1997.

Scarth, John. *Twelve Years in China: The People, the Rebels, and the Mandarins.* Edinburgh: T. Constable, 1860.

Schlegel, G. "On the Invention and Use of Firearms and Gunpowder in China, Prior to the Arrival of the Europeans." *T'oung Pao* 3 (1902): 1–11.

Schurz, William Lytle. *The Manila Galleon.* New York: E. P. Dutton and Co., 1939.

Schwendinger, Robert J. "Chinese Sailors, America's Invisible Merchant Marine 1876–1905." *California History* 57, no. 1 (1978): 58–70.

———. "Coolie Trade: The American Connection." *Oceans* 14, no. 1 (1981): 38–44.

———. *Ocean of Bitter Dreams: Maritime Relations between China and the West.* Tucson: Westernlore Publishing, 1988.

Severin, Tim. *The China Voyage: Across the Pacific by Bamboo Raft.* New York: Addison-Wesley Publishing Company, 1994.

Sing-wu Wang. *The Organization of Chinese Emigration, 1848–1888.* San Francisco: Chinese Materials Center, 1978.

Snow, Phillip. *The Star Raft, China's Encounter with Africa.* New York: Weidenfeld and Nicholson, 1988.

Soan Thao Hon-Hop Boi. *Hai Thuyen Thanh Thu . . . Junk Blue Book.* South Vietnam: Combat Development and Test Center, 1962.

Sokoloff, Valentine A. *Ships of China.* San Bruno, Calif.: Sokoloff, 1982.

"The Song Dynasty Shipwreck Excavated at Quanzhou Harbor." *Wen Wu* (Song Shipwreck group, Department of History, Xiamen University) 10a (1975): 1–18.

Sopher, David Edward. *The Sea Nomads: A Study Based on the Literature of the Maritime Boat People of Southeast Asia.* Singapore: Memoirs of the National Museum, 1965.

Sparling, Tobin Andrews. *The Great Exhibition: A Question of Taste.* New Haven, Conn.: Yale Center for British Art, 1982.

Spencer, J. E. "The Junks of the Yangtze." *Asia* 38 (1938): 469–70.

———. *Junks of Central China: The Spencer Collection of Models at Texas A&M University.* College Station: Texas A&M University Press, 1976.

Steffy, J. Richard. *Wooden Ship Building and the Interpretation of Shipwrecks.* College Station: Texas A&M University Press, 1994.

Steiner, Stan. *Fusang, the Chinese Who Built America.* New York: Harper and Row, 1979.

Storer, Douglas F. Correspondence Between President of *Ripley's Believe It or Not!* and Paul Chow, navigator of junk *Free China*, August 29, 1955, Paul Chow collection.

Sunken Treasures: Underwater Archaeology in China. Conference papers from University of California, Los Angeles, Center for Pacific Rim Studies, October 14, 1995.

Ta Chen. *Chinese Migrations, with Special Reference to Labor Conditions.* Washington, D.C.: Government Printing Office, 1923.

Takaki, Ronald. *Strangers from a Different Shore.* Penguin Books, 1989.

Tate, E. Mowbray. *Transpacific Steam.* New York: Cornwallis Books, 1986.

Teng, Ssu-yu, and John K. Fairbank. *China's Response to the West: A Documentary Survey, 1839–1923.* Cambridge, Mass.: Harvard University Press, 1954.

Teshima Masaki and Arai Yoshio. "Junk Crews in Soochow." In *Transport in Transition: The Evolution of Traditional Shipping in China,* translated by Andrew J. Watson, 57–70. Ann Arbor: University of Michigan, 1972.

Thomas, Nicholas. *Entangled Objects: Exchange, Material Culture, and Colonialism in the Pacific.* Cambridge, Mass.: Harvard University Press, 1991.

Thompson, Laurence G. "The Junk Passage Across the Taiwan Strait: Two Early Chinese Accounts." *Harvard Journal of Asiatic Studies* 28 (1968): 170–94.

Ting, V. K., trans. "Things Produced by the Work of Nature." *Mariner's Mirror* 11, no. 3 (1925): 234–51.

Tomasetti, Rob. "Final Report: A Survey of a Vessel Wrecked at Kona Coast State Park." Unpublished report, University of Hawai'i, 1997.

Tsai, Jung-fang. *Hong Kong in Chinese History: Community and Social Unrest in the British Colony, 1842–1913.* New York: Columbia University Press, 1993.

Tsang, Gerard C. C. *Views of the Pearl River Delta: Macau, Canton, and Hong Kong* (exhibition catalogue). Hong Kong: Hong Kong Museum of Art, 1996.

Urry, John. *The Tourist Gaze: Leisure and Travel in Contemporary Societies.* London: Sage Publications, 1990.

van Leur, J. C. *Indonesian Trade and Society: Essays in Asian Social and Economic History.* The Hague, Bandung: W. van Hoeve, 1955.

Van Loan, Derek, and Don Haggerty. *The Chinese Sailing Rig.* Middletown, Calif.: Paradise Cay Publications, 1993.

Viraphol, Sarasin. *Tribute and Profit: Sino-Siamese Trade, 1652–1853.* Cambridge, Mass.: Harvard University Press, 1977.

Wade, Geoff. *The Pre-Modern East Asian Maritime Realm: An Overview of European-Language Studies,* working paper no. 16. Singapore: National University of Singapore, Asia Research Institute, 2003.

Walker, David E. *The Modern Smuggler.* London: Secker and Warburg, 1960.

Wallace, Ben J., and William M. Hurley. "Transpacific Contacts: A Selected Annotated Bibliography." *Asian Perspectives* 11 (1968): 157–75.

Waller, John H. *Gordon of Khartoum: The Saga of a Victorian Hero.* New York: Atheneum, 1988.

Wang Zhiyi. *Zhong guo jin dai zao chuan shi* (Ship Construction in Ancient China). Beijing: Hai yang chu ban she, 1986.

Warren, James. *The Sulu Zone, 1776–1898: The Dynamics of External Trade, Slavery and Ethnicity in the Transformation of a Southeast Asian Maritime State.* Singapore: Singapore University Press, 1981.

Waters, D. W. "Chinese Junks: The Antung Trader." *Mariner's Mirror* 24, no. 1 (1938): 49–67.

———. "Chinese Junks: The Pechili Trader." *Mariner's Mirror* 25, no. 1 (1939): 62–87.

———. "Chinese Junks—The *Twaqo*." *Mariner's Mirror* 32, no. 1 (1946): 155–68.

————. "Chinese Junks: The Hangchow Bay Trader and Fisher." *Mariner's Mirror* 33, no. 1 (1947): 28–38.

Watson, Andrew J., trans. *Transport in Transition: The Evolution of Traditional Shipping in China.* Ann Arbor: University of Michigan, 1972.

Watson, James L. "Standardizing the Gods: The Promotion of T'ien Hou ("Empress of Heaven") Along the South China Coast, 960–1960." In *Popular Culture in Late Imperial China,* edited by D. Johnson et al., 292–324. Los Angeles: University of California Press, 1985.

Webber, Bert, and Margie Webber. *Amazing Tales of Wrecked Japanese Junks.* Medford, Ore.: Webb Research Group Publishers, 1999.

Weibust, Knut. *Deep Sea Sailors: A Study in Maritime Ethnology.* Stockholm: Kungl. Boktrycheriet, 1969.

Werner, E.T.C. *A Dictionary of Chinese Mythology.* Shanghai: Kelly and Walsh, 1932.

Westerdahl, Christer. "The Maritime Cultural Landscape." *International Journal of Nautical Archaeology* 21, no. 1 (1992): 5–14.

————. "Maritime Cultures and Ship Types: Brief Comments on the Significance of Maritime Archaeology." *International Journal of Nautical Archaeology* 23, no. 4 (1994): 265–70.

White, Walter G. *The Sea Gypsies of Malaya: An Account of the Nomadic Mawken People of the Mergui Archipelago with a Description of Their Ways of Living, Customs, Habits, Boats, Occupations, Etc.* London: Seeley, Service and Company, 1922.

Wiens, Herold J. "Riverine and Coastal Junks in China's Commerce." *Economic Geography* (1955): 248–64.

Wilkinson, Endymion. *The History of Imperial China: A Research Guide.* Cambridge, Mass.: Harvard University Press, 1990.

Winchester, Clarence, ed. *Shipping Wonders of the World.* London: Fleetway House, 1936.

Winterburn, W. G. "The Chinese Junk." *Cassier's Magazine Engineering Illustrated* 21 (1901–1902): 424–30.

Woodman, Richard. *The History of the Ship.* London: Conway Maritime Press, 1997.

Woodside, A. B., "Early Ming Expansionism (1406–1427): China's Abortive Conquest of Vietnam." In *Papers on China* 17 (Seminars at Harvard University). Cambridge, Mass.: Harvard University Press, 1963.

Worcester, G.R.G. *A Classification of the Principal Chinese Sea-Going Junks (South of the Yangtze).* Shanghai: Statistical Department of the Inspectorate General of Customs, 1948.

————. "The Chinese War Junk." *Mariner's Mirror* 34, no. 1 (1948): 16.

————. "The Amoy Fishing Boat." *Mariner's Mirror* 40, no. 4 (1954): 304–9.

————. "Six Craft of Kwangtung." *Mariner's Mirror* 45, no. 2 (1959): 130–44.

————. *The Junkman Smiles.* London: Chatto and Windus, 1959.

————. *Sail and Sweep in China.* London: HMSO, 1966.

———. *The Floating Population of China.* Hong Kong: Vetch and Lee, 1970.

———. *The Junks and Sampans of the Yangtze.* Shanghai: Inspector General of Customs, 1947. Reprint, Annapolis: Naval Institute Press, 1971.

Wortham, Hugh Evelyn. *Chinese Gordon.* Boston: Little, Brown and Company, 1933.

Wright, Arnold, ed. *Twentieth Century Impressions of Hong Kong, Shanghai, and Other Treaty Ports of China: Their History, People, Commerce, Industries, and Resources.* London: Lloyd's Greater Britain Publishing Company Limited, 1908.

Wright, Stanley Fowler. *Hart and the Chinese Customs.* Belfast: W. Mullen, 1950.

Wu, David Y. H. *The Chinese in Papua New Guinea: 1880–1980.* Hong Kong: Chinese University Press, 1982.

Wu Yuey Len. "Extract from the Life and Culture of the Shanam Boat People." *Nankai Social and Economic Quarterly* 9, no. 4 (1937): 1–24.

Xi Longfei. *Zhongguo zao chuan shi* (China Ship Construction). Hubei: Hubei jiao yu chu ban she, 2000.

Xiamen zhi: Fujian sheng (Xiamen gazetteer: Fujian province).

Yinghan hanghai cidian (English-Chinese Maritime Dictionary).

Yonemura, Ann. *Yokohama: Prints from 19th-Century Japan.* Washington, D.C.: Smithsonian Institution Press, 1990.

Yoneo Ishii, ed. *The Junk Trade from Southeast Asia: Translations from the Tosen Fusetsu-gaki, 1674–1723.* Singapore: Institute of Southeast Asian Studies, 1998.

Yu Weichao, Zhang Wei, Zhou Changfa, Tsang Cheng-hwa, Huang Yung-chuan, Liu Benan, Porter Hoagland, and Chou Hung-hsiang. *Sunken Treasures: Underwater Archaeology in China.* University of California at Los Angeles (conference proceedings), 1995.

Zao chuan shi hua (Notes on Ship Construction). Shanghai: Jiaotong University, 1979.

Zhang Jingfen. *Zhongguo gudai de zao chuan he hanghai* (Ship Construction and Navigation in Ancient China). Taiwan: Taiwan shang wu yin shu guan, 1994.

Zhou Shide. "Shipbuilding." In *Ancient China's Technology and Science,* 479–93. Beijing: Foreign Language Press, 1983.

Index

Hans Konrad Van Tilburg was originally introduced to the ocean on board his father's sloop *Brunhilde.* Since then he has worked as a sport diving instructor and a research and commercial diver in California, Louisiana, North Carolina, and Wisconsin. He holds a master's degree in maritime history and nautical archaeology from East Carolina University, and a Ph.D. from the University of Hawai'i, where he focused on the maritime history of Asia and the Pacific. For several years he headed the graduate certificate program in Maritime Archaeology and History at UH. Currently he is the maritime heritage coordinator for NOAA's National Marine Sanctuary Program in the Pacific Islands region.

New Perspectives on Maritime History and Nautical Archaeology

Edited by James C. Bradford and Gene Allen Smith

Maritime Heritage of the Cayman Islands, by Roger C. Smith (1999; first paperback edition, 2000)

The Three German Navies: Dissolution, Transition, and New Beginnings, 1945–1960, by Douglas C. Peifer (2002)

The Rescue of the Gale Runner: Death, Heroism, and the U.S. Coast Guard, by Dennis L. Noble (2002; first paperback edition, 2008)

Brown Water Warfare: The U.S. Navy in Riverine Warfare and the Emergence of a Tactical Doctrine, 1775–1970, by R. Blake Dunnavent (2003)

Sea Power in the Medieval Mediterranean: The Catalan-Aragonese Fleet in the War of the Sicilian Vespers, by Lawrence V. Mott (2003)

An Admiral for America: Sir Peter Warren, Vice-Admiral of the Red, 1703–1752, by Julian Gwyn (2004)

Maritime History as World History, edited by Daniel Finamore (2004)

Counterpoint to Trafalgar: The Anglo-Russian Invasion of Naples, 1805–1806, by William Henry Flayhart III (paperback edition, 2004)

Life and Death on the Greenland Patrol, 1942, by Thaddeus D. Novak, edited by P. J. Capelotti (2005)

X Marks the Spot: The Archaeology of Piracy, edited by Russell K. Skowronek and Charles R. Ewen (2006; first paperback edition 2007)

Industrializing American Shipbuilding: The Transformation of Ship Design and Construction, 1820–1920, by William H. Thiesen (2006)

Admiral Lord Keith and the Naval War Against Napoleon, by Kevin D. McCranie (2006)

Commodore John Rodgers: Paragon of the Early American Navy, by John H. Schroeder (2006)

Borderland Smuggling; Patriots, Loyalists, and Illicit Trade in the Northeast, 1783–1820, by Joshua M. Smith (2006)

Brutality on Trial: "Hellfire" Pedersen, "Fighting" Hansen, and the Seamen's Act of 1915, by E. Kay Gibson (2006)

Uriah Levy: Reformer of the Antebellum Navy, by Ira Dye (2006)

Crisis at Sea: The United States Navy in European Waters in World War I, by William N. Still Jr. (2006)

Chinese Junks on the Pacific: Views from a Different Deck, by Hans K. Van Tilburg (2007; first paperback edition, 2013)

Eight Thousand Years of Maltese Maritime History: Trade, Piracy, and Naval Warfare in the Central Mediterranean, by Ayse Devrim Atauz (2007)

Merchant Mariners at War: An Oral History of World War II, by George J. Billy and Christine M. Billy (2008)

The Steamboat Montana *and the Opening of the West: History, Excavation, and Architecture*, by Annalies Corbin and Bradley A. Rodgers (2008)

Attack Transport: USS Charles Carroll *in World War II*, by Kenneth H. Goldman (2008)

Diplomats in Blue: U.S. Naval Officers in China, 1922–1933, by William Reynolds Braisted (2009)

Sir Samuel Hood and the Battle of the Chesapeake, by Colin Pengelly (2009)

Voyages, The Age of Sail: Documents in Maritime History, Volume I, 1492–1865, edited by Joshua M. Smith and the National Maritime Historical Society (2009)

Voyages, The Age of Engines: Documents in Maritime History, Volume II, 1865–Present, edited by Joshua M. Smith and the National Maritime Historical Society (2009)

H.M.S. Fowey Lost . . . and Found!, by Russell K. Skowronek and George R. Fischer (2009)

American Coastal Rescue Craft: A Design History of Coastal Rescue Craft Used by the United States Life-Saving Service and the United States Coast Guard, by William D. Wilkinson and Commander Timothy R. Dring, USNR (Retired) (2009)

The Spanish Convoy of 1750: Heaven's Hammer and International Diplomacy, by James A. Lewis (2009)

The Development of Mobile Logistic Support in Anglo-American Naval Policy, 1900–1953, by Peter V. Nash (2009)

Captain "Hell Roaring" Mike Healy: From American Slave to Arctic Hero, by Dennis L. Noble and Truman R. Strobridge (2009)

Sovereignty at Sea: U.S. Merchant Ships and American Entry into World War I, by Rodney Carlisle (2009; first paperback edition, 2011)

Commodore Abraham Whipple of the Continental Navy: Privateer, Patriot, Pioneer, by Sheldon S. Cohen (2010; first paperback edition, 2011)

Lucky 73: USS Pampanito's *Unlikely Rescue of Allied POWs in WW II*, by Aldona Sendzikas (2010)

Cruise of the Dashing Wave: *Rounding Cape Horn in 1860*, by Philip Hichborn, edited by William H. Thiesen (2010)

Seated by the Sea: The Maritime History of Portland, Maine, and Its Irish Longshoremen, by Michael C. Connolly (2010; first paperback edition, 2011)

The Whaling Expedition of the Ulysses, *1937–1938*, by LT (j.g.) Quentin R. Walsh, U.S. Coast Guard, edited and with an Introduction by P.J. Capelotti (2010)

Stalking the U-Boat: U. S. Naval Aviation in Europe During World War I, by Geoffrey L. Rossano (2010)

In Katrina's Wake: The U.S. Coast Guard and the Gulf Coast Hurricanes of 2005, by Donald L. Canney (2010)

A Civil War Gunboat in Pacific Waters: Life on Board USS Saginaw, by Hans K. Van Tilburg (2010)

The U.S. Coast Guard's War on Human Smuggling, by Dennis L. Noble (2011)

The Sea Their Graves: An Archaeology of Death and Remembrance in Maritime Culture, by David J. Stewart (2011)

Lightning Source UK Ltd.
Milton Keynes UK
UKHW040632230223
417513UK00004B/176